HELP YOUR KIDS WITH
aDOLeScence

HELP YOUR KIDS WITH
ADOLESCENCE

DK

A NO-NONSENSE GUIDE TO
PUBERTY AND THE TEENAGE YEARS

Lead Editor Amanda Wyatt
Senior Designer Michelle Staples
Project Editor Steven Carton
Editors Niki Foreman, Emma Grundy Haigh
Designer Sean Ross
Editorial Assistant Sophie Parkes
US Editors Kayla Dugger, Lori Hand
Illustrators Edwood Burn, Claire Joyce, Michael Parkin
Managing Editor Lisa Gillespie
Managing Art Editor Owen Peyton Jones
Producer, Pre-production Gillian Reid
Senior Producers Mandy Inness, Anna Vallarino
Jackets Designers Suhita Dharamjit,
Juhi Sheth, Surabhi Wadhwa
Senior DTP Designer Harish Aggarwal
Jackets Editorial Coordinator Priyanka Sharma
Jacket Editor Claire Gell
Jacket Design Development Manager Sophia MTT
Category Publisher Andrew Macintyre
Associate Publishing Director Liz Wheeler
Art Director Karen Self
Publishing Director Jonathan Metcalf

First American edition, 2017
Published in the United States
by DK Publishing
345 Hudson Street,
New York, New York 10014

Copyright © 2017 Dorling Kindersley Limited
DK, a division of Penguin Random House LLC
17 18 19 20 21 10 9 8 7 6 5 4 3 2 1
001-299754-July/2017

A catalog record for this book is available from the Library of Congress.

ISBN 978-1-4654-6184-1

DK books are available at special discounts when purchased in bulk for sales
promotion, premiums, fund-raising, or educational use. For details, contact: DK
Publishing Special Markets, 345 Hudson Street, New York, New York, 10014
SpecialSales@DK.com

Printed and bound in China

A WORLD OF IDEAS:
SEE ALL THERE IS TO KNOW

www.dk.com

CONSULTANT AND CONTRIBUTOR

DR. KAREN RAYNE

Dr. Karen Rayne has worked in sexuality education for almost two decades. She focuses on writing curriculum, training sexuality educators, and writing books. Her most recent book is "GIRL: Love, Sex, Romance, and Being You." She has worked with The Center for Sex Education, the New York Department of Education, Girls Inc, the American Psychological Association, and the UNFPA, among others. She is also the associate editor of the American Journal of Sexuality Education.

OTHER CONTRIBUTORS

LAVERNE ANTROBUS

Laverne Antrobus is a consultant child and educational psychologist. Having trained at the prestigious Tavistock Clinic in London, UK, she then worked in Local Authorities and the UK's National Health Service (NHS). Laverne appears on television, radio, and in print media. She has made programs on childhood for the BBC and currently appears on the CBeebies Grown-ups website.

TERESA DAY MSC, RGN, RMN

Teresa Day trained and qualified as both a general nurse and a mental health nurse. She has spent most of her career working in the field of adolescent health, including carrying out research into relationships and sex education for her Master's dissertation. In her current role she supports and trains school staff, specializing in emotional health and well-being, and relationship education.

PROFESSOR SONIA LIVINGSTONE OBE

Sonia Livingstone is a professor in the Department of Media and Communications at the London School of Economics and Political Science, UK. She's author of 20 books on kids' online opportunities and risks, including "The Class: Living and Learning in the Digital Age." She advises the UK government, European Commission, and Council of Europe on children's rights in digital environments. She directs the projects "Global Kids Online" and "Parenting for a Digital Future" and founded the EU Kids Online research network.

DR. RADHA MODGIL

Dr. Radha Modgil is a practicing NHS doctor in London, UK. She broadcasts across all platforms, online, TV, and radio, including The Surgery on BBC Radio 1. A campaigner for physical and mental well-being, Radha educates in a creative and fun way, encouraging people to stay healthy. She appeared as the medical reporter for "The Sex Education Show" on Channel 4, and "Make My Body Younger" on BBC3. She is a medical expert for BBC Radio 4 Woman's Hour, BBC Radio 5 Live, BBC Asian Network, LBC, and Radio 1's Newsbeat.

SARAH PAWLEWSKI MSC

Sarah Pawlewski is a career adviser with more than 20 years' experience. She runs her own consultancy—career-directions.co.uk—and works with clients of all ages across schools, colleges, universities, and industry. She also teaches career guidance courses at degree level. Sarah holds degrees in career guidance and in psychology. She is the principal author of "The Careers Handbook" published by DK.

PROFESSOR ROBERT WINSTON

Robert Winston is a world-renowned scientist, who has combined groundbreaking academic work with a flair for communicating science to the general public. The icon of many British TV series, his pioneering work in the field of human fertility has helped dozens of childless couples have "miracle babies" and earned him an international reputation. He is Professor of Science and Society and Emeritus Professor of Fertility Studies at Imperial College London. UK. He became a life peer of the House of Lords in 1995.

Foreword

During adolescence few things are constant except for change. The physical, emotional, psychological, social, and the cultural understanding of who we are all evolve between childhood and adolescence. Young people experiencing these changes often need guidance to understand what's currently happening as well as information about what's to come. They may also need to understand how and why their peers are going through those changes in different ways. In certain situations, they may have questions about what their options are, and need support to figure out which paths are best for them.

Parents often think back to their own adolescence, and may be surprised to find that their teens are having different experiences than they had in their youths. They may wonder what is new today and how they can best help their teen make wise choices. This book is written to support both young people and their parents, as kids grow into adolescents and onwards into adulthood. Sometimes parents see themselves as having less influence on their children as they grow up, but research suggests otherwise. The majority of young people say they want to talk with their parents about the big issues in their lives.

Help Your Kids with Adolescence presents information about the changes, challenges, and charms of adolescence in an accessible and relatable way for tweens and teens. Even parents who aren't sure where to start, or what to say as they begin conversations will find that this book supports them, and helps them to understand and support their kids.

As a sexuality educator, I work with young people, and with parents, on some of the most personal, emotional, and potentially influential aspects of life. I see how much healthier and grounded teens are when their parents talk with them openly about a wide range of topics, from sexuality and religion to politics and race, as well as puberty, staying safe online, and peer pressure. I am delighted to have worked on this book with my fellow experts, and to have it as a resource to recommend to families who want to talk about these things, but just aren't sure where to start.

Karen Rayne

KAREN RAYNE

Contents

How to use this book

Being a tween or a teen can be exciting, fun, wonderful, tricky, confusing, and stressful. And being the parent of a tween or teen is equally emotional. This book has been developed as a resource to support teens and guide parents, and to make adolescence a more positive and enjoyable experience. It's been crafted by experts to provide information and ideas to help everyone navigate this complicated time.

Who is this book for?

This book can be read separately by parents or young readers, but it's also designed to be read together. Not everything is suitable for every child, because the book covers a wide range of topics with the hope that it will help families throughout the tween and teen years, and grow with the readers' needs.

Depending on the family, particular pages and chapters of this book will be relevant at different points during adolescence. Some tweens and teens will be ready for, and interested in, certain sections depending on their age and curiosity. Parents are the best judge of what their kids are ready for. Some might prefer to read ahead in order to feel confident and comfortable with what's discussed and shown. Others may want their teens to feel free to absorb everything in their own time. Whether you use this book as a way to ease into awkward conversations, to understand your teen and modern adolescence, or to inform your teen, is entirely up to you.

How the book works

Divided into different sections, this book guides readers through all the physical, emotional, and social changes that adolescence brings. You'll find pages about having a healthy mind and body, puberty, relationships, and school, as well as social media and sexuality.

Biological changes are shown clearly in diagrams, along with labels and scientific explanations. A cast of characters appears throughout the book to reflect a variety of teenagers and families, as well as the different situations that might make up a teen's life.

Tips and hints

Throughout the book, you'll find colored boxes offering extra information and useful, practical advice and tips.

Blue boxes offer **TEEN HINTS** with reassurance and helpful suggestions. Parents may want to read them to better understand a teen's point of view.

TEEN HINTS

Family structures

Sometimes a family structure can change due to a separation, divorce, death, or new marriage, for example. Finding your way in a new family structure can be hard, especially when what was your "normal" has been unexpectedly altered. But change often brings the opportunity to form relationships with new people. These people will never replace the people in your old family structure, but will help you to form, and be a part of developing, a new family structure.

MYTH BUSTER

The truth about smoking

It doesn't look cool. It also comes with bad breath, stinky hair, and a reduced sense of taste.

It won't help you fit in. Never feel that you have to do something dangerous to fit in with friends.

You won't just be able to have one or two. Research suggests that the brains of young people are more vulnerable to nicotine addiction than adults, so even one or two is enough to develop an addiction.

Yellow factboxes are **MYTH BUSTERS** that clarify misconceptions and provide the facts.

PARENT TIPS

Signs of cyberbullying

Many of the signs are similar to those of regular bullying, but may be intensified by electronic devices.

• The way a teen uses their devices might change, such as suddenly not using them, being secretive when using them, or being online obsessively.

• A teen's behavior might change. They might become sad or withdrawn, lash out, or be reluctant to do things they usually enjoy.

Purple boxes give **PARENT TIPS** and offer practical advice on how to support teens. Teens themselves may want to read them to better understand an adult's point of view.

Orange factboxes are **ALERT!** features. These deal with legal issues or risky situations.

GOOD TO KNOW

Good and bad stress

Stress can sometimes be very useful, as it motivates people to keep working under pressure and energizes them to complete tasks they care about. But if it becomes overwhelming, stress can limit a person's ability to function effectively. When you're feeling stressed, try to use it as motivation to tackle a challenge, but if things start to seem unmanageable, seek support.

Green **GOOD TO KNOW** boxes provide interesting background information.

ALERT!

Dangerous selfies

Selfies of people in precarious positions have become widespread on social media. Across the world, creating daredevil selfies is putting people's lives at risk. With teens more prone to risk-taking due to the changes that are taking place in their brains, it is important that they don't buy in to this dangerous trend, in which people have been injured. Instead, a person should be aware and ensure that they're safe before taking a selfie.

Starting conversations

We hope this book will help tweens and teens and their parents understand each other a little more. Many pages suggest ways of initiating conversations, listening to each other, and seeing one another's point of view. These tools will help mold confident, happy teens.

This book is a starting point, but it can't answer every question. Each topic also has suggested cross-references, because many aspects of puberty and adolescence are closely linked to one another. At the end of the book, there are **Find out more** pages with suggestions on where get further information and support.

Growing up

Teen brains

Throughout childhood, the brain grows and develops, and by the time a child is 6 years old, their brain has reached up to 90 percent of its full adult size. During puberty, however, the brain experiences its most dramatic transformation, in ways that can affect a teen's thoughts and behavior.

Changing brains

As children get older, their brains must learn how to cope with life as adults, and so transformations occur in the anatomy and chemistry of the brain. Areas involved in more basic functions, such as processing sensory input, mature first, while the areas responsible for more complex thought, such as planning ahead, develop later. These changes begin during puberty. Although the brain is fully grown by a person's mid-20s, it continues to develop and change for the rest of their life.

GOOD TO KNOW

Making connections

In early life, millions of connections called synapses form between brain cells, and these are what allow a person to learn. Over time, the brain starts to prune the connections that aren't used. This gives more space and "brain power" to those that are needed, making them more efficient. The teen years are a critical period for strengthening and pruning connections, but this process continues throughout a person's life.

◁ **Early childhood**
Connections form quickly, allowing a person to develop new skills.

◁ **Adolescence**
Unused connections fade away, while those that are used frequently become stronger.

Prefrontal cortex
Responsible for rational thinking, problem solving, self-control, and thinking ahead, this is the last part of the brain to mature.

Basal ganglia
The basal ganglia controls movement and decision-making.

Nucleus accumbens
The brain's reward center, this helps form memories in response to positive or negative experiences. Dopamine levels in the nucleus accumbens change during adolescence—teens need more than adults to achieve the "buzz" from pleasure, meaning they'll take more chances to achieve this feeling.

Hypothalamus
This area triggers puberty by releasing the hormone GnRH. It also regulates sleep, body temperature, hunger, and thirst.

Pituitary gland
This controls hormone levels in the body.

Amygdala
Responsible for instinctive behavior, aggression, and risk-taking, the amygdala creates powerful emotions, such as fear and anger. Teens use the amygdala to process information more than adults, making them more prone to extreme emotions.

Being clumsy

During puberty, growth spurts—when a teen grows quickly in a short space of time—can leave the brain struggling to keep up. The brain needs to adapt to the body's longer limbs and different proportions. While the brain adjusts, teens may find that they trip or knock things over more than before.

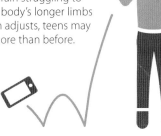

▷ **Self-consciousness**
Teens also become more body-aware during puberty. If they feel self-conscious, it can make them even clumsier.

Corpus callosum
This bundle of nerves connects the two halves—the left and right sides—of the brain. The nerves thicken during adolescence and improve problem-solving abilities.

Risky behavior

Teens are more likely than adults to seek out thrills and to act on impulse. This is because the teen brain matures from back to front, with the prefrontal cortex—which controls impulses and rational thought—maturing last. As a teen's prefrontal cortex matures last, the amygdala—responsible for instinct and risky behavior—takes control in the meantime and allows teens to become more independent from their parents.

△ **Testing boundaries**
Some teens make careless decisions because their brains are more focused on the social rewards of an action rather than the risks.

Cerebellum
Responsible for coordinating the body's movement and balance, the cerebellum adjusts as the body grows.

Brain rest

With the brain and body changing so quickly, teens need an average of nine hours of sleep per night. The changes occurring in the brain also affect their sleep patterns. During adolescence, melatonin (the hormone that encourages sleep) isn't released in the brain until late in the evening, and continues being released in the morning, turning teens into night owls who struggle to wake up early.

Some scientists believe that the human brain today is 10% smaller than it was 20,000 years ago because it has become more efficient.

◁ **Sleep**
Sleep is vital for the healthy development of the brain and body.

Identity

Identity is a complex topic that is personal to each individual. It explores the question, "Who am I?" Working out the answer to this question is a lifelong process that is straightforward for some and more complex for others.

Who are you?

Some aspects of a person's identity, such as nationality, will probably be clear from a very early age. Other parts—for example, personality type and sexual identity—will become gradually clearer over time. With certain elements of their identity, like religion and political views, teens might follow in their parents' footsteps, or instead develop their own ideas throughout their life.

   The make-up of a person's unique identity may also include all sorts of other components, such as the hobbies they have; their likes and dislikes; their friends; or whether they are adopted, or born to parents from different backgrounds. Combined, all these aspects of a person are what make each child, teen, and adult a one-of-a-kind individual.

▽ **Unique combination**
Identity is influenced by a huge variety of factors.

"Today you are you, that is truer than true. There is no one alive who is youer than you."
Dr. Seuss

How identity evolves

Young children usually talk about their identity in terms of their appearance and what they do—for example, their hair color or favorite sport. Older children tend to compare their identities to others. A child might start to feel good about their talents or bad about their perceived weaknesses.

During adolescence, teens generally gain a more complex sense of who they are. They might explain themselves in greater depth—for example, that they are cheerful and optimistic, but that doesn't mean they don't feel down sometimes. Many teens experiment to find out which identity feels real to them. As they encounter new people and new ideas, they learn, and their interests and views develop—all of which contribute to their evolving identity.

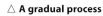

△ **A gradual process**
Although teens think a lot about who they are, their identity is fluid and will continue to change into adulthood.

When identities clash

Although family members may have some things in common, it's also completely normal for them to have very different perspectives on life. Sometimes teens and parents can feel as if they don't understand each other or can't agree on anything. When clashes happen, it's usually due to different personal values that make it hard for each side to understand the other. Acknowledging and accepting the differing values can make it easier to talk things through and get along.

▷ **Changing perspective**
Teens often seek fresh perspectives on topics such as music or politics in an effort to separate themselves from the identity their parents created for them when they were younger.

Thinking independently

During adolescence, rapid brain development means that teens begin to use new ways of thinking. One really important ability is independent thought, which helps to boost a teen's self-esteem and prepares them for the future.

What is independent thought?

When a person is able to think on their own and make informed decisions, without anyone guiding their thoughts or decision-making, they are demonstrating independent thought. People begin to think independently as young children, but it takes time and practice to cultivate the skill. During the teen years, a person's ability to think independently advances quickly, because the parts of the brain responsible for cognition begin to develop rapidly. While their brain function is expanding, teens are continually refining the skills that help them to become independent individuals, learning from examples set by others, and by their own trial and error.

"The essence of the independent mind lies not in what it thinks, but in how it thinks."
Christopher Hitchens— journalist, author, critic

Thinking skills in adolescence

Brain growth in adolescence allows teens to develop complex thinking processes—such as abstract thinking, reason, comparison, and empathy—encouraging independent thought and behavior.

Abstract thinking
This way of thinking considers possibilities and ideas that are not physically present.

Reasoning
This thought process involves a person looking at all the facts of a situation logically and analytically to form their own opinions and ideas, plus questions for further research and understanding.

Comparing different viewpoints
This trait leads to a greater understanding of topics, and provokes questions for debate.

Empathy
This attribute enables a person to see things from another's perspective, and to understand their point of view. It is an important part of healthy and successful relationships.

Independent thinking traits

Independent thought goes hand-in-hand with independent behavior. Teens can show that they are ready for more independence not only in what they do, but in how they think and approach things:

Staying true to oneself and avoiding peer pressure shows strong self-belief and assertiveness.

Considering as many sides of a situation as possible lets a person decide what's right for them, without dismissing other perspectives.

Thinking creatively and using imagination allows teens to find ways of approaching a task that others haven't thought of.

Staying motivated and determined in the face of obstacles and setbacks encourages problem-solving and resilience.

GOOD TO KNOW
Thinking differently

Thinking independently allows a person to make informed decisions and to question the norm in order to consider new ways of doing things. By questioning rather than accepting, a person is able to deduce and logically come to their own conclusions, which may lead to fresh and innovative new ideas.

PARENT TIPS
Encouraging independence

- Give your teen space and autonomy to develop the skills of independent thought within a safe environment.

- Be available to offer help and advice when it is needed, but allow them to make their own decisions.

- Encourage your teen to consider the cause and effect of things that happen in their life, to help them consider different perspectives and encourage critical thinking.

- Show your teen how to admit and learn from their mistakes by discussing your own in front of them, by taking responsibility, and by explaining what you'll do differently in the future.

- Discuss issues and ideas with your teen. Give them space to voice their own opinions, but take care not to criticize them if you disagree. Instead, ask them to explain their thinking.

- Encourage your teen to ask questions.

Developing independent thought

Independent thought isn't simply a person asserting their point of view. It is coming to an informed conclusion following a sequence of thought processes that gather information, assess that information, consider external factors and past experiences—both failings and achievements. Following this critical thinking, a person can feel confident in their own thoughts, and build on them to learn and deduce independently.

◁ **Pulled in different directions**
Making sense of different and conflicting thoughts is one aspect of independent thought.

Mood swings

Teen moods can change in the blink of an eye. From physical transformations to the pressures of growing up and interacting with the world, teens experience mood swings for so many reasons, it can be hard to know what's causing them.

Feeling moody

Unpredictable mood swings are common and normal during adolescence, although not every teen experiences them. They can happen abruptly or pass in phases. For some teens, they are unsettling, leaving them feeling embarrassed, and if other family members are taken by surprise, mood swings can sometimes end in conflict, too.

Teens can be loving by surprise, as well as grumpy.

Ups and downs

During the teen years, it's normal to feel happy and excited one minute, then bored or low the next, often for no apparent reason. Every teen experiences emotions differently, and some express them more intensely than others.

Learning what makes teens feel happy is an important part of discovering who they are during puberty.

Some teens often feel thoughtful, as puberty is a time when teens start to think about different ideas and form new opinions.

Feeling confused during puberty is completely natural, with physical and emotional changes all happening at once.

Stress allows teens to recognize when they care about something. It can provide motivation to prepare well.

Many teens feel self-conscious or awkward as their bodies change and they encounter new situations.

Anger and frustration can be difficult emotions to manage, and sometimes lead to conflict with other family members.

The causes of mood swings

During puberty, parts of the brain mature at different rates. The limbic system, the part responsible for emotions and feelings, develops early on. The prefrontal cortex, which regulates a person's response to their emotions, doesn't develop until later, toward the end of puberty. While the prefrontal cortex catches up with the limbic system, teens tend to experience extreme emotions and are generally less able to control their emotional responses, resulting in mood swings.

Mood swings aren't just down to teenage brain development, however. The pressures of puberty—encountering new situations; feeling self-conscious; coping with peer pressure and increased expectations; and worrying about exams, relationships, and the future—all play a major role in teens' changing moods.

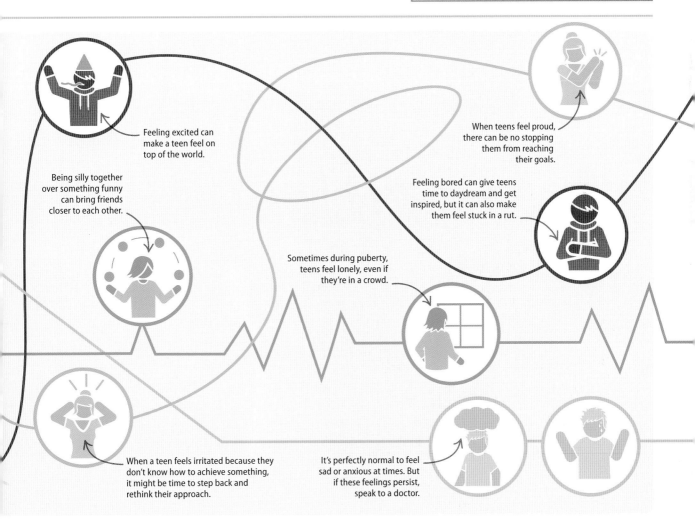

Feeling excited can make a teen feel on top of the world.

Being silly together over something funny can bring friends closer to each other.

When teens feel proud, there can be no stopping them from reaching their goals.

Feeling bored can give teens time to daydream and get inspired, but it can also make them feel stuck in a rut.

Sometimes during puberty, teens feel lonely, even if they're in a crowd.

When a teen feels irritated because they don't know how to achieve something, it might be time to step back and rethink their approach.

It's perfectly normal to feel sad or anxious at times. But if these feelings persist, speak to a doctor.

Self-expression

There are many different ways for people to convey who they are—and appearance is one of them. Teens might find creativity, individuality, and connection with their peers based on how they express themselves through their appearance.

Appearance

When people feel good about their appearance, it can make them feel more positive and confident. Receiving compliments from others can also help to boost confidence. However, sometimes the reactions people get may not be what they'd hoped for. Unfortunately, some people can be prejudiced toward those who do things differently from them—including dressing differently.

It can be easy for teens to fall into the trap of dressing to please other people, rather than themselves, but it is best for people to remain authentic and honest in all that they do—including how they look.

▷ **Looking good**
Self-expression, feeling good, and self-acceptance all go hand-in-hand.

Experimentation

It can be fulfilling to experiment with appearance, as figuring out what makes an individual look and feel their best can take time. After all, going through puberty is a process, and so as teens grow and mature, it makes sense for them to try different looks. There's no harm in an individual playing with the way that they look over time, or even day-to-day. It can allow people to get to know themselves better, which in turn helps others to understand them better, too.

TEEN HINTS

Dealing with disapproval

You might find you often disagree with your parents about what you wear or how you look. This happens because parents generally focus on how others will judge or stereotype a person based on how they look. You, on the other hand, might value creativity, individuality, and being accepted by friends much more highly. If your appearance regularly becomes a topic of conflict, try discussing these different values calmly with each other. Some might be more important than others in different situations.

△ **Trying new things**
Exploring different looks can give teens the chance to figure out not just what they like, but also how they want other people to perceive them.

Means of expression

There are many things an individual can do to personalize an outfit, and the teen years are a great time to try things out and experiment.

Clothes

If a person's clothes feel comfortable and fit well, they will look good, too. It's worth finding a few staple, good-quality items that can be dressed up or down. Some people make their own clothing, which is a clever and fun way to fill a wardrobe.

Make-up

Wearing make-up can accentuate an individual's features, cover up blemishes, and be dramatic or natural. It can help a person to feel more confident in their looks, and is often fun to experiment with—for boys and girls alike. Of course, it can be just as expressive to wear no make-up at all.

Hair

Long or short, curly or straight, styled or natural, the options are endless for how to wear hair. Many people find a style that they like and stick to it, while others experiment day by day. Sometimes, a person's decisions reflect their cultural or religious identity.

▽ **Unique look**
Body art is a way for a person to express their identity through their appearance.

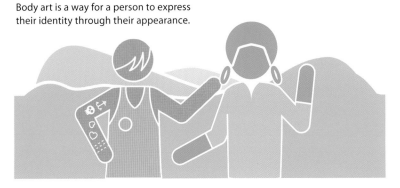

Piercings and tattoos

From ear-piercings to personalized tattoos, body art lets a person be extremely creative in how they look, but the permanence of these can be both a thrill and a problem. As a teen explores their identity during adolescence, they and their tastes change, so it's essential for an individual to think very carefully and take their time when considering getting a piercing or tattoo.

The risks

Piercings:

- can damage nerves if not done properly.

- can get infected if not cared for correctly.

- can close up if taken out for a prolonged period of time.

Tattoos:

- should be done hygienically. There are strict laws on sterilization in regard to tattoos. Using an unlicensed tattooist increases the risk of hepatitis and HIV infection.

- have a minimum age requirement, even with parental consent.

- can only be removed using a painful laser technique that breaks down the ink particles in the skin.

Gender

Many people think of gender as being female or male, and it's often thought to mean the same thing as biological sex (the hormones, sex organs, and genes a person has). In fact, it is much more complicated—a person's gender is determined by more than simply the anatomy they were born with.

SEE ALSO

❰ **16–17** Identity

❰ **22–23** Self-expression

Body image　　　　　**72–73** ❱

Confidence and self-esteem　　**86–87** ❱

Explaining gender

Gender is a concept that works on two levels. On an individual level, it refers to a combination of a person's biological sex, their sense of who they are, and the choices they make about their behavior and appearance. But on a social level, gender is a subject that explores the traditional expectations a society has about how people should look and act.

▽ **What is gender?**
Gender is based on biological sex, gender identity, and gender expression.

Biological sex
This refers to the physical characteristics with which a person is born. Some people are born male, others female. Some are intersex, which means that their biology has both male and female characteristics.

Gender identity
This is whether individuals personally think, feel, and see themselves as a man, woman, or other gender. No one else can tell someone what their gender identity is.

Gender expression
This is the way in which individuals present themselves to society through their appearance and behavior. Gender expression may or may not match a person's gender identity. It may also change depending on who they are with.

A spectrum of genders

Rather than just recognizing female and male, gender can be thought of as a wide spectrum of identities. There are many ways for a person to describe how they identify their gender.

▷ **Diversity**
There are an enormous range of gender identities. This list does not include all of them.

Cisgender
When a person's gender identity matches what their culture expects of them given their biological sex.

Transgender
Someone whose gender identity differs from what society expects given their sex at birth, such as they identify as a woman but were born male.

Agender
This term describes someone who feels they don't belong to either gender; they don't feel like either a woman or a man.

Breaking down gender stereotypes

Most societies encourage people to behave in a certain way, wear appropriate clothes, and do particular things based on conventional ideas about what it means to be a woman or a man, and to be feminine or masculine. Unfortunately, people who do not conform to these expectations may encounter disapproval from society.

Thinking more broadly about gender allows everybody to express themselves more fully. Gender stereotypes regularly appear in the media and may lead someone to feel there are things they can't or shouldn't do, but nobody should feel limited by social norms, regardless of whether they are male, female, neither, or both.

△ **Challenging social norms**
Everyone should feel able to achieve their full potential and make their own choices, free from the constraints of gender stereotypes.

Gender dysphoria

For most people, their gender identity matches their biological sex (cisgender). However, for some, the sex they were assigned at birth may not correspond with how they identify or express themselves. Gender dysphoria refers to the emotional distress a person experiences if their body doesn't match their gender identity.

A person with gender dysphoria may feel very uncomfortable with the assumptions society makes about their gender identity based on their biological sex. To match the way they feel inside, some people choose to change their name, their appearance, or their anatomy to align with how they feel.

TEEN HINTS

If you're confused

- Research other people's experiences and thoughts on gender; you're not alone in your questions.

- Talk to someone you trust—a close friend, school counselor, or support group.

- If you feel ready to share and think your parents will support you, find a time when you can talk to them alone. If you are concerned your parents will react negatively, don't feel pressured to tell them—it's okay to wait.

PARENT TIPS

If your teen needs support

- Puberty can be an upsetting time for a person with gender dysphoria, so it's important to listen carefully and take your teen's concerns seriously.

- Find resources, including books, websites, and people to help you learn more.

- Avoid pressuring your teen to behave differently. Remind them it's okay to act in a way that doesn't conform to traditional expectations.

Questioning
Refers to a person who is reluctant to label themselves while they explore their gender identity.

Genderqueer
This is someone whose gender identity does not fall easily into either woman or man; this term covers a wide range of identities.

Gender fluid
A person whose gender identity includes a range of male, female, masculine, and feminine traits. They don't consider their gender to be fixed.

Androgynous
A gender expression that includes approximately equal aspects of both the feminine and the masculine.

Female puberty

What is puberty?

During puberty, females reach physical maturity and become capable of sexual reproduction. Puberty can be a challenging time as teens transform emotionally and physically.

Reaching maturity

Both males and females begin puberty when the brain produces gonadotropin-releasing hormone (GnRH). This hormone triggers a wide range of physical and emotional changes that take place in stages, over several years, as the body develops. The process is different for everyone, but the key stages are common to all. It can be disorientating for teens, but talking to a trusted adult can help—after all, they once went through puberty, too.

GOOD TO KNOW

Body confidence

Many teen girls feel self-conscious or embarrassed about their body during puberty, but try not to worry—it happens to everyone. It's natural, and it can be exciting.

What to expect

Girls begin puberty earlier than boys do, usually between 8 and 14 years old. During puberty, with so many transformations happening, it's not unusual for tweens and teens to feel as if their body and emotions are out of control. By learning about how the body works, a teen can feel better prepared for what will happen.

Increase in height
One of the first signs of puberty, this can sometimes happen in spurts.

Growing breasts
Small "breast buds" appear under the nipple, and the breasts grow gradually larger.

Pubic hair
The hair above and around the genitals gets thicker, darker, and coarser. By the end of puberty, this hair becomes curly.

Greasy hair
Most teens find their hair gets greasy, and that they have to wash it more regularly than they did before.

Gaining weight
Bones become heavier, and an extra layer of fat stores the energy needed to support growth.

Changing emotions

For some teens, puberty brings new emotions that can be difficult to express. Many teens may be overly sensitive or irritable, or may feel angry, self-conscious, or insecure. These feelings are completely normal, but for the teen, they can sometimes seem overwhelming. Talking openly about new emotions with a friend or parent can help tweens and teens understand and reflect upon how they are feeling.

△ **Mood swings**
A teen's mood can often swing up and down abruptly. Teens might feel grumpy one minute and be laughing the next.

△ **Romantic feelings**
During puberty, teens may start to feel attracted to other people. This can be exciting, but also a bit confusing.

First period
Menstruation is probably the biggest change a young woman experiences during puberty.

Sweat and smells
During the teen years, the body starts to produce more sweat, which can cause body odor and smelly feet.

Armpit hair
Under the arms, the hair gets darker, longer, and thicker.

Pimples
Pimples are a common teenage complaint, caused by clogged pores and trapped bacteria.

Wider hips
The hips widen in preparation for giving birth at some point in the future.

Female hormones

Hormones are chemicals produced in the body that send instructions to cells. Each hormone can only affect specific target cells, which contain the appropriate receptor for that hormone.

Kickstarting puberty

At the start of puberty, gonadotropin-releasing hormone (GnRH) in the brain signals to the body that it's ready to start developing into an adult. GnRH causes an increase in the level of the primary sex hormones in females and males—estrogen in females, and testosterone in males. As puberty continues, these and other hormones regulate and monitor each stage of development.

▽ **Chemical messengers**
Blood vessels transport hormones from the endocrine glands to specific cells around the body, where they stimulate change.

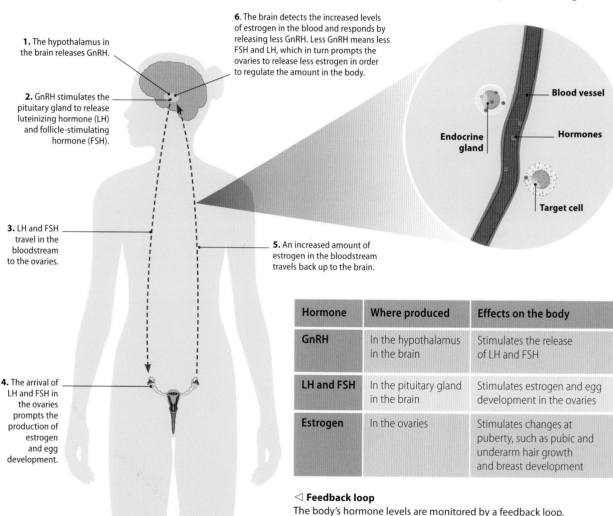

1. The hypothalamus in the brain releases GnRH.

2. GnRH stimulates the pituitary gland to release luteinizing hormone (LH) and follicle-stimulating hormone (FSH).

3. LH and FSH travel in the bloodstream to the ovaries.

4. The arrival of LH and FSH in the ovaries prompts the production of estrogen and egg development.

5. An increased amount of estrogen in the bloodstream travels back up to the brain.

6. The brain detects the increased levels of estrogen in the blood and responds by releasing less GnRH. Less GnRH means less FSH and LH, which in turn prompts the ovaries to release less estrogen in order to regulate the amount in the body.

Blood vessel

Endocrine gland

Hormones

Target cell

Hormone	Where produced	Effects on the body
GnRH	In the hypothalamus in the brain	Stimulates the release of LH and FSH
LH and FSH	In the pituitary gland in the brain	Stimulates estrogen and egg development in the ovaries
Estrogen	In the ovaries	Stimulates changes at puberty, such as pubic and underarm hair growth and breast development

◁ **Feedback loop**
The body's hormone levels are monitored by a feedback loop. The amount of a hormone in the bloodstream signals to the brain whether more or less is required.

Primary female sex hormones

The two primary female sex hormones are estrogen and progesterone. The changing level of each of these hormones prompts sexual characteristics to develop during puberty and regulates the menstrual cycle.

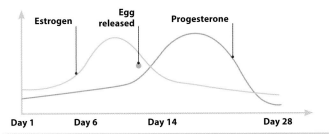

Estrogen

Estrogen is the main female sex hormone at work during puberty. It causes the ovaries to produce eggs and prepare them for the possibility of sexual reproduction. During puberty, estrogen is responsible for promoting the development of sexual characteristics, such as breasts and pubic hair. After puberty, it regulates the menstrual cycle.

Progesterone

Progesterone is present in female and male children at low levels. In females, progesterone comes into effect at the start of the first period. It builds and maintains the lining of the uterus, ready to receive an egg if it's fertilized. If the egg isn't fertilized, progesterone levels drop dramatically, causing the lining of the uterus to be shed during a period.

Shared hormones

Estrogen, progesterone, and testosterone are present in both females and males, but in vastly different amounts. Throughout their lives, females continue to produce low levels of testosterone and males produce some estrogen and progesterone. In females, testosterone is linked to maintaining bone and muscle mass, and contributes to the sex drive. In males, estrogen controls body fat and contributes to the sex drive, while progesterone monitors testosterone production. Hormone levels differ between people and change over a lifetime.

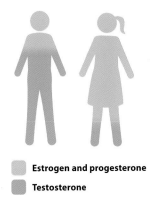

■ Estrogen and progesterone

■ Testosterone

△ **Hormone levels**
Females produce twice as much estrogen and progesterone as males, but ten times less testosterone.

Other hormones

Hormones don't just prompt the start of puberty and the development of sexual characteristics. There are lots of different types at work in everybody, regardless of sex, that control and coordinate many bodily functions to keep the body healthy.

Maintaining a healthy body

- Antidiuretic hormone (ADH) keeps the body's water levels balanced.
- Melatonin allows the body to sleep at night and stay awake during the day.
- Thyroxine determines how quickly or slowly the body metabolizes food.

Managing food processes

- Leptin regulates the appetite by making the body feel full after eating.
- Gastrin triggers gastric acid in the stomach, which breaks down food.
- Insulin and glucagon control how much sugar is released into the blood after eating.

Coping with stress

- Adrenaline raises the heart rate and produces energy when a person is under stress.
- Cortisol manages the brain's use of sugars, providing more energy.
- Oxytocin enables bonds with other people by reducing fear and creating feelings of trust.

Changing body

Puberty can be a challenging time, with the body going through many changes—both inside and out. Everybody goes through puberty, but each teen's experience is unique to them.

What to expect

These are the most common changes that females experience, but they happen at different times for everyone.

▽ **Child**   ▽ **Tween**   ▽ **Teen**   ▽ **Adult**

Getting taller
Growing in height is one of the first signs of puberty, beginning between the ages of 9 and 15 years. When and how much a person grows depends on the individual.

Growing breasts
Small bumps under the nipple, known as "breast buds," start to develop around 9 to 10 years old. Over time the breasts become larger and rounder.

   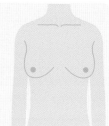

Underarm hair
Coarser, darker hair grows under both arms. Some teens choose to remove this hair as they get older, but doing so is based on personal preference.

Wider hips and pubic hair
During puberty, the hips get wider and curvier, and the thighs gain more body fat. Pubic hair grows longer and thicker to protect the genitals.

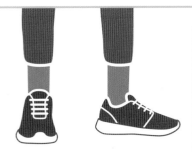

Growth spurts

Between the ages of 11 and 15 years, females grow up to 3 in (8 cm) per year, with periods of rapid growth affecting different parts of the body at different times. The hands and feet usually grow first, followed by the arms and legs, with the spine and torso growing last. The hands and feet usually grow first, followed by the arms and legs, with the spine and torso growing last. These differently timed growth rates can cause clumsiness, as the muscles needed to keep teens balanced play catch-up, and the part of the brain that deals with spatial awareness adjusts to the individual's new height and body proportions.

Puberty problems

The average age for females to start puberty is 11 years old, but it can start at any point from 8 to 14 years old. If someone starts puberty before the age of 8, it's called "precocious puberty." If this occurs, it's best to see a doctor to see why the body has kickstarted puberty so early. It may lead to an early growth spurt that also stops sooner than it should, leaving them shorter than average as an adult. Similarly, if puberty occurs much later than 14 years of age, medical advice should be sought.

▷ **Different rates**
If a teen is concerned about their development, visiting a doctor should help reassure them.

Building body confidence

Feeling confident on the inside makes a big difference when a teen is dealing with the many changes taking place on the outside. The important thing is not to worry about what is happening to other people, because everyone matures differently.

△ **Focus on the positives**
Think about the incredible things the body can do, such as dance, run, and sing.

Embracing change

- Your body lets you participate in exciting activities—focus on what it can do, rather than how it looks.
- Speak to yourself as you would speak to a friend, give yourself compliments, and avoid putting yourself down.
- Choose clothes that make you feel good, and focus on the parts of the body you like best.

Supporting your teen

- Try to make this exciting life stage feel positive, in order to build your teen's self-esteem about who they are becoming.
- Providing your teen with all the information and practical stuff they might need can help them feel better prepared to manage the physical changes when they happen.
- If you're embarrassed about broaching these topics, acknowledge it to your teen – it will help your teen to see that being honest about their body is healthy.

Female sex organs

The female sex organs have two main functions. The ovaries store and release the eggs needed for sexual reproduction, while the uterus supports and carries a baby as it develops during pregnancy.

On the inside

The internal sex organs are located between the bladder at the front of the body and the rectum at the back. They include the uterus, the vagina, and two ovaries. Knowing the function of each part helps teens understand how the female body works and why females have regular periods.

▽ **Internal sex organs**
The primary function of the internal sex organs is sexual reproduction.

GOOD TO KNOW

Vaginal discharge

During puberty, females will start to notice a clear, yellow, or white fluid in their underwear. This fluid, known as vaginal discharge, is produced by the cervix. This discharge helps to clean and moisten the vagina, and to prevent infection. If, however, the fluid changes color, or is smelly, lumpy, or itchy, then speak to a doctor.

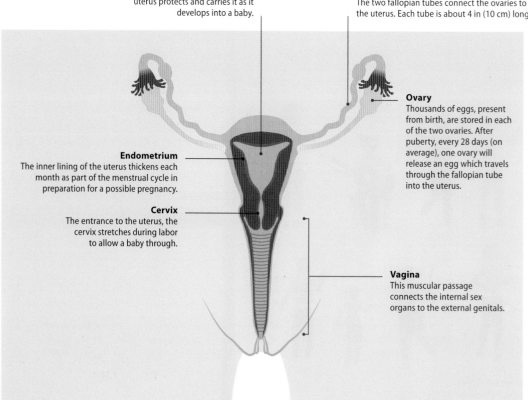

Uterus
The uterus is about 3 in (7.5 cm) long and 2 in (5 cm) wide. If the female sex cell, known as the egg, is fertilized, the uterus protects and carries it as it develops into a baby.

Fallopian tube
The two fallopian tubes connect the ovaries to the uterus. Each tube is about 4 in (10 cm) long.

Ovary
Thousands of eggs, present from birth, are stored in each of the two ovaries. After puberty, every 28 days (on average), one ovary will release an egg which travels through the fallopian tube into the uterus.

Endometrium
The inner lining of the uterus thickens each month as part of the menstrual cycle in preparation for a possible pregnancy.

Cervix
The entrance to the uterus, the cervix stretches during labor to allow a baby through.

Vagina
This muscular passage connects the internal sex organs to the external genitals.

On the outside

The external sex organs, known as the vulva or genitals, are located between the legs. There is a lot of variation in the shape, size, and color of female genitals. Everybody's genitals are unique and a teen should never worry that hers should look a certain way.

The hymen

Females are born with a hymen, a thin membrane of skin covering the vaginal opening, but over time it wears away. Playing certain sports can cause the hymen to disintegrate, but if it hasn't already done so by puberty, hormones cause it to break down to allow vaginal discharge and menstrual blood to leave the body.

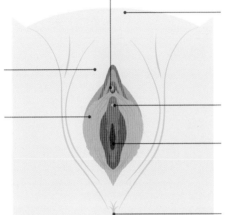

Clitoris
This internal system is actually much bigger than what is visible externally. The clitoris swells during sexual arousal, and its tip contains thousands of sensitive nerve endings.

External labia
The outer lips protect the vaginal opening.

Internal labia
These protective inner folds of skin are often longer than the external labia.

Mons pubis
This fatty tissue over the pubic bones is generally covered in pubic hair after the onset of puberty.

Urethral opening
The urethra connects to the bladder and is where urine is expelled from the body.

Vaginal opening
This opening can shrink or expand during sex or childbirth.

Anus
Situated at the end of the rectum between the buttocks, this is where feces is expelled from the body. It sits close to the genitals but is not part of them.

◁ **The vulva**
This term refers to the external female genitals, which are full of nerves that play a role in sexual arousal.

Shapes and sizes

Each female's genitals are different. Some have a bigger internal labia than external, while for others the opposite is true. The size of the clitoris also varies.

Staying healthy

Practicing good hygiene reduces the possibility of genital infections. After going to the bathroom, girls should always wipe from front to back to avoid spreading bacteria from the anus to the vagina. Washing the genital area every day and patting it dry thoroughly afterward, as well as wearing clean underwear, helps to keep it healthy. The vagina cleans itself, so it's not necessary to wash inside.

Using a mirror

Using a small mirror to look between your legs, it's possible to get to know your genitals and see what part is where. Learn what's normal for you, so that you can recognize if there are any changes down there.

The menstrual cycle

The menstrual cycle is the process that enables a female's body to make a baby. The cycle is counted from the first day of a period to the day before the start of the next period.

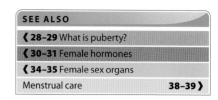

SEE ALSO

❮ **28-29** What is puberty?
❮ **30-31** Female hormones
❮ **34-35** Female sex organs
Menstrual care   **38-39** ❯

How it works

The female hormones, estrogen and progesterone, regulate the menstrual cycle. As the levels of these hormones rise and fall, the menstrual cycle progresses. Its four stages take 28 days on average, but can last from 21 up to 35 days. The length of each stage may vary.

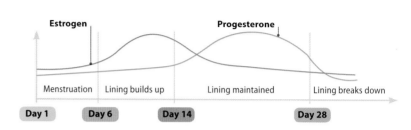

Estrogen | Progesterone

Menstruation | Lining builds up | Lining maintained | Lining breaks down

Day 1 | **Day 6** | **Day 14** | **Day 28**

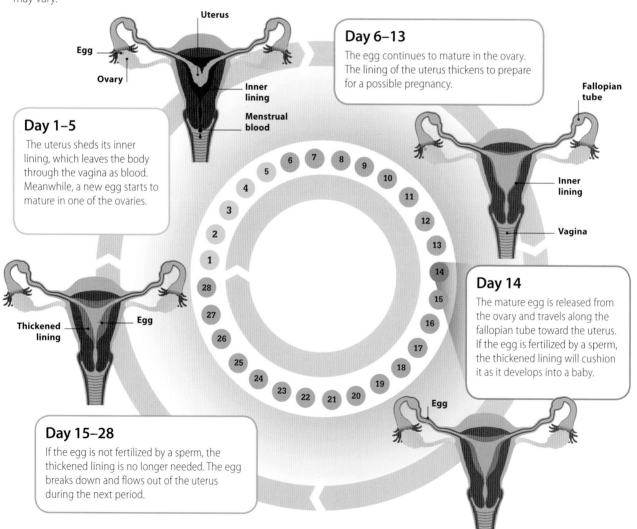

Day 6–13

The egg continues to mature in the ovary. The lining of the uterus thickens to prepare for a possible pregnancy.

Day 1–5

The uterus sheds its inner lining, which leaves the body through the vagina as blood. Meanwhile, a new egg starts to mature in one of the ovaries.

Day 14

The mature egg is released from the ovary and travels along the fallopian tube toward the uterus. If the egg is fertilized by a sperm, the thickened lining will cushion it as it develops into a baby.

Day 15–28

If the egg is not fertilized by a sperm, the thickened lining is no longer needed. The egg breaks down and flows out of the uterus during the next period.

Labels: Uterus, Egg, Ovary, Inner lining, Menstrual blood, Fallopian tube, Inner lining, Vagina, Thickened lining, Egg, Egg

Being prepared

Most girls have their first period, known as menarche, around the age of 12, although it's not uncommon to start earlier or later. Feeling apprehensive is natural, but talking to a trusted adult can help a teen feel more prepared. Once a teen starts noticing vaginal discharge (white or yellow fluid) in her underwear, it's useful to have sanitary protection and spare underwear on hand, as the first period is likely to happen soon.

What to expect

- Your period normally starts about two years after your breasts start developing and about a year after pubic hair starts to grow.

- There probably won't be a sudden gush of blood. In fact, many girls don't notice at first. There might be a feeling of dampness or a few spots of blood in your underwear.

- A period usually lasts three to seven days. The amount of blood lost during a period is very small, typically between 3 and 5 tablespoons, though it may seem like more.

- Menstrual blood can be bright red, dark red, or brown, and is made up of the discarded lining of the uterus.

- Nobody else knows if you have your period, unless you tell them.

Ups and downs

Feeling tired or emotional in the days leading up to a period is completely normal. Some people also experience bloating, breast tenderness, backaches, or cramping and abdominal pain. These symptoms are referred to as premenstrual syndrome (PMS) and are caused by changing hormone levels.

PMS can start up to ten days to two weeks before a period, but everyone is different. Taking painkillers, relaxing with a hot-water bottle, or doing some exercise can soothe physical discomfort.

▷ **Feel-good chemicals**
Exercise releases endorphins, natural painkillers that elevate a person's mood.

Premenstrual syndrome (PMS)

There are ways to make PMS feel more manageable.

- Let people know how you are feeling.

- Eat healthy and get a good night's sleep.

- Stay active and exercise.

- Recognize how PMS affects your mood.

- See a doctor if PMS symptoms are very severe.

Irregular periods

In the first couple of years, the amount of blood lost each period can vary. It is also common for periods to happen irregularly, but over time the menstrual cycle should settle into a pattern.

It's important to see a doctor if periods were once regular but then stop, if they are exceptionally painful, or if the amount of bleeding increases. If a teen has had sex and misses a period, it may be a sign that she is pregnant.

△ **Keeping track**
Making a note on a phone or calendar can help with predicting when the next period might be due.

Living life

Although they can sometimes be uncomfortable, periods shouldn't restrict someone's lifestyle. With sanitary protection, everyone should feel confident and able to do the activities they love.

Menstrual care

Menstrual care products are designed to keep girls and women feeling comfortable during their period. There are many products, but all enable someone who's menstruating to conveniently dispose of their shed menstrual blood in a way that meets their own needs.

SEE ALSO

❰ 28–29 What is puberty?
❰ 30–31 Female hormones
❰ 34–35 Female sex organs
❰ 36–37 The menstrual cycle

Individual choice

There are lots of options available to deal with menstrual blood lost during a period. Many teens start out using menstrual pads and continue to use them, while others try other options, such as tampons and menstrual cups. Whatever product somebody chooses, it can take practice to become familiar with how to use it effectively. It's worth talking to an adult or friend to see what they've found works best for them.

ALERT!

Proper disposal

Menstrual pads can be rolled into the wrapper of the next pad, and tampons into toilet paper, before being placed in a trash can. Empty menstrual cups directly into the toilet before cleaning. Never flush menstrual products down the toilet.

◁ **Many options available**
Choose a product that's comfortable and convenient.

Menstrual pads

Made of a cottonlike material, menstrual pads protect clothes and help avoid discomfort by absorbing the blood of a period and keeping it away from the body. To suit people's needs at different stages of their period, there are three main types of menstrual pad, which come in different sizes and thicknesses. Making a decision about which to use depends on the heaviness or lightness of a period.

▽ **Pads**
These have an adhesive underside to keep the menstrual pad fixed in place.

△ **Panty liner**
These thinner, lighter pads are used when a period is light or very light, known as spotting.

△ **Pad**
These thicker and more absorbent pads are used when the blood lost during a period is medium to heavy.

△ **Pad with wings**
Sticky side panels can be folded over the sides of underwear to improve protection and help users feel more secure.

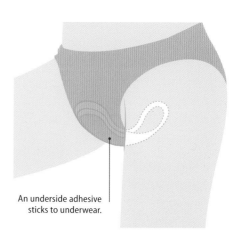

An underside adhesive sticks to underwear.

Tampons

A tampon is a small, compact roll of soft material that is placed inside the vagina to soak up menstrual blood. Tampons must be changed about every four to six hours. There are different sizes and absorbancies available, according to whether a period is light, medium, or heavy.

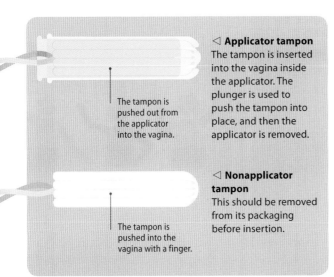

◁ **Applicator tampon**
The tampon is inserted into the vagina inside the applicator. The plunger is used to push the tampon into place, and then the applicator is removed.

The tampon is pushed out from the applicator into the vagina.

◁ **Nonapplicator tampon**
This should be removed from its packaging before insertion.

The tampon is pushed into the vagina with a finger.

Toxic shock syndrome (TSS)

TSS is a rare but dangerous condition that may cause flulike symptoms, a high temperature, and a rash. It is caused by toxins produced by bacteria that can build up in the vagina when using a tampon. To reduce the risk, change tampons every four to six hours, always wash your hands before insertion and removal, and use the lowest size and absorbancy for the heaviness of your period.

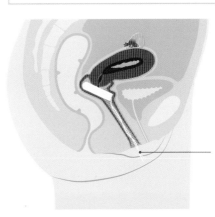

◁ **Position**
The tampon should be placed high up in the vagina, near the opening of the cervix.

The string helps make removing the tampon easier.

Menstrual cups

Made of flexible silicone, a menstrual cup is a reusable product worn inside the vagina to collect menstrual blood, rather than absorb it. During a period, it needs to be emptied, rinsed, and replaced every four to eight hours. At the end of a period, it should be washed with unscented soap and water, and stored in a clean place. The sizes are not related to menstrual flow, but to the user's age and whether or not she has given birth.

The truth about menstrual care

You'll still be a virgin if you use a tampon or menstrual cup. A virgin is a person who hasn't had sex.

A tampon or menstrual cup can't get lost. The cervix is too small for a tampon or menstrual cup to pass through.

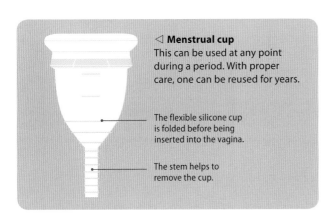

◁ **Menstrual cup**
This can be used at any point during a period. With proper care, one can be reused for years.

The flexible silicone cup is folded before being inserted into the vagina.

The stem helps to remove the cup.

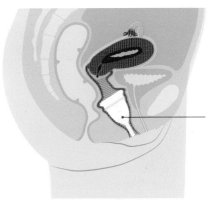

◁ **Position**
These should be placed as low as is comfortable in the vagina, with the stem sitting just inside the vagina.

The cup creates a seal within the vagina to stop blood leaking.

Breasts

On average, females will start to grow breasts between the ages of 9 and 13 years old, and they usually take 5–6 years to develop fully. Some can't wait for their breasts to develop, but others might feel nervous or uncomfortable as their body changes.

SEE ALSO
❮ **28–29** What is puberty?
❮ **30–31** Female hormones
❮ **32–33** Changing body
Bras   **42–43** ❯

How they work

Breasts are made up of glands and fatty tissue, and lie over the pectoral muscles at the top of the torso. They continue up into the armpits. During puberty, female breasts grow bigger and rounder in response to increased levels of estrogen. As males have low levels of estrogen, their breasts do not typically develop.

A primary function of female breasts is to produce milk to feed and nourish a baby, in a process called lactation, which is controlled by the hormone oxytocin. When the baby sucks on its mother's nipple, a network of ducts transport the milk through the breast and out through tiny holes in the nipple.

TEEN HINTS

Love your breasts

There is no standard breast or nipple shape. They come in all different shapes, sizes, and colors and all are perfectly natural. Try to love yours, no matter what they look like!

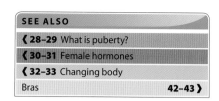

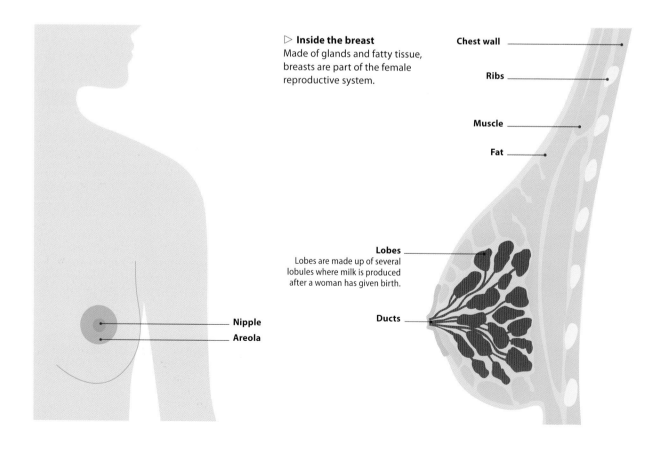

▷ **Inside the breast**
Made of glands and fatty tissue, breasts are part of the female reproductive system.

Chest wall

Ribs

Muscle

Fat

Lobes
Lobes are made up of several lobules where milk is produced after a woman has given birth.

Ducts

Nipple
Areola

Breast development

The breast bud—a small, firm bump that appears under the nipple and surrounding areola—is one of the first signs of puberty. It usually appears between the ages of 9 and 10 due to an increase in the body's level of estrogen, one of the female sex hormones. At first, breast buds might feel tender, or sore, but this should pass.

Over time, as glandular tissue and fatty tissue develop, the breasts grow bigger and rounder. The areola darkens and becomes enlarged. The nipples may start to protrude outward from the breast.

△ **Stages of growth**
Breast development is triggered by the female sex hormone estrogen.

Common concerns

Teens may sometimes worry about their breasts and how they look. Here are the most common concerns:

Developing early or late

Everyone develops at different times. How fast breasts grow is not related to what they will eventually look like.

Asymmetrical breasts

Most of the time breasts will gradually become more even, but natural breasts are not completely symmetrical.

Tenderness

Some teens experience breast tenderness in the days leading up to a period, but this should end with the period.

Inverted nipples

Some teens find their nipples go into the breast. They may pop out eventually, but some never do. This is nothing to worry about.

Hairy nipples

Hair around the nipples is completely normal. Plucking the hair is fine if a person doesn't like the way it looks.

Stretch marks

Breast tissue may grow faster than the skin on the surface. This can cause fine lines, called stretch marks, to appear, but they will fade over time.

Self-checks

Girls and women should check their breasts regularly and get to know how they feel at different times in their menstrual cycle. This will allow them to notice any changes sooner. If there are any changes, or if there is pain or discharge, it's best to see a doctor as quickly as possible.

1. Stand in front of a mirror and look at both breasts for any changes in shape, size, or asymmetry.

2. Clasp hands behind the head and press hands forward to tense the muscles. Check for changes in the skin or nipple, and for discharge.

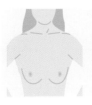

3. Press hands firmly on hips and bow slightly forward. Look for any visible changes.

4. Lie down with one arm above the head. Press small circles all around the flesh of each breast, including the nipple and armpit. Feel for any changes in the breast tissue.

Bras

Wearing a bra provides support for the breast tissue and makes some girls and women feel more comfortable. There are many different styles, colors, and designs available.

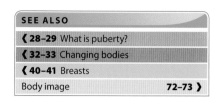

SEE ALSO
❮ 28–29 What is puberty?
❮ 32–33 Changing bodies
❮ 40–41 Breasts
Body image   72–73 ❯

Getting measured

Choosing the correct bra size is very important, as a poorly fitting bra can affect posture and potentially cause back pain. It is possible to work out the right bra size at home, but in order to ensure a bra fits properly, it's best to get fitted in a store by a bra-fitting expert. It's okay to feel embarrassed, but it helps to remember that professional bra fitters are experienced and regularly measure people for their first bra. They should be kind and understanding.

▷ **Measuring for a bra**
To work out the correct bra size, two measurements are needed.

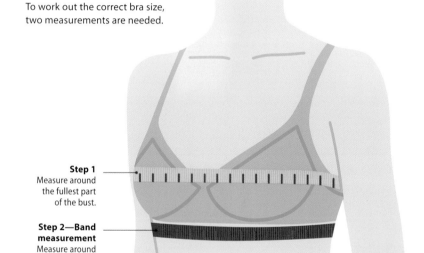

Step 1
Measure around the fullest part of the bust.

Step 2—Band measurement
Measure around the body just under the breasts.

Step 1
Measure around the fullest part of the bust, in line with the nipples. The measuring tape should be straight across the back. Record this number in inches.

Step 2—Band measurement
Measure around the body underneath the breasts, next to the rib cage, again making sure the measuring tape is straight across the back. Record this number in inches. This is the band measurement.

Step 3
Subtract the second measurement from the first. The difference between the two measurements indicates the cup size.

A = Up to 1 in (2.5 cm)
B = Up to 2 in (5 cm)
C = Up to 3 in (8 cm)
D = Up to 4 in (10 cm)
DD = Up to 5 in (13 cm)
E = Up to 6 in (15 cm)

When to get fitted

The average age to start wearing a bra is 11 years old, but everyone develops at different rates. A girl might feel she needs more support when breast buds appear or when some sports start to feel uncomfortable. At that point, it is worth starting to think about getting measured. There are training bras and crop tops available for those who might not have developed yet but want to wear a bra.

The right fit

Getting the right fit is essential for breast and back health. A bra should be so comfortable it feels like a part of the body and should give a teen confidence. It's important to keep reassessing the size of the breasts throughout life, as they can be affected by changing hormones during pregnancy and menopause.

▷ **Front fitting**

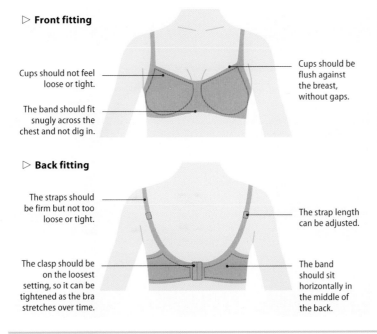

Cups should not feel loose or tight.

The band should fit snugly across the chest and not dig in.

Cups should be flush against the breast, without gaps.

▷ **Back fitting**

The straps should be firm but not too loose or tight.

The clasp should be on the loosest setting, so it can be tightened as the bra stretches over time.

The strap length can be adjusted.

The band should sit horizontally in the middle of the back.

The wrong fit

Up to 70–80 percent of women are thought to wear the wrong bra size. Uncomfortable, badly fitting bras fail to give support and can cause the breasts to move or lead to backaches.

◁ **Straps too tight**
The strap at the back should be horizontal and not ride up. Loosen the straps to the correct length.

◁ **Overspilling**
The breasts should sit comfortably within the cup. A larger cup size may be needed to fully enclose the breast.

◁ **Underfilling**
There shouldn't be a gap between the breast and bra cup. A smaller cup size may help.

Types of bras

Bras have different purposes depending on the wearer's needs. They can also come in all sorts of styles. It can be hard to know what to choose at first, so asking for help is a great way to explore options.

Training bra or first bra

These lightweight bras are useful when breasts first start to grow, but are not yet big enough to fit a standard bra. They usually look like crop tops.

Underwire

These bras have a wire underneath to give the lining of a bra added support and structure.

Sports bra

These bras are higher cut and extra supportive, thereby minimizing discomfort caused by movement during exercise.

Soft cup bra or T-shirt bra

These bras are wire-free with soft cups. They are good for everyday use.

Male puberty

What is puberty?

During puberty, males reach physical maturity and become capable of sexual reproduction. With emotional and physical changes all happening at once, puberty can be a challenging time for teens.

Reaching maturity

For males and females, puberty starts when the brain produces gonadotropin-releasing hormone (GnRH). This hormone kickstarts a number of emotional and physical changes that happen in stages, over several years. Everyone experiences puberty differently, but there are key stages common to all. The transformation can be disorientating for teens, but talking it over with a trusted adult can help—after all, they once went through puberty, too.

GOOD TO KNOW

Body confidence

It's normal to feel self-conscious or embarrassed about your body during puberty. Try not to worry—it's a natural process that everyone goes through, and it can be fun.

What to expect

On average, males start puberty a year later than females, normally between the ages of 9 and 14. During puberty, with so many changes happening, it's not unusual for tweens and teens to feel as if their body and emotions are out of control. In order for teens to feel better prepared for puberty, it helps to learn about how the body works and what to expect.

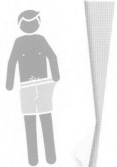

Body hair
Thicker, darker, and coarser hair starts growing in the pubic region and on the legs and chest. By the end of puberty, this hair becomes curly.

Sweat and smells
A teen's body starts to produce more sweat, which can cause body odor and smelly feet.

More testosterone
Increased testosterone makes males stronger, but can influence mood and disturb sleep patterns.

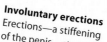

Involuntary erections
Erections—a stiffening of the penis—start to occur. They can happen during sleep, throughout the day, or when a person sees someone they fancy.

Bigger genitals
Over the course of puberty, the penis lengthens, and the testicles grow larger.

Changing emotions

For some teens, puberty brings new emotions that can be difficult to express. Teens often have periods when they feel overly sensitive, irritable, angry, self-conscious, or insecure. These feelings are completely natural, but for the teen, they can sometimes seem overwhelming. To help tweens and teens cope with the emotional side of puberty, talking to a friend or adult can provide an opportunity to reflect on new feelings.

△ **Aggression**
Extra testosterone can dramatically affect a teen boy's mood, and may lead to mood swings and increased aggression.

△ **Romantic feelings**
One exciting but confusing change at puberty is the onset of romantic feelings toward other people.

Pimples
The skin begins to produce an oily substance known as sebum, which can lead to pimples.

Wet dreams
The testicles start to produce sperm, which is released sometimes from the penis in a fluid called semen, during sleep. This is often called a "wet dream".

Growing bigger
Teens get taller, by up to 3.5 in (9 cm) in a year, and testosterone and other hormones cause their muscles and bones to develop.

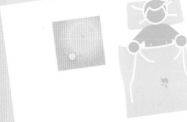

Deeper voice
An increase in the body's testosterone levels causes the larynx (or "voice box") to enlarge and change shape. This results in the voice becoming deeper, or "breaking."

Facial and armpit hair
Soft hair starts to appear on the face and in the armpits. Many boys choose to shave off their facial hair.

Male hormones

Hormones are chemicals produced in the body that send instructions to cells. Each hormone can only affect specific target cells, which contain the appropriate receptor for that hormone.

Kickstarting puberty

At the start of puberty, gonadotropin-releasing hormone (GnRH) in the brain signals to the body that it's ready to start developing into an adult. GnRH causes an increase in the level of the primary sex hormones in males and females—testosterone in males, and estrogen in females. As puberty continues, these and other hormones regulate and monitor each stage of development.

▽ **Chemical messsengers**
Blood vessels transport hormones from the endocrine glands to specific cells around the body, where they stimulate change.

6. The brain detects the increased levels of testosterone in the blood and responds by releasing less GnRH. Less GnRH means less FSH and LH, which in turn prompts the testicles to release less testosterone in order to regulate the amount in the body.

1. The hypothalamus in the brain releases GnRH.

2. GnRH stimulates the pituitary gland to release luteinizing hormone (LH) and follicle-stimulating hormone (FSH).

3. LH and FSH travel in the bloodstream to the testicles.

5. An increased amount of testosterone in the bloodstream travels back up to the brain.

4. The arrival of LH and FSH in the testicles prompts the production of testosterone and sperm.

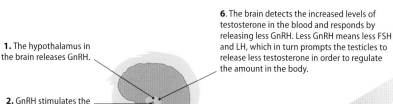

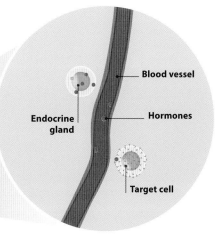

Blood vessel

Hormones

Endocrine gland

Target cell

Hormone	Where produced	Effects on the body
GnRH	In the hypothalamus in the brain	Stimulates the pituitary gland to release LH and FSH
LH and FSH	In the pituitary gland in the brain	Stimulates testosterone and sperm production in the testicles
Testosterone	In the testicles	Stimulates changes at puberty, such as the enlargement of the testicles and penis

◁ **Feedback loop**
The body's hormone levels are monitored by a feedback loop. The amount of a hormone in the bloodstream signals to the brain whether more or less is required.

Testosterone

Testosterone is the game changer during puberty. It is converted in the testicles to dihydrotestosterone (DHT)—the active form of the hormone—and is regulated by low levels of progesterone.

It is DHT that causes the changes to a male's body during puberty. DHT works on target organs to help the genitals to grow, as well as to develop pubic, body, and facial hair. It also helps the prostate gland to grow, helping semen production. The amount of testosterone in the body controls the levels of DHT.

△ **Getting bigger**
Different levels of testosterone cause males to mature at different rates.

Shared hormones

Estrogen, progesterone, and testosterone are present in both females and males, but in vastly different amounts. Throughout their lives, males produce some estrogen and progesterone and females continue to produce low levels of testosterone. In males, estrogen controls body fat and contributes to the sex drive, while progesterone monitors testosterone production. In females, testosterone is linked to maintaining bone and muscle mass, and contributes to the sex drive. Hormone levels differ between people and change over a lifetime.

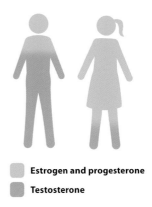

■ **Estrogen and progesterone**

■ **Testosterone**

△ **Hormone levels**
Males produce ten times more testosterone than females, but only half the amount of estrogen and progesterone.

Other hormones

Hormones don't just prompt the start of puberty and the development of sexual characteristics. There are lots of different types at work in everybody, regardless of sex, that control and coordinate many bodily functions to keep the body healthy.

Maintaining a healthy body

- Antidiuretic hormone (ADH) keeps the body's water levels balanced.
- Melatonin allows the body to sleep at night and stay awake during the day.
- Thyroxine determines how quickly or slowly the body metabolizes food.

Managing food processes

- Leptin regulates the appetite by making the body feel full after eating.
- Gastrin triggers gastric acid in the stomach, which breaks down food.
- Insulin and glucagon control how much sugar is released into the blood after eating.

Coping with stress

- Adrenaline raises the heart rate and produces energy when a person is under stress.
- Cortisol manages the brain's use of sugars, providing more energy.
- Oxytocin enables bonds with other people by reducing fear and creating feelings of trust.

Changing body

Puberty can be a challenging time, with the body going through many changes—both inside and out. Everybody goes through puberty, but every teen's experience is unique to them.

SEE ALSO	
❮ 46–47 What is puberty?	
❮ 48–49 Male hormones	
Testicles	52–53 ❯
The penis	54–55 ❯

What to expect

These are the most common changes that males experience, but they happen at different times for everyone.

▽ **Child** ▽ **Tween** ▽ **Teen** ▽ **Adult**

Getting taller

Growing in height is one of the first signs of puberty, beginning between the ages of 10 and 16 years. When and how much a person grows depends on the individual.

Facial hair

Testosterone triggers hair growth on the face. At first, the hair is sparse and thin, but it becomes thicker and more prominent over time.

Broader chest and shoulders

The chest broadens and becomes wider as a male matures. The chest muscles also start to develop and become more pronounced. Some males also grow chest hair.

Bigger penis and testicles

The penis and testicles increase in size, the scrotum darkens, pubic hair grows, and the testicles start to produce sperm.

Puberty problems

The average age for puberty to start in males is 12 years old, although it can be anytime between the ages of 9 and 14. If puberty starts before 9 years old, it is called "precocious puberty." If this occurs, it's best to see a doctor to find out why the body has triggered puberty early. It may lead to an early growth spurt that then also stops sooner than it should, leaving a person shorter than average as an adult. Similarly, if puberty occurs much later than 14 years of age, with no testicular development, medical advice should be sought.

GOOD TO KNOW

Gynecomastia

Gynecomastia, otherwise known as "man boobs" or "moobs," may be caused by changing hormone levels, which can make a male's "breasts" swell. This is a common, temporary occurrence that usually resolves itself between six months and two years. However, if the swelling persists or there are any asymmetrical changes in breast size, or lumps or bumps on the chest, see a doctor.

Growth spurts

Between the ages of 12 and 15 years, males grow an average of 3–3.5 in (7–9 cm) per year, with periods of rapid growth affecting different parts of the body at different times. The hands and feet usually grow first, followed by the arms and legs, with the spine and torso growing last.

These differently timed growth rates can often cause clumsiness in teens, as the muscles needed to keep them balanced play catch-up, and the part of the brain that deals with spatial awareness takes time to adjust to the individual's new body proportions.

Building body confidence

Feeling confident on the inside makes a big difference when a teen is dealing with the many changes taking place outside the body. The important thing is not to worry about what is happening to other people, as everyone matures differently.

△ **Focus on the positives**
Think about the incredible things the body can do, such as dance, run, and sing.

TEEN HINTS

Embracing change

- Your body lets you participate in exciting activities—focus on what it can do, rather than how it looks.

- Speak to yourself positively. Give yourself compliments as a friend would, and avoid putting yourself down.

- Choose clothes that make you feel good, and focus on the parts of your body you like best.

PARENT TIPS

Supporting your teen

- Try to make this exciting life stage feel positive, to build your teen's self-esteem about who they are becoming.

- Providing your teen with all the information and practical stuff they might need can help them feel better prepared to manage the physical changes when they happen.

- If you're embarrassed about broaching these topics, acknowledge it to your teen—it will help your teen to see that being honest about their body is healthy.

Testicles

Testicles are part of the male reproductive system. Each testicle is a factory producing sperm, the male sex cells. Testosterone, the hormone that controls the development of male puberty, is also made in the testicles.

How they work

Two testicles are housed in a protective pouch of skin called the scrotum. The scrotum helps keep the temperature of the testicles slightly cooler than the body's core temperature of 99°F (37°C). The testicles hang outside the body, because they produce sperm best at about 95°F (35°C). To stop them bumping into each other, it's common for one testicle to hang lower than the other. It's also perfectly normal for them not to be symmetrical.

▽ **Sperm**
Each sperm contains genetic information from the male, and its function is to move toward and fuse with an egg, the female sex cell, during sexual reproduction. Sperm live only for a few days.

Midpiece
This contains mitochondria, which release energy that helps the sperm to move.

▽ **Inside the testicle**
The average testicle is small, oval-shaped, and about 2 in (5 cm) in length from end to end. After puberty starts, each testicle continues making around 3,000 sperm per second, until the end of a man's life.

Acrosome
The caplike coating of a sperm helps it to enter the egg during sexual reproduction.

Vas deferens
This is a long, wide tube through which sperm travels from the epididymis to the penis.

Nucleus
The nucleus contains 23 chromosomes, which carry genetic information.

Epididymis
Sperm mature in the epididymis by developing the ability to move and to fertilize an egg.

Tail
The tail allows the sperm to propel itself forward.

Seminiferous tubules
Sperm are produced in the seminiferous tubules. These tubules account for about 95 percent of a testicle's volume.

Scrotum
Muscles in the scrotum pull the testicle up into the body and wrinkle the scrotal skin to prevent heat loss when it's cold.

Self-checks

Although testicular cancer is uncommon in young people, it's important for a person to get into the habit of examining their testicles once a month from the age of about 15. This is to check that they're healthy. It's easy to do, and takes just a few minutes. The best time to examine the testicles is after a shower or bath, as the warm water relaxes the scrotum, making it easier to feel inside.

1. The testicles
Gently roll each testicle between thumb and fingers. Apply a little pressure at times. Feel for any pain, lumps, or swelling.

2. The epididymis
Inspect the epididymis, the comma-shaped cord behind each testicle. It's important to learn what the epididymis feels like, as it can be mistaken for a lump or swelling.

3. The vas deferens
The vas deferens feels like a firm, moveable, and smooth tube that runs behind each testicle. Try to run thumb and forefinger along its length, in both testicles, feeling for lumps or tenderness.

Looking after the testicles

In order to keep the testicles as healthy as possible, they should be cleaned regularly and protected against the risk of injury.

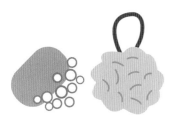

△ **Cleaning thoroughly**
Ensuring teens clean around and underneath the testicles helps to avoid body odor and infection.

△ **Proper protection**
It can be extremely painful to get hit in the testicles, so when playing any sport, it's a good idea to use a protective cup to decrease the risk of injury.

The penis

The penis has two main functions. It's the male body part used for urination, and is for sexual pleasure and sexual reproduction. During sex, the penis ejaculates a fluid called semen, which contains millions of the male sex cell, sperm.

SEE ALSO

❮ **46–47** What is puberty?
❮ **48–49** Male hormones
❮ **50–51** Changing body
❮ **52–53** Testicles

Anatomy of the penis

The penis is made up of several parts, including the glans, urethra, corpora cavernosa, and the corpus spongiosum. Knowing the function of each part helps teens to understand how the male body works.

GOOD TO KNOW

Keeping clean

Keep your penis clean by washing it daily with warm water and soap. If you have a foreskin, be sure to wash underneath it to avoid a build-up of smegma (a smelly substance made of dead skin cells and oils).

▽ **The penis**
Most of the time, the penis hangs loosely, and is soft or "flaccid." The length and width of a penis can vary greatly, and it's normal for them to curve left, right, or upward.

Seminal vesicle
This secretes the fluid that makes up 70% of semen.

Bladder
Urine from the kidneys is stored here before it is expelled from the body.

Vas deferens
Sperm travels from the testicles to the seminal vesicle and prostate gland via the vas deferens.

Prostate gland
A milky fluid that makes up 30% of semen is secreted from the prostate gland.

Corpora cavernosa
This pair of spongy tissues on the top side of the penis fills with blood during an erection.

Corpus spongiosum
This region of spongy tissue below the urethra fills with blood when the penis is erect.

Urethra
This tube carries urine and semen to the glans of the penis.

Testicle
Sperm, the male sex cell, is produced in the two testicles.

Foreskin
A retractable fold of skin over the glans.

Epididymis
Sperm matures in the epididymis.

Glans
The end, or "head", of the penis.

Shapes and sizes

It's common for teens to worry about the shape and size of their penises, and to compare themselves to others. The important thing to remember is that the size of a penis when it's flaccid does not affect its size when erect.

Circumcision

The operation to remove the foreskin is known as circumcision. About one-third of all males are circumcised, and it usually happens for religious or cultural reasons, although it can be recommended on medical grounds if the foreskin is too tight or if it regularly becomes infected. A general or local anesthetic is usually administered before the procedure is carried out. Circumcision does not affect how the penis works or how the penis looks when erect.

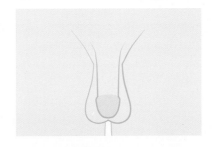

△ **Circumcised penis**
The foreskin has been removed and the glans of the penis is exposed.

△ **Uncircumcised penis**
The foreskin forms a retractable hood over the glans of the penis.

Erections

An erection happens when the penis fills with blood and becomes stiff. About 0.2 pt. (100 ml) of blood floods into the corpora cavernosa on the top side of the penis, and the corpus spongiosum on the under side. Most penises point upward when erect, but they can also point to the side, straight, or downward.

Though erections usually happen when a male is sexually aroused, they can also happen spontaneously, or during sleep.

△ **Spontaneous erections**
During the teen years, spontaneous erections are likely to occur more frequently—this can be embarrassing, but it's best to laugh it off.

Ejaculation

An ejaculation occurs when semen, a milky fluid containing sperm, is expelled from the penis. The process begins in the testicles, where sperm is produced, before being stored for a short time in the epididymis. From there, sperm travels via the vas deferens, combining with seminal fluid from the seminal vesicle and prostate gland to create semen. During an ejaculation, signals are sent to the muscles at the base of the penis, which contract to push the semen out of the erect penis.

The ejection of semen usually happens during masturbation or sexual intercourse and is a pleasurable experience, but it can also happen involuntarily during sleep – this is known as a "wet dream".

GOOD TO KNOW

Wet dreams

An ejaculation that happens during sleep is commonly known as a "wet dream." Wet dreams tend to be a regular occurrence during the teen years, although they happen to some people more frequently than others.

Teens are likely to feel embarrassed, but it's a natural part of growing up. Cleaning the penis and testicles thoroughly and changing the bedsheets first thing in the morning is a good idea.

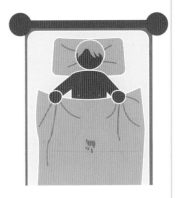

Breaking voices

During puberty, the voices of both males and females change to a lower pitch than that of pre-puberty. The deepening in females' voices is hardly noticeable, but some males' voices drop dramatically. When this happens, people say a male's voice is "breaking".

SEE ALSO
❮ 46–47 What is puberty?
❮ 48–49 Male hormones
❮ 50–51 Changing body
Confidence and self-esteem   86–87 ❯

How the voice works

The larynx, often known as the "voice box," combines with a system of cavities in the face and throat to enable people to manipulate the sounds they make to talk and sing.

When air is pushed out of the lungs, it rushes up the trachea, or "windpipe," and through the larynx. Stretched across the larynx are two vocal ligaments, or "vocal cords," which are a bit like elastic bands. They vibrate when air passes between them—much like when a guitar string is strummed—and produce the sound of the voice.

The impact of puberty

During puberty, testosterone makes the cartilage in the voice box grow. The vocal cords become 60 percent longer and thicker, and so vibrate at a lower frequency than before—reducing from 200 times per second to as low as 130 times per second. This makes the voice sound much deeper.

It's not clear why this change to the voice occurs. In other animals, males develop deeper voices to attract a mate and to frighten off predators and competing males more effectively. It may be that the human voice changes for the same reasons.

Vocal cords
The V-shape vocal cords, which stretch across the larynx, are "strummed" by air rushing past them to produce the sound of a person's voice.

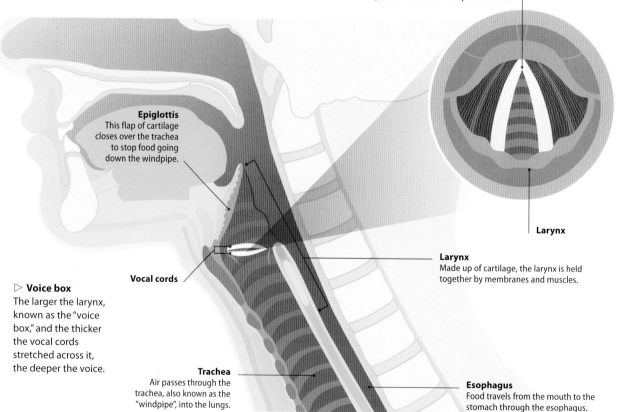

Epiglottis
This flap of cartilage closes over the trachea to stop food going down the windpipe.

Vocal cords

Larynx

Larynx
Made up of cartilage, the larynx is held together by membranes and muscles.

▷ **Voice box**
The larger the larynx, known as the "voice box," and the thicker the vocal cords stretched across it, the deeper the voice.

Trachea
Air passes through the trachea, also known as the "windpipe", into the lungs.

Esophagus
Food travels from the mouth to the stomach through the esophagus.

Changing face shape

Just as the cartilage of the voice box is sensitive to testosterone, so, too, are the facial bones. As the facial bones increase in size, they cause air-filled spaces—known as cavities—in the skull to increase in size, too. Larger cavities give the air molecules that have rushed through the vocal cords more space to bounce around, or resonate, deepening the voice further.

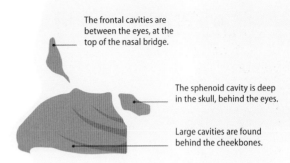

The frontal cavities are between the eyes, at the top of the nasal bridge.

The sphenoid cavity is deep in the skull, behind the eyes.

Large cavities are found behind the cheekbones.

▷ **Bigger cavities**
The different-size cavities within a person's facial structure create the different tones and pitches of the voice. Each person has different-size cavities, which is why everyone has different sounding voices.

The larynx resonates to a small degree, mainly when a person is making higher-pitched sounds.

Squeaks and croaks

During puberty, the changes to males' voices usually start once the penis has finished its rapid growth spurt. Voice changes are usually gradual, as the larynx and facial bones grow relatively slowly. However, in some people, the growth is sudden. With this sudden change can come squeaks and croaks when the teen tries to speak, as the body adjusts to the enlarged voice box. This "breaking voice" can't be controlled, but will pass within a few months, once the larynx stops growing.

What to expect

- The average age for the voice to change is 15, but it can happen earlier or later—every individual's progress through puberty is different. Voices usually break toward the end of puberty, but most males' voices don't fully mature until they're in their twenties.

- You may feel concerned or embarrassed about the sound of your voice, but it's perfectly normal, and people understand. Remember that many others are going through the exact same thing. It will pass within a few months, or even weeks.

- As the voice box grows, it also tilts slightly, and can sometimes protrude from a person's throat as a so-called Adam's apple (laryngeal prominence). This happens to some teens and not to others.

◁ **Highs and lows**
The sounds a teen's voice makes while the vocal mechanisms change can waver between high-pitched squeaks and husky croaks.

Healthy body

Keeping clean

Having a daily hygiene routine, in addition to eating healthy and getting regular exercise, keeps a teen's body clean and free from smells. Additionally, good hygiene improves a teen's mental well-being and can boost confidence, too.

Personal hygiene

Poor personal hygiene can be unhealthy, and can increase the risk of infection, so it's a good idea for teens to get into healthy habits as soon as possible.

▷ **Unpleasant smells**
Making good hygiene a habit during puberty can help teens to avoid potentially embarrassing situations.

Hair

During puberty, the overproduction of sebum (oil) at the root of hair follicles can make hair greasy and lank, or bind dead skin cells together, causing dandruff.

To avoid these afflictions, wash hair regularly with a small amount of shampoo and rinse thoroughly. Some people need to wash their hair every day, while others can go a week or more before they need to wash theirs.

Use the pads of the fingers to rub shampoo into the scalp. Avoid using the nails as this can break the skin.

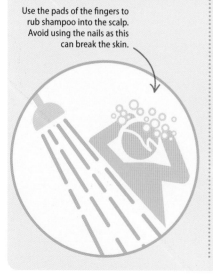

Eyes

Washing the hands before touching the eyes reduces the risk of conjunctivitis, also known as "pink eye," as well as other infections. Visiting the optician regularly for a check-up is important, particularly if a teen wears contact lenses or glasses.

To help avoid spreading infections, such as conjunctivitis, never share eye make-up with friends.

Skin and nails

Skin is the body's largest organ so it's essential to keep it healthy. Exfoliating once a week, using a gentle scrub, will remove dead skin cells, but avoid doing this any more frequently as it could cause dryness and irritation. Moisturizing regularly keeps skin hydrated. Use a short-bristle brush to keep the nails and toenails clean.

Cleaning nails regularly using a nail brush gets rid of dead skin cells and reduces the risk of infection.

Washing

Knowing how to wash clothes without help is an essential life skill for a teen to learn.

Separating clothes into darks, lights, and colors before putting them in the washing machine or handwashing them keeps fabrics looking their best. Clothes should be completely dry before they are put away, so they don't get moldy.

Choosing the right products

Paying attention to whether a product is suitable for sensitive, oily, or dry skin or for people with allergies can help with avoiding skin irritation. Similarly, hair products can be designed for use by people with dry or greasy hair, and curly, straight, fine, or thick hair, or people of different ethnicities.

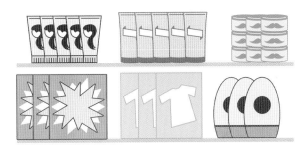

◁ **Lots of options**
There's no need to spend a lot of money. Inexpensive products can work as well as more expensive options.

Teeth

To keep the mouth healthy, it's best to brush teeth and gums at least twice a day. Using floss to remove any trapped food between the teeth will help to prevent tooth decay. Sweets and sugary drinks should be limited to an occasional treat.

Keep the toothbrush clean, stand it upright to dry out, and replace it every three months to avoid bacteria building up.

Armpits

The armpits are full of sweat-producing glands. Tucked under the arms, this warm environment is ideal for bacteria to break the sweat down, which can lead to unpleasant smells in this part of the body.

To minimize body odor, wash the armpits every day with warm water and mild soap. Most people use deodorant daily to help limit the amount they sweat, and cover up any unpleasant smells.

Washing the armpits every day keeps bad smells at bay.

Feet

There are more sweat glands on the soles of the feet than anywhere else on the human body, which is why they are often the smelliest part.

Wash feet with warm, soapy water and dry them thoroughly, especially between the toes, to prevent fungal infections, such as athlete's foot.

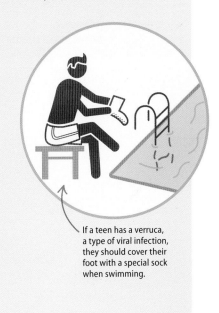

If a teen has a verruca, a type of viral infection, they should cover their foot with a special sock when swimming.

Sweat and smells

During puberty, the body produces more sweat, and more smells. As teens sweat much more than children, maintaining good personal hygiene will help to reduce self-consciousness about being sweatier or smellier than before.

SEE ALSO

❮ 60–61 Keeping clean

Healthy eating 68–69 ❯

Body image 72–73 ❯

Exercise 74–75 ❯

Explaining sweat

Sweat is produced by two types of sweat glands, which are long, coiled tubes in the skin. Active from birth, eccrine glands cover most of the body and produce a clear fluid that empties directly onto the skin. As this fluid evaporates from the skin, it cools the body's temperature.

Apocrine glands are found in the armpits and genital regions. These glands produce a thick, milky fluid when a person is nervous or stressed. This substance is full of proteins that are broken down by bacteria on the skin, causing bromhidrosis, known as "body odor" or BO.

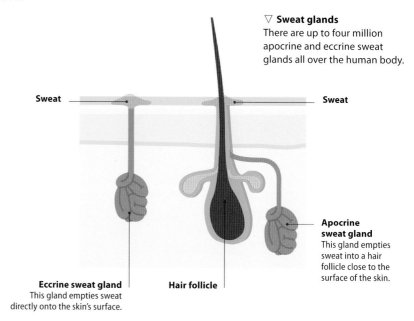

▽ **Sweat glands**
There are up to four million apocrine and eccrine sweat glands all over the human body.

Sweat

Sweat

Eccrine sweat gland
This gland empties sweat directly onto the skin's surface.

Hair follicle

Apocrine sweat gland
This gland empties sweat into a hair follicle close to the surface of the skin.

Sweating

Sweating is caused by:

- high temperatures
- exercise and physical activity
- emotional distress
- eating hot or spicy foods
- hormonal changes.

Some people sweat more or less than others, and it's worth seeing a doctor if a teen is concerned.

Sweaty teenagers

The apocrine glands only become active once puberty starts, which is why teens find that they sweat more at this time. The hormonal changes of puberty can also make a person more sweaty. It can take a while to get used to sweating more and to learn how to deal with it, but it's important to remember that it's a natural bodily function. Whether a person's being active or inactive—everyone sweats throughout the day.

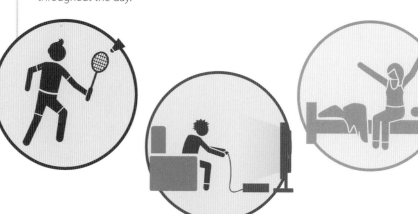

▷ **Daily sweats**
Some activities will make you sweat more than others, as will certain feelings, such as anxiety.

Body odor

Sweat is odorless. It's only when sweat is broken down by the bacteria that live on skin and hair that odor is created. Everyone has body odor and learns how to handle it. Daily washing decreases the amount of bacteria on the skin, and so reduces the likelihood of body odor.

▷ **Finding a routine**
Showering regularly reduces the number of odor-creating bacteria on the skin.

Dealing with body odor

- Wash every day and as soon as possible after exercising, focusing on the areas you sweat from the most, such as your armpits.

- Use a deodorant or antiperspirant. Deodorants are perfumed substances that disguise the smell of body odor. Antiperspirants reduce the amount you sweat by blocking the pores of the skin.

- Wear fresh clothing, including socks and underwear, every day. Choose clothes made of breathable, natural fibers, such as cotton.

Bad breath

Bad breath (halitosis) has several causes, but one of the most common is food trapped between the teeth. Bacteria in the mouth attach to and break down these food remnants, releasing a smelly gas as they do so. Regular brushing and flossing helps to remove any trapped food, reducing the chances of bad breath and tooth decay.

▷ **Bacteria buildup**
Switching to a new toothbrush every three months stops the buildup of bacteria.

Solving bad breath

- Brush your teeth and gums for 2–3 minutes at least twice a day. Clean your tongue regularly, too. Floss to remove any food debris trapped between the teeth.

- Drink water with meals to wash out the mouth.

- Avoid smoking. This can make bad breath worse.

- Pay regular visits to a dentist.

Stinky feet

The feet's sweat glands are eccrine glands, which produce sweat that is less likely to be broken down by odor-creating bacteria. However, feet can still start to smell if the sweat is unable to evaporate from the skin—such as when they are cooped up in socks and shoes for long periods. If shoes become damp with sweat, it creates the perfect climate for bacteria to breed and break down the sweat to produce a smelly odor.

▷ **Breathable shoes**
Shoes need to dry out between wears to avoid bacteria buildup from sweaty feet. A foot deodorant can help reduce and hide foul smells.

Coping with smelly feet

- Thoroughly wash and dry your feet every day.

- Wear fresh socks every day.

- Avoid wearing the same shoes two days in a row. If possible, alternate between pairs of shoes so they have 24 hours to dry out.

Body hair

During the teen years, rising hormone levels in the body cause hair to darken and thicken. The color, texture, and amount of hair usually depends on a person's genetic makeup. Some people have lots of body hair, while others have less.

SEE ALSO	
❰ 22–23 Self-expression	
❰ 60–61 Keeping clean	
Body image	72–73 ❭
Peer pressure	192–193 ❭

The function of hair

Human hair has lots of different functions. The fine, light-colored hair that covers most of the body traps air to help humans regulate their body temperature. Hair on the head also allows the body to retain heat and helps protect the scalp, while hair around the eyes and in the nose protects these body parts from foreign objects entering. Pubic hair protects the genitals and may also play a part in attraction between males and females.

▽ **Puberty changes**
Hair grows in new places, and becomes darker and thicker in others. The color of body hair may be different to the hair on a teen's head.

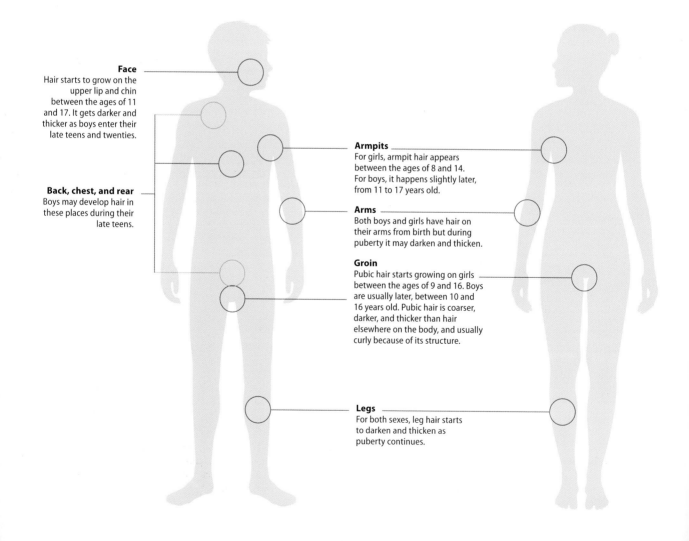

Face
Hair starts to grow on the upper lip and chin between the ages of 11 and 17. It gets darker and thicker as boys enter their late teens and twenties.

Back, chest, and rear
Boys may develop hair in these places during their late teens.

Armpits
For girls, armpit hair appears between the ages of 8 and 14. For boys, it happens slightly later, from 11 to 17 years old.

Arms
Both boys and girls have hair on their arms from birth but during puberty it may darken and thicken.

Groin
Pubic hair starts growing on girls between the ages of 9 and 16. Boys are usually later, between 10 and 16 years old. Pubic hair is coarser, darker, and thicker than hair elsewhere on the body, and usually curly because of its structure.

Legs
For both sexes, leg hair starts to darken and thicken as puberty continues.

Body hair choices

Some people prefer to remove their body hair, while others decide to keep it or trim it. There are no rules about what to do with body hair, nor is there any medical reason to remove it.

▽ **Personal preference**
Deciding what to do with body hair is all about personal preference. There are advantages and disadvantages to each option.

	How it works	Advantages	Disadvantages
Hair removal creams	• Chemicals dissolve hair at or slightly below the skin surface	• Effective over large areas • No stubble	• Can irritate the skin
Keeping	• Leaves the hair natural	• No cost, fuss, or effort	• Armpit hair can trap bacteria and encourage body odor
Plucking	• Removes hair at the root, using tweezers	• Can reduce regrowth • Lasts about a week	• Can be painful, or cause irritation of hair roots and scarring
Shaving	• Cuts off hair at the skin surface	• Painless • Cheap, easy, and quick	• Can result in skin irritation or cuts
Waxing	• Removes hair at the root, using wax strips	• Lasts three to six weeks • Can reduce regrowth	• Can irritate the skin • Can be painful • Can be expensive

Shaving facial hair

When thicker hairs begin to appear on a boy's chin and upper lip, he might start thinking about shaving. Whether or not a boy shaves is down to personal preference, but a trusted adult can help with the decision.

Don't push too hard with the razor.
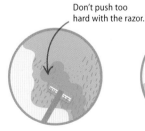

△ **1.** Choose a razor or electric shaver. Shaving after a bath or shower is best, as the skin is soft and hydrated.

△ **2.** If using a razor, apply a shaving cream or gel first—this reduces the risk of cuts.

△ **3.** Shave in the same direction as hair growth. Going the opposite way can irritate the skin.

△ **4.** Wash with soap and water, then apply moisturizing lotion to avoid skin dryness.

△ **5.** If using a razor, change the blades regularly so they stay sharp.

Pimples

Pimples occur when dead skin cells and oil clog the pores of the skin. Also known as acne or zits, pimples can make teens feel self-conscious, but they are a normal part of growing up.

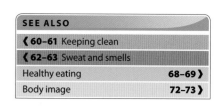
▷ **Blackheads**
When a plug of dead skin cells and oil clogs up a pore, it is called a blackhead. A blackhead is not filled with dirt—rather, the dark spot is caused by skin pigmentation. It can contain bacteria.

▷ **Whiteheads**
Whiteheads happen when a thin membrane of skin traps a plug of dead skin cells, oil, and bacteria. They can get bigger as the sebaceous gland continues to produce oil, which builds up underneath the skin.

▷ **Pustules**
These red bumps with a pus-filled center are what most people think of when they think of acne. They appear when there is an infection of the pore, which causes pus to form.

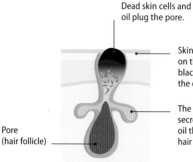

Dead skin cells and oil plug the pore.

Skin pigmentation on the surface of a blackhead causes the dark spot.

The sebaceous gland secretes sebum, an oil that lubricates the hair and skin.

Pore (hair follicle)

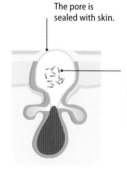

The pore is sealed with skin.

Bacteria, which help keep the skin healthy, also get trapped with dead skin cells and oil.

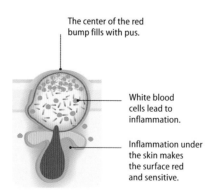

The center of the red bump fills with pus.

White blood cells lead to inflammation.

Inflammation under the skin makes the surface red and sensitive.

Acne

Acne is the umbrella term for minor outbreaks of blackheads, whiteheads, and other types of pimples. Acne begins when pores (hair follicles) get blocked by dead skin cells and oil (sebum). It can help to know what type of acne a teen has in order to treat it effectively.

> **MYTH BUSTER**
>
> ## The truth about pimples
>
> **Poor diet doesn't cause skin problems.** No foods cause acne, but eating healthfully can help to prevent it.
>
> **Pimples aren't caused by uncleanliness.** Pimples start beneath the skin's surface, so aren't caused by a lack of washing.
>
> **Menstruation may lead to pimples.** Changing hormone levels before and during a period have only a minor impact, but this tends to be temporary.

Infection

When bacteria build up in a blackhead or whitehead, it can lead to infection. The body's immune system then sends in white blood cells to attack the infection, which causes the redness and swelling that makes pimples painful.

There are four types of pimples that can develop: papules, pustules, nodules, and cysts. Papules and pustules are red bumps, with pustules having pus-filled tips. Nodules and cysts are larger and form deep under the skin. Nodules are solid, while cysts are liquid-filled.

Preventing pimples

Taking steps to prevent pimples is easier than trying to treat them once they appear. Maintaining a regular skin-care regime even during pimple-free periods will help teens' skin to stay healthy.

Look for treatments with soothing antiseptic ingredients, such as tea tree oil.

Keep hair off the face.

Use a lightweight moisturizer every day.

Wash the face using lukewarm water and hands no more than twice a day, to avoid drying out the skin.

Avoid covering pimples with make-up, as it might make them worse. If a teen still wants to use make-up, try to find oil-free options.

Drink plenty of water and aim to eat a healthy diet.

Gently exfoliate once a week to get rid of dead skin cells.

Feeling self-conscious

The important thing to remember about pimples is that, though they may make a teen feel self-conscious or ashamed, most people won't notice. Even if anyone does notice, they will most likely have had pimples themselves, and sympathize.

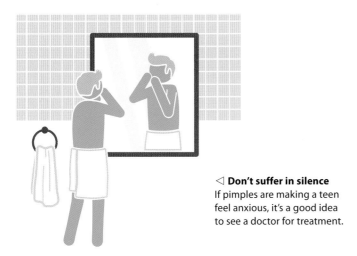

◁ **Don't suffer in silence**
If pimples are making a teen feel anxious, it's a good idea to see a doctor for treatment.

Popping pimples

No matter how much you want to get rid of them, it's best to leave pimples alone. Popping them can spread bacterial infection and may lead to scarring. However, if the temptation becomes too much to resist, it's essential to wash your hands thoroughly beforehand, use only the fingertips, and if it doesn't pop or any blood is drawn, stop immediately.

▷ **Resist the urge**
Although tempting, popping pimples can often make them worse.

Healthy eating

During puberty, the teen body needs extra energy and nutrients to support all the changes it's going through. Developing good eating habits during adolescence can make living a healthy life easier, as these habits often stick into adulthood.

Balanced diet

A balanced diet means eating foods from each of the different food groups, and in the right proportions. Meals and snacks should contain lots of colorful fruit and vegetables, to ensure a teen is getting all the essential nutrients.

GOOD TO KNOW

Different choices

Some people don't eat certain meats, or prepare their food in a specific way, for religious reasons. For ethical reasons, pescatarians eat fish but no meat, while vegetarians and vegans eat neither fish nor meat. Instead, they find nutrient-rich options from the rest of the food groups to ensure the body still receives everything it needs.

▷ **Eating well**
Aim to eat a well-balanced diet that covers all the food groups, every day.

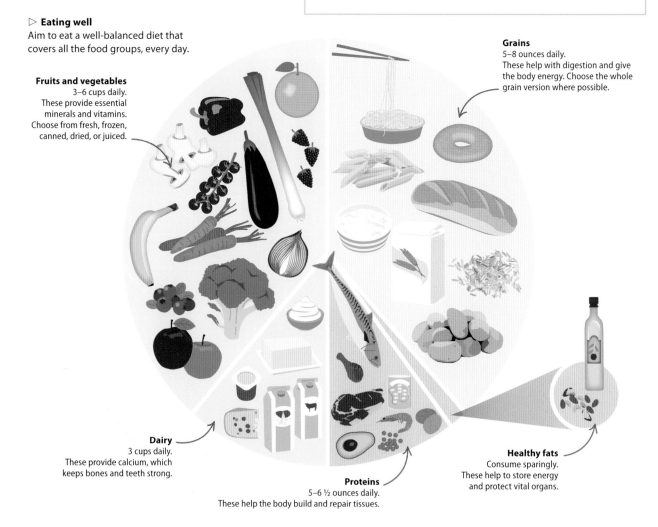

Fruits and vegetables
3–6 cups daily.
These provide essential minerals and vitamins. Choose from fresh, frozen, canned, dried, or juiced.

Grains
5–8 ounces daily.
These help with digestion and give the body energy. Choose the whole grain version where possible.

Dairy
3 cups daily.
These provide calcium, which keeps bones and teeth strong.

Proteins
5–6 ½ ounces daily.
These help the body build and repair tissues.

Healthy fats
Consume sparingly.
These help to store energy and protect vital organs.

The benefits of eating well

Eating healthy gives a teen more energy, better concentration, and a general sense of well-being. It's easy for teens to take small steps to improve their diet.

Healthy habits

There are lots of things teens can do to make sure they are eating healthy. Here are just a few.

△ **Staying hydrated**
Drinking 6–8 glasses of liquid per day is recommended. Water is best, so try to limit fruit juice and smoothies to half a cup (150ml) per day.

△ **Eating breakfast**
Breakfast means "breaking the fast" after a night's sleep. It energizes the brain and body ready for the day ahead.

△ **Healthy snacking**
Healthy snacks can be just as quick as sugary snacks to put together. They also keep the body feeling full longer.

△ **Controlling portion size**
For carbohydrates, proteins, and vegetables, a serving should measure about the size of a person's fist.

△ **Dining regularly**
To sustain the body throughout the day, eat meals and snacks at regular times.

△ **Getting enough fruits and vegetables**
Eat a selection of 3–6 cups fruits and vegetables every day.

Not so healthy

Teens should be conscious of unhealthy habits in their everyday diet. Having treats in moderation is the best way to stay healthy.

Fast food

Fast food can often be tasty and quick, but it's typically high in calories, saturated fat, salt, and sugar. Fast food should only be consumed as an occasional treat.

Sugary treats

Chocolate, ice cream, fizzy drinks, and sweets can seem a more appealing snack than healthy fruit. However, too much of these can increase the risk of diabetes, cause tooth decay, and lead to weight gain.

Detox diets

Teens should avoid diets encouraging them to "detox," "cleanse," or anything that recommends skipping meals or eating just one type of food. Dieting in this way can be dangerous, and may cause a teen to develop an eating disorder.

Eating disorders

Eating disorders are a range of conditions characterized by abnormal, unhealthy, or even dangerous eating habits. They affect people regardless of their gender, race, or background.

Relationships with eating

Eating enables people to stay physically and mentally well, and mealtimes allow for bonding and socializing with loved ones. But when a person's relationship with food dominates their thinking, or becomes unhealthy or harmful, it's known as an eating disorder.

Eating disorders occur when a person's relationship with food becomes the source of internal pressure or a means of exerting control over their situation. They can develop for many reasons, including feeling pressure to look a certain way, or experiencing a stressful life event.

△ **Food and socializing**
Food is a big part of the daily routine, and mealtimes can be a struggle for someone with an eating disorder.

Types of eating disorder

The characteristics of an individual's eating disorder can change over time and people can have more than one at once. These are the most commonly recognized disorders.

Anorexia Nervosa

This disorder involves a distorted perception of being overweight, leading to eating very little, missing meals, or regular fasting.

Other characteristics include being very underweight, obsessive weighing and calorie counting, over-exercising, and using laxatives.

Complications include dizziness and fainting, dry skin, fatigue, hair loss, impaired memory, infertility, irregular menstruation, muscle loss, risk of kidney and liver damage, and weak bones.

Bulimia Nervosa

This condition is a cycle of overeating (known as bingeing) to cope with stress or emotional anxiety, followed by vomiting in order to purge the body of food and to avoid weight gain.

Other characteristics include fasting or over-exercising after bingeing, anxiety, and guilt caused by failing to meet impossible dietary restrictions.

Complications include dehydration, irregular menstruation, mineral deficiency, stomach ulcers, swollen saliva glands, risk of bowel and heart problems, and tooth decay.

Binge Eating Disorder

This disorder consists of repeated episodes of compulsive binge eating in private, to cope with negative feelings.

Other characteristics include anxiety and depression; feelings of guilt, shame, or loss of control; and buying certain foods in advance before a binging session.

Complications include being overweight or obese, diabetes, high cholesterol, osteoarthritis, painful or swollen joints, risk of heart problems, and bowel or breast cancer.

Warning signs

There are some common signs to look out for that may indicate a person has an eating disorder:

- Rapid weight loss, or frequent weight changes.

- Disordered eating behaviors, such as eating very little or excessively.

- Repeated weighing and obsessive calorie counting.

- Refusing to eat with other people or in public.

- Saying negative things about the body.

- Feeling tired or low energy.

- Wearing baggy or oversize clothing to hide the body.

- Extreme exercise habits.

- Secretive behavior or disappearing to the bathroom after meals.

Seeking help

The health problems caused by eating disorders can be fatal if left untreated, so it's essential to address the issue as soon as possible. Helping a loved one can be a challenge, especially if they are in denial or act defensively. After seeing a doctor, it may be necessary for them to be referred to a specialized eating disorders clinic for further support.

▷ **First steps**
Seeing a doctor is the first step toward treatment and recovery.

Helping a loved one

- Stay calm and avoid passing judgement, blame, or criticism. Instead, build their self-esteem with praise.

- Try not to be pushy with advice—rather, ask what support they need. Talk to them about how they feel.

- Be prepared for the person to reject help or to respond negatively.

- Avoid talking about appearance or weight in front of them.

- Keep trying to include the person in activities, even if they don't want to socialize.

- Encourage them to get professional help, either through their doctor or by calling a helpline.

Treatment

Eating disorders often disguise other problems, such as anxiety, depression, or feelings of isolation. Consequently, treating an eating disorder is not simply about helping a person reach a healthy weight. It also involves addressing the underlying emotional and psychological issues behind the behavior. Recovery can be a slow process as the person with an eating disorder gradually rebuilds their relationship with food and the body. Some people may relapse, but with the right support and time, eating disorders can be successfully treated.

△ **Treatment methods**
Treatments differ for everybody, but can include medication, counseling, or family therapy.

Body image

A person becomes more aware of their body image during the teenage years when their appearance may start to become more important to their sense of identity. If a teen is unhappy about how they look, it can affect their confidence and self-esteem.

Explaining body image

Body image is how a person perceives how they look, as well as the thoughts and feelings associated with this perception. These feelings can be positive, negative, or a bit of both. How people perceive their body doesn't necessarily equate to how they really look.

> Body image is not about how teens look, but how they feel about how they look.

Influencing body image

Puberty can be a turbulent time for a tween or teen and their body image. Throughout adolescence, some young people feel constantly self-conscious. In addition to the physical transformations experienced during puberty, other things can affect body image:

Media manipulation

Teens are introduced to unrealistic "ideal" body shapes or standards of beauty through celebrity culture and digitally manipulated images in the media. The pressure to conform to these standards can lead teens to adopt unhealthy behaviors, such as dieting.

△ **False "perfection"**
It is important to remember that images in the media are typically altered to give a false impression of "perfection."

Body shaming

Body shaming is when people criticize the appearance of others or themselves directly, through gossip, online, or in person. It is a type of bullying that involves making people feel bad about the way they look, and can directly result in poor body image and low self-esteem.

△ **Teasing**
Even for outwardly confident teens, hurtful comments about their appearance can be humiliating and upsetting.

Difficult life events

Facing any kind of upheaval, such as moving to a new school or going through a breakup, can make teens feel vulnerable about how they look. Teens might become very self-critical as a way of channeling stress and coping with a challenging situation.

△ **Upheaval**
Encountering people in new situations can also cause a teen to worry about how they are perceived.

Body dysmorphic disorder (BDD)

BDD is an anxiety disorder that involves obsessive thoughts which distort a person's view of how they look. People with BDD may spend a lot of time in front of the mirror, perhaps focusing on one or more parts of their body, or constantly compare their appearance to that of others. Often other people don't see the problem, yet the self-perceived flaw causes so much concern for the BDD sufferer that it can restrict their enjoyment of life.

△ **Feelings, not facts**
Low body confidence can cause teens to see themselves in a distorted way.

GOOD TO KNOW

Bigorexia

"Bigorexia" (muscle dysmorphia) is a particular type of BDD. It usually affects boys and men. People with this condition see themselves as small and weak, despite being big and muscular. People with bigorexia exercise excessively to build muscle, neglect friendships in order to work out, and may even use steroids in pursuit of their ideal body shape.

Negative body image

Many teens aren't even aware that they have negative opinions about their own bodies, which crop up in either their thoughts or in conversation with others. Developed over time, it often becomes a habit that is hard to break.

A good first step, however, is to recognize the pattern behind the negative comments. Directly addressing such feelings begins the process of figuring out where they come from.

PARENT TIPS

Supporting your teen

- Speak positively about your own body image, especially around your teen.

- Encourage them to focus on being fit and healthy, rather than on achieving a goal weight or shape.

- Make clear that images in the media are usually enhanced, and that there is no such thing as a perfect body.

- Be supportive of your teen's changing body, but let them take the lead in conversations, to ensure they feel at ease.

Improving body image

It's possible to improve a teen's body image. It can take time, because it's really about changing their self-perception. This can make a big difference to how good a person feels about themselves. The most important thing is for a teen to learn to embrace their uniqueness as, over time, this will reinforce a healthy body image and strong self-esteem.

▷ **Unique you**
Teens should focus on something they like about their appearance each time they look in the mirror.

TEEN HINTS

Boosting body confidence

- Speak to yourself as a friend might and point out every day three compliments they would give to you about your body—and your personal qualities, too.

- Moving your body makes you feel good. Figure out what's fun for you, such as running, swimming, or dancing.

- If negative feelings become overwhelming, talk about them with an adult you trust.

Exercise

Exercise is good for the body and the brain. It keeps teens' bodies healthy, improves memory and sleep quality, and boosts confidence.

Being active

Teens should try to include some form of physical exercise in their day, every day. They should aim for a mix of activities throughout the week, at varied intensity levels, in order to build muscle and bone strength and maintain cardiovascular fitness.

▷ **Recommended amounts for teens**
Teens should aim to get at least 60 minutes of some form of physical activity every day.

Finding balance

During stressful periods, such as when homework starts to pile up, finding the time to exercise can be hard. But, in fact, exercise can be a great stress reliever. If setting aside a chunk of time to exercise is tricky, fitting a small amount of physical activity into the day can still make a difference, such as using the stairs instead of taking the elevator.

Physical inactivity: in small doses
Limit the amount of physical inactivity in a day.

Try activities that improve both muscle and bone strength, such as swimming.

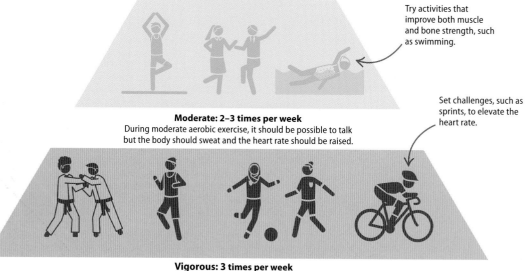

Moderate: 2–3 times per week
During moderate aerobic exercise, it should be possible to talk but the body should sweat and the heart rate should be raised.

Set challenges, such as sprints, to elevate the heart rate.

Vigorous: 3 times per week
Vigorous exercise includes anything that raises the heart rate and gets a teen breathing heavily. It shouldn't be possible to talk easily.

Light physical activity: daily
Many everyday physical activities that keep a teen moving about can help them stay healthy, too.

Enjoying variety

Exercise is more than just going to the gym, although it can take time for a teen to figure out what physical activity they like best. When it's enjoyable, exercise often doesn't feel like exercise at all.

Trying new things can be a great way to stay interested in exercise. Going to an observation session with a friend can provide much-needed support if a teen's nervous about trying out something new. As with everything, practice makes perfect, so if teens feel they aren't making progress at first, they shouldn't give up.

▽ **Keep it varied**
Trying out lots of activities and learning new skills will help teens find out what they most enjoy.

Getting motivated

People have more energy, and tend to enjoy it more, if they exercise often. Finding time to exercise regularly, such as after school, and a friend to exercise with, makes sticking to it easier and more fun. The main goal shouldn't be about competing, but rather aiming to enjoy how it makes you feel. Setting goals may also motivate you—for example, meeting new people, getting healthier, or feeling less stressed.

△ Running builds muscle, increases cardiovascular strength, and improves endurance.

△ Cycling is a healthy way to get around, builds muscle, and improves cardiovascular strength.

△ Climbing strengthens bones and muscles and challenges problem-solving skills.

△ Team sports boost confidence and provide a regular exercise routine.

△ Boxing builds coordination, discipline, and strength.

△ Dancing improves coordination, rhythm, and stamina.

△ Yoga increases flexibility and muscle strength, and helps to relieve stress.

△ Group activities are a great way to make friends through teamwork.

△ Pilates strengthens core muscles and improves flexibility.

Sleep

Teens need eight to nine hours of good-quality sleep every night to develop their bodies and brains. A good night's sleep reenergizes the body, and improves learning and memory.

The importance of sleep

Sleep is vital, especially during puberty, when a teen's body and brain are undergoing massive changes. Sleep functions as a period of rest, and also as a time for the body to carry out a number of processes. Good-quality sleep strengthens the immune system, aids muscle development, maintains hormonal responses, and boosts mental well-being.

◁ **Bedtime**
Having a regular routine before going to bed, with comfortable clothes and comfort objects, will encourage tweens and teens to feel tired.

▽ **An early night**
Good sleep is not just about the number of hours a teen gets each night, but also the quality of their sleep. To improve sleep quality, the bedroom should be a serene space, free from clutter.

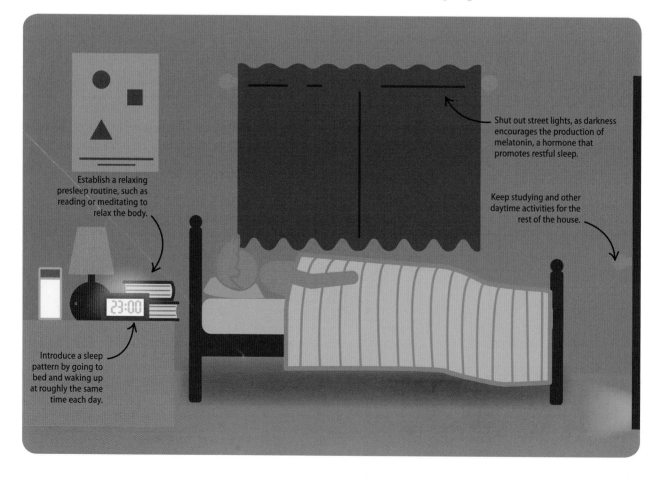

Establish a relaxing presleep routine, such as reading or meditating to relax the body.

Introduce a sleep pattern by going to bed and waking up at roughly the same time each day.

Shut out street lights, as darkness encourages the production of melatonin, a hormone that promotes restful sleep.

Keep studying and other daytime activities for the rest of the house.

23:00

The circadian rhythm

The circadian rhythm is a hormone cycle responsible for creating feelings of wakefulness and sleepiness in humans. It's linked to the body's level of melatonin, a hormone produced by the brain, and also influenced by exposure to light. When the sun goes down, the brain raises melatonin levels, causing tiredness. When it's light again, melatonin levels fall, prompting a person to wake up.

The differences between a teen's rhythm and an adult's help to explain why many teens struggle to wake up early. Teen brains start releasing melatonin later than adult brains do, around two to three hours later, meaning they feel don't feel tired until late in the evening. Furthermore, a teen's brain continues to produce melatonin for about three hours after an adult's, meaning that waking up for school can often feel like waking up in the middle of the night.

GOOD TO KNOW

Insomnia

Having difficulty falling or staying asleep is known as insomnia. People who have insomnia often wake up feeling unrefreshed, find it hard to nap even when they feel tired, and are often unable to concentrate in the daytime. Insomnia can be caused by a multitude of things, including anxiety and stress, other health conditions, lifestyle factors, or bad sleeping habits.

Avoiding caffeinated drinks for a few hours before going bed and limiting the use of electronic devices in the evening might help, but it's worth seeing a doctor if insomnia persists.

▽ **Bad habits**
Poor-quality or too little sleep affects mood and makes it harder to concentrate, in addition to increasing the risk of long-term health problems.

Loud noises activate adrenaline, which makes it harder to get to sleep.

Bright outside light signals to the brain that it's time to wake up.

Stressful activities, such as studying for exams, produce cortisol, which keeps the brain awake.

Going to bed too late or at different times every night stops the body from settling into a routine.

Screens emitting blue light disrupt the body's circadian rhythm.

Stimulants, such as caffeine found in tea, coffee, and energy drinks, reduce sleep quality.

A messy room distracts the brain, stopping it from resting.

Teen ailments

Changing hormones, anxiety over tests, and close physical contact with peers are just a few of the factors that make teens particularly susceptible to some infections and medical conditions.

SEE ALSO

❰ **68–69** Healthy eating

❰ **74–75** Exercise

❰ **76–77** Sleep

Stress   **92–93** ❱

Potential problems

The ailments listed here can affect teenagers. This is because teens' bodies are going through many changes, and teens spend much of their time in group environments.

A person's immune system works hard to protect them against the constant barrage of infectious pathogens, such as bacteria, viruses, fungi, and parasites, that come with living a normal life. But it sometimes needs help, so it's important to be aware of these ailments, to take steps to reduce the chances of infection, and to seek medical advice if necessary.

Mononucleosis

A viral infection that affects mostly young people

Complications: Enlarged lymph nodes, prolonged tiredness, sometimes a decrease in blood cells, damage to spleen, neurological problems

Causes: Epstein-Barr virus, often spread through saliva, such as by kissing, sharing toothbrushes, sharing utensils

Symptoms: Extreme tiredness, fever, sore throat, swollen glands in neck

Diagnosis: Blood test

Treatment: Fluids, painkillers, rest

Tips for prevention: Avoid sharing drinks or eating utensils, avoid kissing people if they're ill

Measles

A viral illness, recognizable by its rash, that is highly contagious

Complications: Eye, liver, lung, or neurological damage; can be fatal

Causes: The measles virus

Symptoms: Cold-like symptoms, fever, light sensitivity, red and sore eyes, skin rash, whitish spots on the inside of the mouth

Diagnosis: Blood or saliva sample, clinical diagnosis

Treatment: Fever relief, painkillers; symptoms usually improve on their own within 7–10 days

Tips for prevention: Vaccination

Meningitis

Inflammation of the meninges—the membranes around the spinal cord and brain

Complications: Neurological damage, loss of limbs; can be fatal if not treated quickly

Causes: Bacterial (more dangerous) or viral (more common) infection, often spread through sneezing, coughing, kissing, or sharing utensils

Symptoms: Aching muscles, blotchy rash that doesn't fade when a glass is rolled over it, drowsiness, fever, headache, sensitivity to light, seizures, vomiting

Diagnosis: Blood tests and testing fluid from around the spinal cord and brain

Treatment: Immediate hospital treatment, with fluids, intravenous antibiotics, and oxygen (bacterial meningitis); viral meningitis tends to resolve itself within 7–10 days

Tips for prevention: Vaccination—several available

Migraines

A severe or moderate headache, usually on one side of the head, sometimes with warning signs beforehand like visual disturbances; occasionally, no headache but other symptoms

Complications: Sometimes vomiting, nausea
Causes: Unknown, may be due to abnormal nerve signals affecting chemicals and blood vessels in the brain
Symptoms: Blurred vision, headache, increased sensitivity to light and sound, vomiting, nausea
Diagnosis: Clinical diagnosis, pattern of symptoms
Treatment: Migraine medication, painkillers, rest
Tips for prevention: Avoiding or reducing known triggers, taking preventative medications

Mumps

A contagious viral infection that causes painful swellings at the side of the face under the ears

Complications: Damage to pancreas, infertility (rarely), meningitis, swollen ovaries or testicles
Causes: Viral infection, spread through saliva
Symptoms: Fever, headache, joint pain, swelling of parotid salivary glands on face under ears
Diagnosis: Saliva swab
Treatment: Cold compress for swollen glands, fluids, mild painkillers, rest; infection usually resolves itself within 2 weeks
Tips for prevention: Vaccination

Sexually transmitted diseases (STDs)

A variety of bacterial, parasitic, and viral infections

Complications: Fertility issues, skin problems, neurological damage
Causes: Bacteria, viruses, parasites
Symptoms: Sometimes none; sometimes changes to menstrual bleeding, genital discharge, itching, rashes, urinary and bowel problems
Diagnosis: Blood tests, genital swabs, urine tests
Treatment: Dependent on infection; antibiotic, antiviral, or antiparasitic medication, currently no cure for HIV but medications can help a person live a long, healthy life
Tips for prevention: Regular STD checks, ask sexual partners if they've had an STD check, practice safer sex

Urinary tract infections (UTIs)

Bacterial infection of the bladder, called cystitis

Complications: Kidney damage with recurrent UTIs
Causes: Bacterial infection
Symptoms: Blood in urine, painful and/or frequent urination, smelly urine
Diagnosis: Urine sample
Treatment: Antibiotics, fluids, rest
Tips for prevention: Staying hydrated, females should wipe from front to back after going to the toilet

Vaccinations

Infectious agents such as bacteria and viruses are called pathogens. Vaccinations help the human body fight infections by exposing it to a harmless version of a particular pathogen. This triggers the immune system to produce the antibodies needed to fight that pathogen should it be encountered in the future. Vaccination programs help to prevent and reduce infection from many deadly diseases.

Recommended vaccinations

A number of vaccinations and booster shots need to be given to teens between the ages of 11 and 18. It's important for every teen to have a record of the shots that they've received, and to keep it updated. Booster shots are just as important as the initial immunization and should be administered at the right time to maintain immunity.

Healthy
mind

Positive mental health

Mental health is a person's emotional and social self, their inner well-being. People look after their physical health through exercising, and by eating and sleeping well. It's just as important to take time to look after their mental health, too.

Feeling positive

Positive mental health consists of four main elements: the ability to recognize emotions, dealing with those emotions, practicing healthy mental habits, and establishing strong support networks. When a person has these four things in place, it is easier to feel mentally positive. And when someone feels mentally positive, they are able to live life to their full potential while handling any hurdles and hiccups that life sends their way.

PARENT TIPS

Supporting your teen

- Talk to your teen about the qualities you admire in them, such as their thoughtfulness toward friends and family.

- Model thoughtfulness for your teen. When you are frustrated, talk about how it makes you feel and the positive steps you plan to take to resolve the issue.

- Encourage your teen to take time do things they enjoy, even during exam time. This will prevent them from getting overwhelmed, which will help their performance.

A healthy mind

Even if a person feels on top of the world, it's important that they take time to do something for their inner well-being. When a person is mentally healthy, they're aware of what makes them feel positive and what gets them down. Paying attention to their mental health helps teens to become better equipped to acknowledge what they're feeling and to keep a balanced perspective on both life and themselves.

Appreciate your talents

When a person takes time to acknowledge and appreciate their own talents and accomplishments, it can help ward off negative thoughts and feelings, such as not feeling good enough or comparing their own achievements with those of others. Everyone is different, with their own unique talents and ways of doing things. Acknowledging that can help teens to celebrate their own.

Attempt mindfulness

Mindfulness is a technique that encourages a person to focus their attention on the present moment, and to their immediate thoughts and feelings. By acknowledging each individual thought, they stop feeling down or overwhelmed. This gives them a sense of control. Breathing exercises help with mindfulness.

▷ **Positive thinking strategies**
There are many ways to build positive mental health—in good times and bad.

Talking about it

If teens are feeling overwhelmed, and negative thoughts are hard to escape, checking in with a friend or parent and talking about how they feel can help. An outside perspective can help a person see that they're actually managing a situation better than they think. Keeping in mind the positive comments made by friends or parents can make a big difference the next time things are feeling difficult.

▷ **Not alone**
It can be hard to open up about feeling sad or low, but talking about it with someone else usually helps put things in perspective.

Build positive relationships
Supportive friends can give a person confidence, and push them to meet their potential. Good friends reinforce a person's positive thoughts, celebrate each other's achievements, and offer support in hard times, which can be invaluable to a person's inner well-being.

Help others
Helping friends and noticing their needs can help people feel good about themselves and their friendship.

Be kind to yourself
People are often kinder to others than they are to themselves. Self-talk is the way people speak to themselves. While people tend to find it easier to believe negative things about themselves, it is important that teens catch any negative self-talk and replace it instead with more positive and compassionate thoughts. This will help a person to feel confident and in control.

Learn new skills
Developing skills outside of a teen's comfort zone can test and develop their resilience, as well as give them a chance to meet and become friends with new and different people.

Stay active
Exercise releases endorphins—the body's natural mood elevator—benefiting both body and mind.

Set goals and ambitions
Having goals—big or small—focuses the mind on a task. Staying on track and focused when working toward a goal is an important part of building resilience. Hard work and setbacks are part of the journey and make successes even sweeter.

Meditate
People have used meditation for thousands of years as a way to manage thoughts and feelings, and to relax a busy mind. It is similar to mindfulness, but uses different methods to encourage feelings of calm.

Relax
Whether it's watching a new film, listening to a favorite band, or reading a book, making time for oneself to relax and just "be" is important for well-being.

Emotions

Emotions are instinctive, physical reactions to things that happen to or around a person. They're triggered by chemicals released in the brain and lead to a person's mental response—feelings. Emotions are universal, while feelings are individual and personal.

SEE ALSO

❰ **20–21** Mood swings
❰ **82–83** Positive mental health
Resilience **90–91** ❱
Anxiety and depression **94–95** ❱

Explaining emotions

Emotions are natural human responses that help people interpret what they're experiencing and how to react. Babies can sense their own emotions and respond to the emotions of others through actions such as smiling, laughing, or crying—even if they can't explain why they feel the way they feel. As children and teens grow, the physical reactions—laughing when happy, sweating when nervous, reddening when angry—remain largely the same, but they become better able to understand and express their emotions. This is because the parts of the brain responsible for rational thought develop during puberty.

▷ **Emotions and memory**
Emotions and memory are connected. This is why when a person thinks of a fun holiday, for example, they are likely to feel happy.

The purpose of emotions

Emotions are a major part of a person's survival instinct. Fear, anger, disgust, and surprise all play a role in avoiding or responding to danger, triggering instinctive responses to fight, flee, or mentally shut out the threat. Although "positive thinking" is often promoted as part of a person's mental well-being, humans' great emotional range helps people to respond to the world, both physically and mentally.

△ **Basic emotions**
How a person reacts to the emotions they experience is personal to the individual.

GOOD TO KNOW
Universally recognizable

A person's emotional state is conveyed to others through facial expressions, and is recognizable regardless of culture and language. In the 1960s, psychologists observed that there are six basic and universal emotions: fear, anger, disgust, joy, sadness, and surprise. Some psychologists concluded there are only four emotions because anger and disgust, and fear and surprise are very similar. Others argue that there are many more.

Teen emotions

Teens tend to behave more recklessly when surrounded by their peers than when with adults, and can be especially affected by social feedback, praise, and what others think of them. In part, this is because the prefrontal cortex—the part of the brain that regulates emotional balance, risk-taking, and self-awareness—is one of the last areas to develop. It may seem counterintuitive, but this delay has biological benefits. One such benefit is that an inability to recognize risks allows developing teens to step away from the security of their parents and become independent.

▷ **Over-the-top reactions**
As the prefrontal cortex develops, some teens may react to minor incidents in ways that seem out of proportion to the situation.

△ **Seeking thrills**
Feelings of excitement are accompanied by the release of feel-good hormones, such as dopamine. This can result in risk-taking and thrill-seeking behavior.

Evolving reactions

Teens are likely to feel emotions more intensely than children or adults because the prefrontal cortex, the "thinking" part of the brain, develops later than the parts of the brain that trigger emotional response. Until the prefrontal cortex catches up, they are less able to identify or control their emotional responses to situations or actions.

The good news is that the prefrontal cortex is able to make room for change, such as developing emotional control—and unlike emotions themselves, which are instinctive, emotional control can be learned, even before the prefrontal cortex has finished developing.

Managing feelings

Sometimes emotions can take over and lead people to behave in ways that they later regret once their "thinking" brain reengages. This can happen more frequently during the teen years.

> If possible, remove yourself from the situation (for example, go into a different room).

> Concentrate on your breathing and count to ten, very slowly.

> Recognize and accept your emotions, then work out how to react to them constructively.

> Exercising, listening to music, or even just writing things down can be positive ways to focus your mind.

PARENT TIPS

Helping teens to manage feelings

- When your teen is feeling emotionally overwhelmed, give them space for their emotions to settle before trying to discuss the cause.

- Try to recognize and respond to the emotion they are experiencing.

- Talk about any issues that need to be resolved once they have their emotions back under control.

- Seeking new opportunities helps teens to become independent. You can support your teen by encouraging them to be bold but thoughtful at the same time.

Confidence and self-esteem

Confidence and self-esteem are often thought to be the same thing, but they are actually very different. Confidence describes how teens feel in specific situations, while self-esteem is related to about how teens feel about themselves.

Confidence

Someone's confidence is all about their trust and belief in themselves to do something well. Confidence is also specific to a situation—a person might be confident in their abilities to wow a crowd with a speech, but not confident in writing an essay.

A self-confident person, someone who believes in their own abilities, is more likely to embrace new challenges and responsibilities. Self-confidence is a positive trait that helps a person to make the most of their talents and develop new ones.

Onward and upward

When someone feels confident, they are more likely to tackle challenges with determination and spirit, which increases their chances of achieving their goals and ambitions. A lack of confidence can actually curb a person's progress, making small obstacles feel daunting. Obstacles are a part of life, but they shouldn't stop a person from doing what they want.

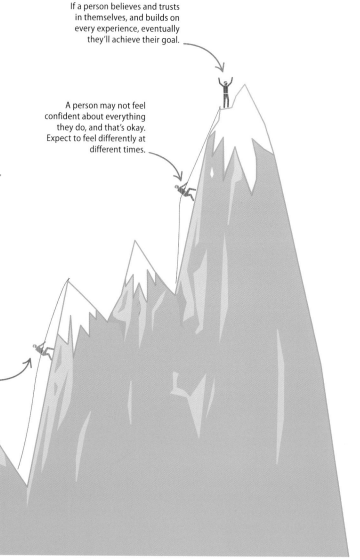

▽ **Overcoming obstacles**
Maintaining confidence when faced with challenges can be a challenge in itself, but small steps can lead to big achievements.

If a person believes and trusts in themselves, and builds on every experience, eventually they'll achieve their goal.

A person may not feel confident about everything they do, and that's okay. Expect to feel differently at different times.

Sometimes it can feel like an uphill battle. Be persistent and remember why these goals are important—this will help a person to keep going.

The first step to overcoming an obstacle is a person's belief that they can do it.

"The fact that **I'm me** and no one else is one of my **greatest assets**."
Haruki Murakami

Building self-esteem

Self-esteem affects almost every part of a person's life, from their relationships with others to academic and work performance, so it is essential to value yourself and give yourself the recognition that you deserve.

- Think and say positive things to yourself, about yourself, every day.
- Don't say mean things to yourself—treat yourself like you would your best friend, with kindness and respect.
- Accept compliments from other people.
- Each day, write down three things you accomplished.

Leading by example

Teens pick up a lot from their parents—even when their parents don't realize it. It's important that teens learn positive self-esteem, and so you can aim to encourage this.

- Let your teen hear you congratulate yourself when you do something well, and say good things about yourself.
- Highlight and repeat your teen's qualities and achievements.
- Encourage resilience by talking about your own challenges with self-esteem. This will help them realize that we all struggle with self-esteem from time to time.

Self-esteem

Self-esteem relates to the way that people feel about themselves. It's their inner sense of their own importance, value, and worth. Confidence is specific to an aspect of a person's life, and it's okay not to be confident in everything—but to have low self-esteem affects more than a person's goals and abilities: it affects their mental health.

People with low self-esteem are extremely critical of themselves, and this constant stream of negative thoughts can lead to anxiety or depression. The good news is that people can choose what to think and say about themselves, and so can kick the negative thoughts, and replace them with positive opinions that are kind and affirmative.

Shyness

Shyness is when people feel uncertain or awkward during social encounters, especially with new people. It can influence how they behave or feel around others, and make them uncomfortable, self-conscious, or nervous. Shyness can also lead to physical responses, such as blushing, sweating, breathlessness, or being unable to speak.

Shyness is quite common, but it isn't a problem unless it causes a person emotional pain and stops them from achieving their full potential. If this occurs, it is advisable to talk to friends and family, or to see a counselor.

△ **Conversation topics**
Thinking about what to talk about with new people in advance can help conversation flow, and alleviate any awkward feelings.

Introversion and extroversion

Whether teens prefer hustle and bustle or peace and quiet, small groups or large, knowing their preferences empowers them to make their way in the world—on their own terms.

SEE ALSO
❮ **82–83** Positive mental health
❮ **86–87** Confidence and self-esteem
Anxiety and depression **94–95** ❯
Speaking up **124–125** ❯

Temperaments and traits

One way to think about people's personalities is whether they're introverts (people who tend to focus on the internal world) or extroverts (people who prefer the external world). Whether a person is one or the other is based on how much social interaction they feel comfortable with. Introverted people typically prefer socializing one-on-one or with smaller groups of people, and feel the need for some time alone to recharge after social situations. People who are extroverted feel energized and stimulated by big groups, as well as new people and situations.

Introversion and extroversion are two extremes, and the complexity of personalities means that while some people identify simply as one or the other, many others are a mix of the two. This type of mixture is known as ambiversion.

"The secret to life is to put yourself in the right lighting. For some, it's a Broadway spotlight; for others, a lamplit desk."
Susan Cain, author

Introversion Ambiversion Extroversion

Introversion
Introverted people enjoy quiet settings with limited stimuli. Due to these preferences, they often choose solitude and small groups. They tackle tasks deliberately and with focus, they listen more than they talk, and they think before speaking.

Ambiversion
Ambiverted people fall somewhere between introversion and extroversion. They tend to be comfortable, motivated, and enjoy interacting in social situations, but also seek out quieter settings and complete tasks thoughtfully.

Extroversion
People who are extroverted prefer hustle and bustle. They feel excited about the outer world, and are motivated by it. Extroverts tend to enjoy meeting people in large groups, take risks, and tackle life with haste and ferocity.

An extroverted world

In today's world, there is a general trend toward promoting extrovert values. Schools and workplaces encourage group learning and team tasks. It can be easy for an introverted person to feel uncomfortable or overwhelmed.

Whatever the trend, the important thing to remember—for introvert, extrovert, and ambivert alike—is that everyone thrives and struggles in different scenarios. Accepting this enables people to learn, build, and execute ways to focus on their different strengths in different scenarios.

MYTH BUSTER

The truth about introverts and extroverts

Extroverts aren't necessarily good at public speaking. Some are, but some aren't. Public speaking is a skill that needs to be learned and practiced. Extroverts may be less nervous, but what they say still needs to be carefully crafted—which is a skill associated with introverts.

Introversion is not the same thing as shyness. Whether someone is introverted or extroverted has no bearing on if they are shy or socially confident.

◁ **Thriving side by side**
While extroverts may shine in a school world that is geared to their ideals, introverts can thrive in their own ways, such as through using those steadfast traits of focus and concentration to block out distractions.

Explaining the science

Some images of extroverts' brains show messages traveling along direct routes when they're being processed. This may help to explain why extroverts enjoy jumping to the next new topic or experience. The longer pathway for introverts may explain why they like to think through things more and take time to process.

△ **Introvert pathway**
An introvert's more complex message route is processed by many parts that deal with memory, planning, and problem-solving.

△ **Extrovert pathway**
An extrovert's message takes a more direct route and is mostly processed by the brain's sensory decoder, which may show why extroverts crave new inputs.

PARENT TIPS

Supporting your teen

Knowing your teen's personality means you can support them whether they are introverted or extroverted.

If they're an introvert:

• give them time to think things through before making decisions.

• respect their private nature, and allow them to be quiet in social situations, as well as at home.

• appreciate their need to work alone, and praise their discipline and focus.

If they're an extrovert:

• let them jump in feet first and find their own way.

• encourage their enthusiasm and allow them to voice their thoughts to think.

• let them multitask, even if it means things take longer.

Resilience

Resilience is the ability to bounce back after disappointment and to learn from mistakes. It can determine a person's ability to cope with pressure, setbacks, and stress, and to persevere through tough times.

SEE ALSO	
❮ 82–83 Positive mental health	
❮ 86–87 Confidence and self-esteem	
Stress	92–93 ❯
Goals and ambitions	112–113 ❯

Managing adversity

Life is full of ups and downs—and the pressures and stresses of everyday life, as well as more traumatic life events (such as bereavement or illness), affect a person's happiness and sense of well-being. A big part of growing up is learning to manage adversity and become stronger than before.

▷ **Tools for life**
Resilience enables a person to avoid feeling overwhelmed, anxious, or depressed in the wake of a challenging situation.

Learning to fail

Trying new things or taking risks can be scary and, when things go wrong, it can be distressing or embarrassing, particularly if others are unsupportive. Yet, it's important not to feel too disheartened—there is actually a lot to be gained from failure.

The experience of failure teaches teens that they can cope with setbacks and improves their ability to adapt and solve problems. With more knowledge of the task, its requirements, and themselves, teens are better placed to achieve their goal in the future.

▽ **Have confidence**
Failure makes success that much sweeter.

"It is **impossible** to live without **failing at something**, unless you live so cautiously that you might as well not have lived at all—in which case, you fail by default."
J. K. Rowling

Negative thinking

When something goes wrong, negative thought patterns can hinder a person's ability to deal with a problem or setback.

Ignoring a problem

Although distraction can provide temporary relief, ignoring a problem will not make it go away. Plan time to tackle the issue and ask for support if needed.

Blaming oneself

Thinking incessantly about a mistake only makes it worse. Instead, recognize what went wrong, and plan what you'd do differently next time.

Catastrophizing

When something goes wrong, it can seem as if it's impossible to fix, or as if everything else is falling apart, too. Try to put things into perspective by asking a friend to give you a more objective point of view.

Building resilience

Over time and with practice, teens can learn new behaviors and ways of thinking to help them keep going when things get tricky.

Encourage yourself

Don't give yourself a hard time. Instead, think positively and praise yourself when you achieve something, no matter how small.

Know your strengths

Thinking about what you're good at reminds you of what you have to offer.

Ask for help

Seek out people in a similar situation who may be able to support you. There is nothing wrong with asking for help.

Remember past challenges

Try to remember another time when you felt this way, what you did, and how you felt afterward.

Learn from others

Some of the greatest athletes, inventors, and writers suffered many disappointments and failures before achieving success. Take inspiration from their persistence.

Work toward a goal

Having a clear goal can give you something to work toward and focus your attention.

Behave proactively

Taking active steps to change a situation can give you a sense of control. Try doing things differently if it didn't work out the first time.

Build a support network

Friends and family can listen and help with your concerns, or provide a great distraction.

Think positively

Try out a different perspective. Aim to be more optimistic—a little humor can help.

Acknowledge your feelings

Reflect on and try to understand how you're feeling. In doing so, it might become clear what steps you need to take to change things.

TEEN HINTS

Adapting to change

As a teen, it's common to encounter new situations where you may not feel entirely comfortable. Part of being resilient is being able to cope with the feelings caused by such changes. It's okay to notice yourself being a bit anxious—anxiety helps you recognize when something is valuable to you. Try rehearsing the situation in advance or making a plan to help you feel more confident and prepared.

Stay healthy

Eating well and doing regular exercise can improve your mental state and strengthen your ability to cope with a difficult situation.

Appreciate the good things

Even the small things count, like listening to a favorite song or reading a good book.

Stress

Whether it's related to exams or frustration with family, everyone feels stressed sometimes. Stress can be a positive thing, motivating teens to work well under pressure, but too much of it can have a harmful effect on a person's emotional and physical health.

SEE ALSO

❰ 82–83 Positive mental health

❰ 86–87 Confidence and self-esteem

❰ 90–91 Resilience

Anxiety and depression   94–95 ❱

Fight or flight

When the body feels stress, it goes into "fight or flight" mode, releasing a mixture of hormones that prepares the body for action. These hormones increase energy and divert blood away from the brain and into the muscles. This stress response works well when a human's life is in danger, but it's less helpful when it's triggered for something that isn't life-threatening, such as taking an exam.

△ **Fight**
The "fight" mechanism prepares the brain and body to defend itself.

△ **Flight**
The "flight" mechanism leads a person to look for a way to escape the situation.

Triggers

A "trigger" is anything that is the initial cause of stressful feelings. While most triggers are external—meaning they are in response to things happening outside the person, such as exams or difficult family events—some are internal, resulting from pressures that people put on themselves.

▽ **Identifying triggers**
There are many different things that can cause teens to feel stressed.

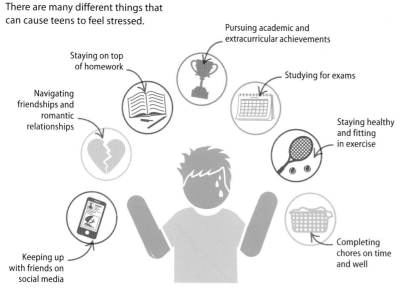

Staying on top of homework

Pursuing academic and extracurricular achievements

Navigating friendships and romantic relationships

Studying for exams

Staying healthy and fitting in exercise

Keeping up with friends on social media

Completing chores on time and well

TEEN HINTS

Figuring out stress

Sometimes it can be hard to work out what it is that's causing stress—especially if everything seems to be happening at once. Take time to think through and write down what is bothering you. This could give you ideas about the practical changes you could make to help you manage stressful feelings.

GOOD TO KNOW

Good and bad stress

Stress can sometimes be very useful, as it motivates people to keep working under pressure and energizes them to complete tasks they care about. But if it becomes overwhelming, stress can limit a person's ability to function effectively. When you're feeling stressed, try to use it as motivation to tackle a challenge, but if things start to seem unmanageable, seek support.

Signs of stress

People experience stress in different ways, but there are quite a few common symptoms. Some people experience these at the same time—such as feeling tired and emotional. Sometimes, one symptom can cause another to happen. The symptoms of stress add to the overall feeling of being stressed by preventing people from feeling rested and clear-minded, which in turn may make them feel even more stressed.

△ **Tiredness**
Stress tires out the mind and muscles, and can affect sleep, making it harder to concentrate.

△ **Feeling emotional**
Panic attacks and sudden crying are signs of the acute anxiety that stress can bring.

△ **Vomiting**
Stress can cause an upset stomach, loss of appetite, constipation, and diarrhea.

△ **Anger**
Some people become irritable, frustrated, and angry when stressed.

△ **Headaches**
Migraines and headaches can be a debilitating aspect of stress.

△ **Chest pains**
Chest pains and heart palpitations can be triggered by stress.

Dealing with stress

There are no immediate solutions to stress, but there are a number of things that can reduce its effects over time. Though they might seem basic, they can help a person feel calm, rested, and supported, and give back a sense of control.

> "The greatest weapon against stress is our ability to choose one thought over another."
> **William James, philosopher**

Take a break

Try to get some time away from thinking about your problem, as it can refresh your perspective and calm you down.

Get enough sleep

Though it might be difficult when stressed, a good night's rest is a massive factor in overcoming stress and anxiety.

Talk

Talking to those around you is a great way of releasing some tension and may help you find solutions to your stress.

Exercise

Physical activity helps you feel calmer, but also improves the quality of your sleep.

Anxiety and depression

Anxiety and depression are the two most common forms of mental illness. These conditions last longer and are more severe than feeling worried or sad about something.

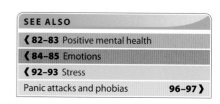
Anxiety

Feeling anxious is a normal response to any type of stress. It describes the thoughts and feelings associated with being worried or afraid. Although it usually feels unpleasant, anxiety is related to the "fight or flight" response, a biological reaction to life-threatening situations that humans, like all other animals, have in order to cope with danger.

◁ **Fight or flight**
When threatened, the body releases hormones that prepare it to fight or flee. The heart beats faster and the brain becomes more alert.

When anxiety is a problem

For some people, however, these anxious feelings do not go away once the stressful event is over. If feelings of anxiety are very strong or overwhelming, last for a long time, or have an impact on their lifestyle, a teen's anxiety may have become unmanageable.

▷ **Getting help**
If anxious feelings start to restrict a teen's lifestyle, it's best to see a doctor.

Managing anxiety and depression

Just as there are ways to keep the body healthy, there are many different steps teens can take to keep their minds healthy, too:

Mindfulness

Yoga and meditation can teach teens to focus on the present.

Go outside

Being outside in nature can help elevate a teen's mood.

Friends and family

Connecting with others is a great way to improve mental well-being.

Exercise and sports

Exercise causes the brain to release endorphins, a natural antidepressant.

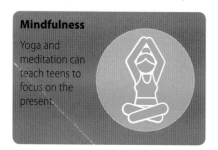

Be creative

Making things and doing creative or crafty activities boosts mood and gives a sense of satisfaction.

Stay healthy

An active, healthy lifestyle helps keep the mind healthy and interested, too.

Depression

People often say "I'm depressed" when they are sad. But in fact, depression lasts longer than the feeling that comes when something or upsetting has happened. Depression may be triggered by experiencing a traumatic event, such as the loss of a loved one, moving to a new home, or changing schools, but sometimes it can happen for no reason at all. People who are depressed feel persistently down and usually experience one or more of the following symptoms.

Symptoms

Constantly feeling sad, low, or worthless; sometimes irritable or tearful

- Losing interest or pleasure in normally enjoyable things
- Having difficulty concentrating and making decisions
- Feeling unable to fall asleep, and sleeping less or more than usual
- Changes in appetite and subsequent weight loss or gain
- Headaches, tiredness or loss of energy, and feeling restless

ALERT!

Suicidal feelings

Suicide is the act of intentionally ending your own life. Sometimes people with depression, or those experiencing intolerable feelings, can start to feel that their life isn't worth living. This feeling is usually temporary, but it's essential to seek help immediately if you feel this way.

For some people, it helps to speak to someone they don't know. There are phone helplines available 24 hours a day, every day of the year, or counselors that can be reached by text or email.

If you're worried for a friend, encourage them to talk about their feelings and listen carefully. Advise them to get help as quickly as possible. They may seem to push you away or appear indifferent at first, but stick by them and offer your support.

What to avoid

There are some pitfalls to avoid if a teen is feeling anxious or depressed.

See the doctor

A nurse or doctor will be able to help if further support is needed.

Counseling

Talking is one of the first and best steps to get help with anxiety and depression.

Medical treatment

When anxiety and depression persist, the doctor may prescribe medication.

Cognitive Behavioral Therapy (CBT)

CBT is a method of changing negative thought patterns.

Too much time online

Be smart about online time. Too much, especially on social media, may worsen a teen's mood.

Alcohol or drugs

Don't rely on these for a mood boost. They make anxiety and depression worse.

Panic attacks and phobias

A panic attack is when intense anxious feelings come on very suddenly. Similar feelings of overwhelming anxiety can also be triggered by the fear of something specific, known as a phobia.

SEE ALSO

❮ **82–83** Positive mental health

❮ **90–91** Resilience

❮ **92–93** Stress

❮ **94–95** Anxiety and depression

Panic attacks

Panic attacks are feelings of extreme anxiety that come on in unpredictable attacks. They may cause a sufferer to feel as if they're about to faint, have a heart attack, or die. A panic attack usually lasts for about 10 minutes. The feelings gradually go away without causing any harm, but a sufferer can feel exhausted afterward.

Panic attacks can happen for no apparent reason, or be caused by a trigger, though the reason may not always be clear. If a teen has had an attack at a particular place and time, being in the same situation again might trigger another.

△ **Jumping or racing heart.**

△ **Shaking, sweating, or trembling.**

△ **Dizziness or nausea.**

△ **Ringing in ears or sensitivity to noise.**

△ **Difficulty breathing normally.**

△ **Tingling hands and feet.**

△ **Panic attack symptoms**
The symptoms might feel scary, but they will not cause any physical harm.

TEEN HINTS

Helping a friend

- Stay calm yourself. Don't rush them; reassure and remind them it will pass. Never say "pull yourself together" or "get over it."

- Get them to focus on their breathing. Ask them to breathe in and out slowly. Do it with them and count in for three, and out for three.

- March on the spot with them to release stress, or ask them to name five things they can see around them.

Reducing the risk of panic attacks

There are ways to help reduce the likelihood of a panic attack:

Realize

- A panic attack is caused by the body's "fight or flight" response, evolved by all animals, including humans, to protect themselves when confronted with danger.

- The symptoms are scary, but they won't cause any physical harm.

Be prepared

- Plan how to respond if an attack happens. Then, if one is about to start, or if a trigger situation occurs, there is a routine and everyone knows what to do.

Slow down

- Try breathing exercises, as well as meditation and mindfulness (focusing on the present moment).

- Have calming music available that can be accessed quickly.

Phobias

People who have phobias tend to feel very anxious about one thing in particular. The thing they feel anxious about may not be dangerous or troublesome to anyone else, but it can make the sufferer feel very nervous and panicky.

Obsessive compulsive disorder (OCD)

Some people who are anxious have obsessive compulsive disorder (OCD). To control their anxiety, they feel compelled to do certain things and may have repeated negative thoughts—for example, that something bad might happen or that they themselves might do something bad. The aim of a sufferer's compulsions is usually to try to combat negative thoughts, and can include things like arranging objects, checking things repeatedly, cleaning, or counting.

▷ **Common phobias**
These are the most common phobias, but there are many more.

Name	Fear of
Acrophobia	Heights
Agoraphobia	Open or public spaces, which makes it difficult for someone to go outside
Arachnophobia	Spiders
Claustrophobia	Confined spaces, which can make it hard to use elevators
Mysophobia/ germophobia	Germs
Ophidiophobia	Snakes
Pteromerhanophobia	Flying
Social phobia	Social situations, which can make a person very isolated
Trypanophobia	Needles and injections

Other mental illness

Mental illnesses affect the way people think, feel, or behave. They range from common problems, such as anxiety and depression, to rarer conditions, such as bipolar disorder and schizophrenia. They often start to develop during the teenage years, at a time when many changes are taking place in the brain. Like any illness, consulting a doctor is often the first step toward treating them.

Stigma

Sometimes people find it much more difficult to admit to having problems with their mental health than they would if it was their physical health. This can be because there is a stigma about mental illness.

Mental illness, however, is in fact very common, and it's important to talk about it openly with friends and family. Being frank about mental illness enables those who are experiencing it to get the treatment and support they need.

◁ **Treatment and medication**
There are many treatments available, from counseling to medication.

Self-harm

Someone self-harms when they do something to hurt their body. They might do this as a way of dealing with very difficult feelings or situations. There is no single cause, but for many who self-harm, it's a physical response to some overwhelming stress or sadness.

SEE ALSO

❮ **82–83** Positive mental health
❮ **86–87** Confidence and self-esteem
❮ **92–93** Stress
❮ **94–95** Anxiety and depression

What is self-harm?

Self-harm is the act of deliberately hurting oneself. People may do this in a variety of ways. The most common is cutting, but other methods include burning, hair-pulling, ingesting harmful substances, pinching, punching walls or doors, and scratching. Taking dangerous risks, not looking after oneself, and exercising obsessively might also be considered forms of self-harm.

MYTH BUSTER

The truth about self-harm

It isn't just girls who self-harm. Although it's more widely known among girls, boys also self-harm. Some self-harm behaviors may not be identified as such—for example, punching a wall or taking risks that result in injury.

Self-harm isn't attention-seeking. In fact, self-harm is often kept secret.

Most people who self-harm don't want to end their life. For most, it's actually a coping mechanism.

Self-harm isn't a mental illness. However, self-harm is associated with some mental ilnesses, such as anxiety, depression, eating disorders, and post-traumatic stress.

▷ **Dangerous risks**
While cutting or hair-pulling are more commonly acknowledged as self-harm behaviors, teens taking dangerous risks may also be seeking to hurt themselves.

Why people self-harm

There can be many reasons why someone would self-harm. It is sometimes described as a "relief valve"—a way to cope with emotions that might otherwise feel unbearable. For some, physical pain provides an escape or a distraction from emotional distress, while others self-harm to express low self-esteem or to punish themselves. It may also be a suicide attempt.

▽ **Overwhelming feelings**
Self-harm often happens during times of anger, distress, depression, fear, low self-esteem, or worry. It can become a cycle that is hard to break, as the harmful behaviors used to relieve difficult or painful feelings in turn lead to feelings of guilt or shame.

Periods of high stress and pressure, such as exams	Relationship difficulties, arguments, and breakups	Traumatic events, such as a bereavement or family breakdown, and their anniversaries	Wanting to escape from something
Feeling rejected, powerless, anxious, angry, or depressed	Finding it hard to communicate or express emotions	Bullying, controlling friendships, or controlling relationships	Witnessing or being subjected to physical, sexual, or emotional abuse

Acknowledging the problem

Self-harm is an unhealthy coping mechanism that can be difficult to admit to other people. It often remains a secret because the person who is self-harming fears the reactions of others. Challenging stigma, and being open and nonjudgmental about self-harm in general, will make it more likely for a person who self-harms to seek support.

TEEN HINTS
Getting help

- Talk to someone you can trust, or, if you prefer to talk to someone you don't know, call a support helpline.

- Sometimes it's easier to talk when you're both doing something else, such as cooking a meal or driving. Writing a list or letter in advance can help you tell them exactly what you need them to know.

- Think about what you want to happen next and what support you need.

- Consider seeking professional help, such as from a doctor or school counselor.

PARENT TIPS
Supporting your teen

- Be aware of the behavioral signs, such as becoming isolated or withdrawn, changes in eating habits and weight, depression, drinking or drug-taking, low self-esteem, or wearing long clothing or refusing to wear a swimsuit or sports uniform, in order to hide any injuries.

- Self-harm is typically carried out secretly, so any physical signs might not be obvious. Look for bald patches, bruises, burns, and cuts.

- Encourage your teen to talk, and listen calmly without passing judgment. Agree together what will happen next.

- Seek professional help if you feel you don't know what to do.

Other ways of coping

Understanding what triggers self-harm can help when trying to find an alternative coping strategy—hitting a pillow really hard might help to vent anger, or doing a breathing exercise can help restore a sense of control.

▽ **Finding distractions**
If talking to a safe person isn't an immediate option, there are all sorts of alternative strategies to help teens cope with overwhelming feelings.

△ Squeeze an ice cube until it melts.

△ Draw and paint on the skin.

△ Flick a hair band on the wrist.

△ Take a cold shower.

△ Play sports or do some exercise.

△ Play relaxing music.

△ Scream loudly.

△ Write down feelings, then scribble them out.

Achieving potential

School life

From setting an alarm, packing lunch, and being on time, to managing schoolwork, keeping up with homework, and making new friends, school is full of exciting activities, challenges, and opportunities.

SEE ALSO

❮ 90–91 Resilience

Tests and studying   104–105 ❯

Goals and ambitions   112–113 ❯

Bullying   150–151 ❯

Ways of learning

Some teens may be particularly fond of one way of learning over another, but most will use a mixture of approaches, depending on the subject, type of work, and where they are when studying.

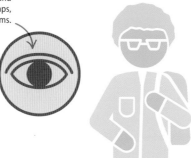

Aural
Aural learners like to understand things by listening, and might read notes aloud or make recordings of work.

Visual
Visual learners prefer to learn about something by seeing it and are likely to draw mind-maps, sketches, and diagrams.

Physical
People who lean toward learning by doing something are called physical learners. They might copy out their notes or walk about when studying.

▷ **Trying different approaches**
Knowing what works best for them and for a particular subject helps teens to study more easily and effectively, so it's worth experimenting with different approaches.

Time management

Time management involves thinking about how much time a task will take and working out how much time is available before a deadline. Thinking carefully about these aspects helps people to work out a realistic schedule, and plan and organize their time efficiently and effectively.

Planning and prioritizing

Planning a schedule for busy periods makes daunting tasks feel more achievable. Write out a list of everything that needs to be completed over the next day or week. Then prioritize the list to avoid wasting time on less important things.

Say "no"

Learning to say "no" is important for time management. When teens take on too much, it can make them feel disorganized and stressed. Learning to prioritize emotional and physical health is part of good time management.

Break down each task

When adding big tasks to a to-do list, divide them into three or four smaller parts, then work through each one-by-one. This makes a big task feel much more achievable and less overwhelming.

Schedule time to relax

Scheduling regular breaks is essential to staying motivated about schoolwork. Relaxing, exercising, doing hobbies, and meeting friends also helps teens to unwind.

Homework tips

Homework can sometimes seem like a chore, even to the most enthusiastic student. Keeping on top of it helps to reduce stress levels and encourages good time management.

- Keep a homework schedule and stick to it.
- Get started on homework right after school.
- Ask the teacher which topics should be prioritized.
- Tell the teacher as soon as possible if homework is going to be late.
- Study outside the house, such as in a library, where there are no distractions.

△ **Being organized**
Having good homework habits keeps it from becoming stressful.

Liking and disliking subjects

It can be easy for students to focus on subjects they really like at the expense of those they find less engaging. However, it's important that students don't neglect any area of study, even if some topics feel harder than others. One strategy to make these subjects feel more appealing is to study with other people, especially someone who really likes the subject. Other ways might include watching videos of experts talking about the subject or visiting an attraction related to the subject.

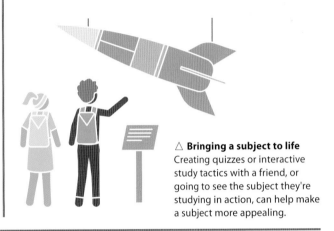

△ **Bringing a subject to life**
Creating quizzes or interactive study tactics with a friend, or going to see the subject they're studying in action, can help make a subject more appealing.

Changing schools

Most people change school at some time, and the experience can seem intimidating. There are new classmates, new teachers, and a whole new routine to figure out, all at the same time. Thankfully, there are some simple things teens can try to help them settle more quickly and make the experience feel easier.

△ **Make new friends**
Smiling and being open to conversation with people sitting nearby is a great way to make some new friends.

△ **Take part**
Joining a team or club, or participating in a school activity, helps people feel involved in school life and learn where things are.

△ **Talk to adults**
Teens should keep their parents informed about how the change is going, as well as who to talk to in the new school if there is a problem.

△ **Be yourself**
Don't feel the need to boast or impress others to fit in. New classmates prefer it when people are themselves.

Tests and studying

There are many different types of tests, but all are designed to review a teen's knowledge and understanding of a subject under timed conditions. While every teen is different, having a study schedule and plenty of time to prepare can help build confidence.

SEE ALSO

❰ 90–91 Resilience
❰ 92–93 Stress
❰ 102–103 School life
Goals and ambitions 112–113 ❱

Studying for a test

Tests can be challenging, especially when several are scheduled to take place in a short period of time. Effective studying starts months in advance of a test, when students first start to learn about and take notes on a subject.

▽ **Keep things varied**
How a teen studies is as important as how much time they spend studying. There are a variety of methods teens can try.

TEEN HINTS
Study environment

Where you study can affect how well you study. Choose a quiet, well-lit place that's free from distractions. Make sure your chair is comfortable. If possible, try not to work in your bedroom, so that you associate your room with relaxing.

Reading notes

When studying, reading over class notes helps teens to improve their understanding and identify areas for further study. Writing notes out using different colors, reducing them down to key points, drawing mind-maps, and annotating hand-outs are all great ways to make the most of class notes.

Memorizing

People have different ways of committing information to memory. Some students organize their notes using a color-coding system to pick out themes or topics. Some visualize the information on the page or associate ideas with pictures or diagrams. Others record themselves or somebody else reading the notes out loud to listen to. Others still create mind-maps or diagrams to make the connections between things clear.

Drafting model answers

Using past test papers, if it's possible to get them, is a useful way of recreating testlike conditions. It's also a chance to practice the style of the test, as well as to time how long each question will take to answer. Students can check their own answers against sample answers, and even ask their teacher to look at their work and provide feedback.

Study schedule

Planning a study schedule that includes the dates of all tests can help teens to feel in control and well-prepared. Starting studying as early as possible in advance allows for more flexibility if a particular topic needs more time and attention.

Construct a chart with days of the week split into morning, afternoon, and evening.

Be sure to include time for relaxing and exercising, too.

▷ **Color-coded timetable**
Using different colors for each topic may help teens to see at a glance what needs to be done and when.

Months before

Construct a timetable that covers all test topics. Find out what type of questions will be asked in the test to help guide study methods.

Weeks before

Ask the teacher for extra help, if needed. Be sure to include time to relax to ensure you stay healthy and motivated. Try answering questions from past papers.

Night before

Avoid last-minute cramming. Instead, put the books away and do something relaxing. Prepare any equipment and note paper and set an alarm for the morning.

On the day

Start the day with breakfast. Arrive as early as possible. Read each question carefully and divide time between each one according to how many points it's worth.

Staying focused

Tests are important, but good mental health is essential. There are lots of strategies a teen can use to reduce stress and boost motivation.

Taking breaks

Even a short break helps to rejuvenate and refocus the mind. If a teen finds their mind is starting to wander while they study, it's probably a good time to take a break.

Staying physically healthy

Exercising regularly is good for the body and allows the mind to recharge. Getting enough sleep is vital, as it improves concentration and decision-making.

Eating well

Eating regular meals and healthy snacks keeps teens going throughout the day. Sugary snacks and "energy" drinks can be tempting, but their quick boost is followed by an energy crash. Drinking plenty of water is important, too.

Getting support

Tests can be stressful, especially if they happen all at once. Sometimes having a lot to do can lead to feelings of stress or anxiety. If it all starts to feel overwhelming, talking things over with a friend or trusted adult is essential.

Problem solving

Whether it's a flat tire or torn clothes, tricky schoolwork or difficult life events, being able to identify a problem and come up with a solution is an important life skill.

SEE ALSO

❮ **18–19** Thinking independently
❮ **90–91** Resilience
❮ **104–105** Tests and studying
Goals and ambitions **112–113** ❯

Overcoming obstacles

People encounter challenges, problems, setbacks, and obstacles all the time. Some problems are small, others are big, some are easy to resolve, and others are quite tricky. People with strong problem-solving skills can see a difficult situation clearly, analyze the facts, and come up with ideas that lead to a solution.

TEEN HINTS

Feeling overwhelmed

- Try to think of a problem as an opportunity to change and improve something.

- Take a step back to see the reality of the situation—it might not be as bad as you think.

- If a problem is making you anxious, speak to friends or family who can support you.

◁ **Stay calm**
Many problems can leave teens feeling fed up or frustrated, but staying calm and thinking things through will help them find a solution faster.

Steps to take

When something goes wrong, it's easy to get discouraged, but the most practical and productive reaction is to take active steps toward working out a solution to the problem. Often the first attempt may not succeed, but failing is a great way to learn what doesn't work. Teens shouldn't feel disheartened, as everyone makes mistakes or fails at some point, and the knowledge they gain will help with the next attempt.

▽ **Find a solution**
These steps will help teens to figure out how best to approach and overcome their problems.

Identify the problem

Think about the situation and work out exactly what it is that you want to change. Know what a successful resolution of the issue would look like to you.

Think of possible solutions

Come up with as many ideas as possible; don't stop at the first. Think about, or write a list of, the pros and cons for each idea. Think about the amount of time it would take, the cost, who you need to speak to, if it is realistic, and whether or not you would need help.

Choose the best option

Think carefully about the facts of the situation, and based on the pros and cons, choose the most suitable solution for the problem. Speak to someone you trust if you're still not sure. Keep in mind a back-up option, in case the first attempt doesn't work out.

Different approaches

There is more than one way to tackle every problem. Being flexible and open to new ideas and approaches increases the chances of finding the best solution.

Take logical steps
Think through the problem step-by-step, and don't move onto the next step until the previous one works or makes sense.

Inspiration all around
Don't be afraid to take ideas and inspiration from things that aren't strictly related to the problem. You could use ideas from one class to resolve a problem you have in another subject, for example.

Think creatively
Try playing around with the problem: start at the end and work backward, use sticky notes to put possible solutions on the wall, or draw a mind-map of ideas. Working in a new way can help you to creatively solve the problem.

Find a different way
Instead of tackling the problem in the most obvious way, there is likely to be another solution. Sometimes, thinking "outside the box" can lead to more ways to get past a problem.

Think like a detective
Ask as many questions as you can, and don't accept anything as fact that can't be proven. One question, and its answer, might lead to a breakthrough.

Visualize success
Visualization is when you imagine how something will look in the future in order to work out how to get there. It can give you confidence and motivation to continue, and a clear goal to aim for.

A problem shared ...
Asking someone else for their input is a great way to solve problems. Sometimes it's easier for a person outside the situation to see things more clearly, and parents, teachers, and friends are often ready to help.

Move around
If you're stuck, distract yourself. Go for a walk or play a video game. Having a break and returning to a problem later can help you look at it with fresh eyes and new enthusiasm.

Hobbies and interests

Hobbies improve self-confidence, create new experiences, and often involve meeting new people. They also relax the body and engage the mind. Most importantly, they should be fun.

SEE ALSO

❰ **74–75** Exercise

❰ **86–87** Confidence and self-esteem

❰ **102–103** School life

Getting a job **122–123** ❱

Choosing hobbies

People usually choose a hobby based on what's important to them. Some people choose a hobby that will help them develop a skill, others because they are curious about a particular topic. The best advice for anyone looking to develop a new interest is to take time to try out new things. The teen years are a perfect time to explore and experiment.

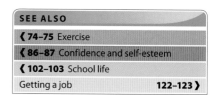

△ **Be led by what you enjoy**
Teens should think about what they enjoy or what interests them. It could be something from childhood, or totally new. An enjoyable hobby is an easy one to keep up.

△ **Ask others**
When teens think they might like to try something, it's a good idea to talk to people who already do that activity to find out what it's like and what time commitment is involved.

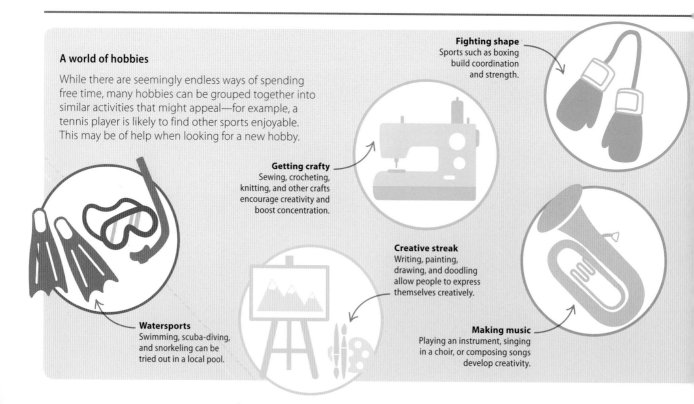

A world of hobbies

While there are seemingly endless ways of spending free time, many hobbies can be grouped together into similar activities that might appeal—for example, a tennis player is likely to find other sports enjoyable. This may be of help when looking for a new hobby.

Fighting shape
Sports such as boxing build coordination and strength.

Getting crafty
Sewing, crocheting, knitting, and other crafts encourage creativity and boost concentration.

Creative streak
Writing, painting, drawing, and doodling allow people to express themselves creatively.

Watersports
Swimming, scuba-diving, and snorkeling can be tried out in a local pool.

Making music
Playing an instrument, singing in a choir, or composing songs develop creativity.

Feeling unsure

When trying out new things, it's normal to be uncertain or feel nervous about it, but it's important not to let that stop you. If you're having fun, keep at it. The more you do it, the more confident you'll become.

△ **Try it out**
The best way to explore a new hobby is to get involved by giving it a try. People might not feel confident to begin with, but should keep trying as their abilities will improve.

△ **Practice makes perfect!**
To get the most out of the hobby, a teen should schedule time for it. For a lot of hobbies, the real fun comes from putting the work in and seeing the improvements over time.

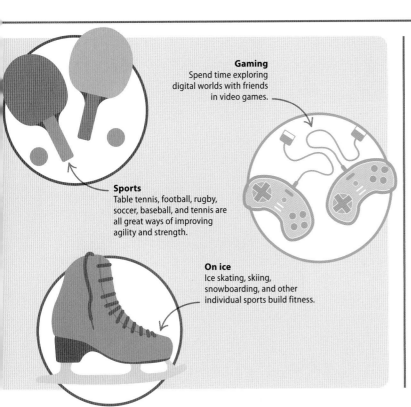

Gaming
Spend time exploring digital worlds with friends in video games.

Sports
Table tennis, football, rugby, soccer, baseball, and tennis are all great ways of improving agility and strength.

On ice
Ice skating, skiing, snowboarding, and other individual sports build fitness.

Other considerations

When selecting a hobby, it's important to think about the practicalities, such as cost, equipment, and space needed, and how much time it requires. A hobby must fit in with everything else that goes on in life—from school to social events. It should help to ease life's stresses, not add to them.

Money matters

Adolescence is a great time to learn how to take responsibility for personal money. Teens can start to earn an allowance for chores or get a part-time job, so it's a good idea to learn how to set a budget, have a bank account, and start saving.

Making a budget

A budget is an estimate of how much money will be coming in and going out in the future. A good budget is based on realistic predictions. Teens should start by working out and writing down what money they receive from an allowance and any part-time jobs they have. They should then write down purchases that are essential, such as school supplies. If there is money left over after these expenses, this can be saved up for things that count as luxury purchases, such as video games or music.

TEEN HINTS

Allowance

An allowance is a great way to start gaining financial independence. Ask your parents if you can earn some money by doing chores at home. Then, once you've started earning, work out a budget and try to stick to it. If your budget works properly, you should be able to save money and buy yourself the things you really want.

▽ **Compare prices**
Try to be savvy when making purchases by shopping around—price comparison websites are quick and reliable, and can save users money.

Free things to do

People don't have to spend a lot of money to have fun. There are many things teens can do that won't cost anything. Spending time in the local library, swapping clothes with friends, visiting galleries and museums, window shopping at the mall, going to free concerts in public spaces, or playing in the park are just a few ideas.

Part-time jobs

Getting a part-time job can be a great way for teens to gain work experience, make new friends, and take the first steps toward financial independence. There are laws about when teens can legally start work and how many hours they are allowed to do each week. A part-time job should not interfere with the teen's school life, especially during test time.

▷ **Paper route**
Doing simple jobs teaches teens about responsibility and can help them develop people skills.

Bank accounts

A bank account is a place where a person can store their money and take it out when they want it. There are many different options available when opening a bank account. Some accounts may charge fees for maintaining the account, while others pay interest on positive balances or have an overdraft (the ability for the account to be in debt).

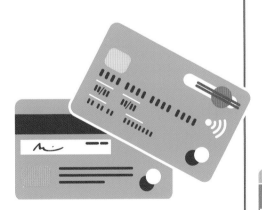

△ **Debit cards**
Most bank accounts will offer a debit card, which allows users to take out money that is already in the account.

Savings

Saving any spare money can help teens to afford things they need or want in the future. Many banks offer simple savings accounts for teens, but it's a good idea to shop around for the best rates and perks. Setting up a regular payment to a savings account can take the hassle out of saving.

▽ **Saving up**
If teens want to buy something expensive, such as an electronic device or driving lessons, a savings plan can help them to achieve their goal eventually.

PARENT TIPS

Setting a good example

- If you're the type of person who budgets and saves, your teen is likely to learn this from you.

- If you've had financial problems in the past, it can be useful to talk about this to your teen, so they understand how mistakes can be made and what to avoid.

- A great way to encourage and educate your teen about money is to include them in some of your financial decisions, such as shopping around for car insurance or vacations.

Goals and ambitions

Goals and ambitions help to give people a sense of direction and focus. From achieving at school, succeeding at sports, or getting a particular job, a person's goals and ambitions are hopes for the future that inspire and excite them.

SEE ALSO	
❮ **86–87** Confidence and self-esteem	
❮ **102–103** School life	
Career advice	**114–115** ❯
Types of career	**116–117** ❯

Looking forward

A goal or ambition is a strong desire to do or to achieve something. Some are small and can be achieved sooner, while others are much longer term, such as going to college or having a career in a particular industry. This type of goal or ambition usually includes lots of smaller activities along the way, which can be thought of as stepping stones—specific hurdles to overcome in order to achieve the long-term aim.

△ **In the short term**
Acting in a school play involves short-term goals that require a teen to learn their lines and scenes in a short period of time in order to succeed.

△ **In the long term**
Planning ahead, such as for becoming an actor, requires teens to imagine their future so they can start working toward it.

Setting goals and ambitions

The best way for teens to set goals and ambitions is to think about what interests, inspires, and excites them. These ideas can be very personal and can be kept private if a person prefers.

"You must expect great things of yourself before you can do them."
Michael Jordan, basketball player

School achievements

Being motivated to attain a particular position—for example, being the best at a subject—is a common aim for teens who want to achieve big things.

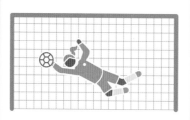

Perfecting a skill

Focusing on perfecting a skill, such as diving for the ball in soccer, is something some teens strive for.

Trying things out

Other teens enjoy a variety of challenges, and prefer to pursue many goals at once, perhaps learning an instrument, training for sports, and studying all at the same time.

Taking action

Goals and ambitions should stretch a person, but at the same time, it's a good idea to think carefully about how realistic they are before throwing everything into pursuing them. Dividing a big ambition into smaller goals, actions, and targets helps to make it feel more achievable. Ambitions can change over time, so it's important for teens to reassess their plans now and then to see if they need or want to do things differently.

▷ **Aim high**
A goal or ambition can be achieved with persistence, dedication, and hard work.

Not feeling sure

Some teens have a very strong sense of what their goals and ambitions are, but for many, it takes a lot longer to work out what excites them. This is completely normal, and there is no pressure to decide. Keeping your options open and trying out lots of different things allows you to find new interests and to discover in time what you feel passionate about, even if that doesn't happen until you're older.

Staying motivated

If a goal or ambition is the destination, then motivation is the fuel that keeps people going, even when things get tough. It's normal to feel frustrated or disheartened occasionally, but there are things people can think about to inspire and energize themselves.

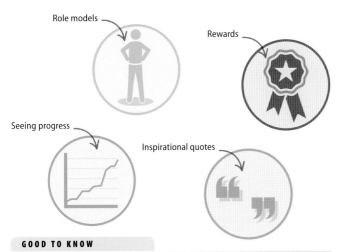

Role models

Rewards

Seeing progress

Inspirational quotes

Visualization

- Visualize your goal in as much detail as possible. This can help you to see what practical steps you need to take to get there.

- Imagine how you might feel once you've achieved your goal, when things get tough. This can provide motivation.

▷ **Celebrating victories**
Whether achievements are big or small, they are a reason to be proud and to feel confident.

Celebrating success

Working toward and achieving a goal or ambition can be very satisfying. Knowing that it's possible to work hard, overcome challenges and obstacles, and accomplish something exciting can all help to boost confidence and self-esteem. If a person is working toward a big goal or ambition, it's important for them to celebrate the smaller successes along the way, too.

Encountering failure

Falling short of achieving a goal or ambition can be very disappointing. Let your teen know that it may take longer than they'd like, but by learning from their mistakes, working out how to improve, and being persistent, they will get there in the end.

Career advice

A career is a job a person does for a significant amount of time that involves opportunities to progress and learn new skills. Building a career begins when teens start to dream about what their future might look like and to explore how to turn their ideas into reality.

Thinking about the future

A career is a journey, with many lessons, opportunities, and challenges to be experienced along the way. Some people have a good idea of what they want to do from an early age, but for many, it's a process of exploring the options available and trying things out to see what fits best for them. It's okay for teens not to know what career they might like to pursue, and there is no rush to decide.

▷ **Different options**
With an enormous number of jobs to choose from, deciding on a potential career can be challenging for some.

Understanding yourself

Each person has a unique combination of skills, talents, interests, values, and goals. Reflecting on these attributes, as well as what motivates them, can give teens insight into the roles and industries that might appeal to them.

▷ **Questions to ask**
Thinking about these questions can help teens to make decisions about the direction of their future career.

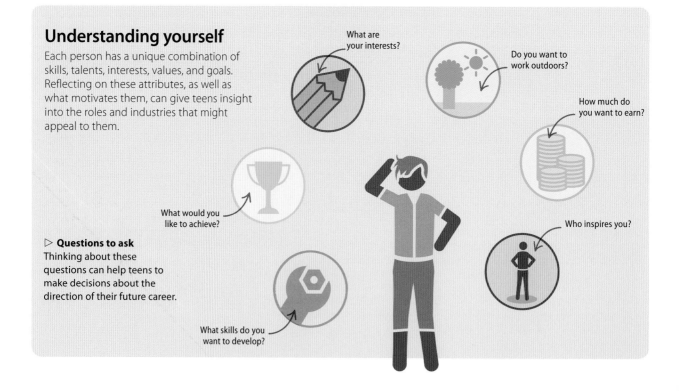

What are your interests?

Do you want to work outdoors?

How much do you want to earn?

Who inspires you?

What would you like to achieve?

What skills do you want to develop?

Thinking about careers

When researching the roles and industries that appeal to them, teens should also consider the qualifications and experience that future employers might be looking for, as well as what opportunities are available. This can help them make a decision about what subjects to study at school or college, and what work experience opportunities to pursue.

Changing careers

It was once common for someone to stay in the same career for their entire working life, but now it's much more normal for people to move around and change industries. This can happen when people develop new interests and skills, or face changes in the job market that create new jobs or cause older jobs to disappear.

Qualifications

It's worthwhile investigating what educational qualifications are required to work in certain areas. Some job areas require people to have studied certain subjects or to have a degree.

Experience

Most jobs require some previous experience. When starting out, the best way to gain experience is through completing an apprenticeship or volunteering.

Opportunities available

The working world can be very competitive. Knowing in advance how likely they are to be able to secure work and develop skills in the future, may be a factor in a teen's thought process.

Work experience

To get a sense of what might appeal, teens can get a taste for different roles through apprenticeships or internships. These opportunities give teens the chance to show enthusiasm, interest, and willingness to potential future employers and to get great experience for their resume, as well as insight into the working world.

Getting work experience

One way to get an apprenticeship is to approach people in your family or community who work in industries that interest you. Alternatively, if your school has one, ask your career adviser if they have any contacts that they can pass on to you. Finally, try contacting companies directly to ask about any opportunities they have available.

▷ **Learning on the job**
Apprenticeships and internships also give teens the chance to experience what working environments suit them best.

Types of career

With so many potential career options available, deciding what steps to take next can be confusing. Finding out what jobs link to the subjects that interest them can help teens decide.

Making decisions

Choosing a future career path is a big decision. Talking to career advisers, teachers, and family, and doing online research are all great ways to learn more about what different jobs entail, but ultimately, it's up to the teen to think about their goals, interests, and skills and how they could one day fit into the world of work.

"Find out what you like doing best, and get someone to pay you for it."
Katharine Whitehorn, journalist

Arts

Artistic people tend to be very creative and imaginative. They are "ideas people," and like to use their talents to create new sounds, images, designs, and messages. Jobs in the arts include being actors, musicians, costume designers, and events managers.

Arts subjects

- Fine art
- Graphic and product design
- Media studies
- Drama
- Dance
- Music

△ **Actor**
Portraying other people in films, TV shows, and in theater, actors need to be interested in literature, be able to memorize lines, and "inhabit" the roles they play.

Humanities

People who study human culture, a set of disciplines that are known as the humanities, tend to enjoy reading, analyzing material, and debating arguments. Careers in the humanities include becoming teachers, historians, translators, and journalists.

Humanities subjects

- History
- Geography
- Philosophy
- Classics
- Languages
- Literature
- Religious studies

△ **Teacher**
A good teacher seeks to inform and inspire students, to help them to reach their full potential in the world.

Vocational

Vocational subjects are usually for physically active people who enjoy being outdoors or hands-on activities. They tend to relish making or fixing things, participating in sports, or working with animals. In these jobs, being able to come up with new ideas and solve problems is essential. Vocational sector jobs include being mechanics, farmers, carpenters, and police officers.

Vocational subjects

- Sports
- Catering and hospitality
- Construction
- Woodworking and metalworking
- Uniformed services
- Farming
- Mechanics

△ **Mechanic**
Fixing and maintaining machinery is a wide field, so mechanics specialize in an area, such as cars, airplanes, or industrial machinery.

Sciences

People who enjoy the sciences tend to be logical and analytical, and have inquiring minds. They like to conduct experiments, design and build prototypes, and test out new theories. Science roles include becoming doctors, scientists, researchers, and computer engineers.

Sciences subjects

- Biology
- Chemistry
- Physics
- Math
- IT
- Engineering
- Environmental science

△ **Doctor**
Diagnosing and treating illnesses and injuries are among a doctor's main tasks, but they also give advice on health matters and preventative measures.

Social sciences

Social scientists are interested in how people interact with their wider society and how decisions made by a government affect the people it governs on a day-to-day basis. Social science covers areas such as the law and economics. Jobs in this field include being lawyers, politicians, entrepreneurs, and sociologists.

Social sciences subjects

- Psychology
- Sociology
- Politics
- Economics
- Business studies
- Finance
- Law

△ **Lawyer**
Lawyers advise and represent their clients in legal matters. They construct legal arguments that take into account the law and the circumstances of a case.

Going to college

Going to college isn't just about getting a degree. It's an exciting chance to study different subjects, have unique experiences, and make new friends.

SEE ALSO

❮ **102–103** School life

❮ **114–115** Career advice

Alternatives to college **120–121** ❯

Getting a job **122–123** ❯

Weighing options

As well as gaining qualifications and enhancing job prospects, many teens find college a great opportunity to make new friends, try out new hobbies and interests, and gain independence, but there are disadvantages to consider, too.

Advantages: ✓

• *Gain a degree, a qualification valued by employers*
• *Learn skills that are transferrable into a workplace*
• *Expand knowledge about a favorite subject*
• *Gather life skills and experience by living independently*
• *Have lots of fun!*

Disadvantages: ✗

• *Fees and living expenses can be costly*
• *No guarantee of a job at the end*

▷ **Pros and cons**
Choosing whether or not to go to college can be a big decision.

Choosing the right college

There are lots of things to consider when deciding what colleges to apply to. For many teens, the biggest factors to think about are whether a college offers the course they want to study and if they meet its entry requirements.

▽ **Making a decision**
There are so many colleges that picking which ones to apply to can be hard. Here are the main things to consider.

Subjects

Are traditional academic subjects or vocational subjects of more interest?

Future career

How easy it is to get a job with this degree after graduation?

Entry requirements

Which college has the most realistic entry requirements? It's best to apply to a range of colleges.

Reputation

What reputation does the college have? How important is this to you?

Location

Is there somewhere you've always wanted to live? Do you prefer big cities or small towns?

Assessment methods

Are essays and projects, exams, or tutorials used to assess grades?

Applying to college

Once a teen has decided on a course of study, it's time to start applying and getting familiar with the information each college requires—closing dates, for example. Most colleges require a personal statement, and drafting it early gives teens time to consider carefully what they want to say. Some colleges also interview prospective students.

> "An investment in knowledge pays the best interest."
> **Benjamin Franklin, scientist**

△ **Open houses**
Visiting colleges and attending open houses can help teens decide where they want to go. Talk to undergraduates there to get a sense of their experience.

△ **Applications**
Well-written, engaging, and original applications cover what teens hope to gain from the course, and what they'll bring to the college as a student.

△ **Housing**
There are usually lots of housing options, such as rented rooms or apartments, or accommodations on campus.

Studying abroad

Some students have the opportunity to study at college abroad through an exchange program. Others study for their entire degree abroad. This can be a great opportunity for a teen to experience another culture, learn a language, and add an international dimension to their resume.

Student finance

Many students take out loans and therefore need to budget carefully. Some students also take on a part-time job to help with their costs. Students can apply for any scholarships or awards that might be associated with their course, but competition for these is usually fierce.

△ **Life skills**
Parents often worry that their teen won't look after themselves at college, but the experience offers them a chance to learn vital skills, such as budgeting, staying healthy, and time management.

Alternatives to college

There are plenty of exciting routes for people who feel that college isn't for them. Some options teach teens skills needed in the working world, while others provide exciting life experiences that teens will never forget.

Options for teens

While some teens feel college is right for them, others prefer to take a different route to achieving their goals. There are many different options and opportunities available. Teens can learn job-specific skills at college or through an apprenticeship or internship. Some teens plan to volunteer, others want to travel, and some start building their career by entering the world of work right away. Each route offers its own mix of advantages and disadvantages, so teens should carefully consider their options before making a decision.

TEEN HINTS

Differing views

All of these options are exciting and provide great experience for a resume, but sometimes people disagree about what the future should hold. If you and your parents don't agree on your future plans, it's a good idea to schedule time to sit down as a family when everyone is calm and has thought about what they want to say in advance. Reassure them that you have thought carefully about the pros and cons of each option, and that you've taken their views into account.

Studying at college

Colleges and vocational schools (also called trade schools) train people in pratical, work-related skills that are associated with a particular job. Originally, these schools focused on training people for technical subjects, such as metal working or plumbing, but some colleges now offer academic subjects.

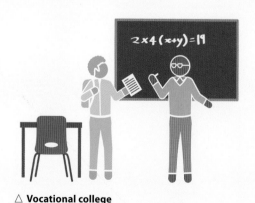

△ **Vocational college**
These colleges offer teens the chance to study a variety of subjects at a higher level.

Being an apprentice

Working with a company or organization as a full-time employee means teens receive formal, on-the-job training that can lead to work-based qualifications. Some apprenticeships can lead to degrees and professional qualifications.

△ **Learning on the job**
Earning money and learning new skills at the same time is a great opportunity to build independence.

Becoming a volunteer

Volunteering involves working for an organization for free. Most volunteering opportunities are with charities, and these give teens an opportunity to gain work experience and learn useful skills while contributing to a cause they believe in. Volunteering is a great idea for teens who want to help people, animals, and the environment.

△ **Helping others**
Serving others can develop a teen's sense of purpose and interest in the community.

Traveling

Traveling provides teens with opportunities to see the world, as well as to work in different places and learn or improve knowledge of another language. Understanding foreign cultures and gaining new insights can be fun and a valuable experience for entering the world of work later. Working while traveling can also help teens save money.

△ **New experiences**
Traveling is a great way to make friends, explore new cultures, and learn about the world.

Completing an internship

Internships allow teens to work for a company on specific projects or tasks, and gain new skills and work experience for a short period. It's a great opportunity to try out different industries to see which one fits best, and can improve a teen's resume for applying to other roles. Some internships are paid, but many are not. Getting a job at the end of the internship is not guaranteed, but if an opportunity comes up and an intern has performed well, the internship might lead to a permanent job offer.

△ **Trial run**
Working for different companies for a short period allows teens to find out which type of industry appeals most, and gives them great experience for their resume, too.

Finding employment

Going straight into the working world offers teens the ability to gain job-specific skills earlier, as well as earn money, independence, and employment perks while they learn. Teens may want to start their own business, turn their part-time job into a full-time one, or gain experience working for someone they know.

△ **Helping hand**
Grants may be available to young people who want to start a new business.

Getting a job

When applying for and interviewing for a job, a strong cover letter and a clear resume can make an employer take notice.

Finding vacancies

Finding a vacancy can seem like a job in itself, but there are lots of ways to go about it. Jobs are typically advertised in newspapers, on recruitment and company websites, and on social media. Networking to gather contacts in companies, by talking to people face-to-face or online, is a great way to get noticed, as is volunteering and work experience or internships.

TEEN HINTS

Social media

Use social media to your advantage by researching employers and searching for vacancies. You can also build and promote your own professional online brand, but be careful about what you post—potential employers might see it.

◁ **How to search**
Newspapers, websites, and job search apps are invaluable when job hunting.

Applying for a role

Most applications consist of a cover letter and a resume. A job description tells an applicant the sort of skills an employer wants. Knowing this allows the applicant to think about what skills they have—such as communication, teamwork, or adaptability—and how these are suited to the role for hire.

▽ **Good preparation**
Tailoring the resume and cover letter to the job and thoroughly checking the spelling and grammar of both will improve a person's chances.

A cover letter should include:

- contact information—name, address, email, and phone number

- an opening greeting and job reference number, if there is one

- the reason for the application and how a person's experience, knowledge, qualifications, and skills match the employer's requirements

- the reason why working for this company appeals

- a formal sign-off, such as "Sincerely" or "Best regards"

A resume should include:

- contact information—name, address, email, and phone number

- a personal profile with key points

- qualifications

- previous experience (employment, volunteering, and internships all count)

- skills

- achievements

- hobbies and interests

Attending an interview

An interview can be a bit nerve-wracking, but it's a great opportunity for a person to decide whether or not they want to work for the employer. Interviews usually take place in person, but they can also happen over the phone or via a webchat. Whatever the format, a good interview is all about preparation.

Preparing for an interview

Research the company and prepare responses for possible questions. Study the job description, as well as your cover letter and resume.

Before an interview

Most interviewers expect candidates to dress smartly. Aim to be early to get familiarized and avoid getting flustered with the venue.

At an interview

Be clear and concise when answering questions, and maintain eye contact. Smile and thank the interviewer at the end, and be ready to shake hands.

Accepting an offer

Being offered a job is exciting, but it's good to think about the commitment and any other opportunities available before accepting it. If a teen is still keen to learn skills and work for that particular organization, it could be the perfect role to accept. If an offer is made over the phone, it's a good idea to ask for it to be put in writing. An official job offer (by letter or email) and contract should include information on when the job starts and the salary.

◁ **Saing "yes"**
Be sure to check that you are happy with the terms of the contract.

Dealing with rejection

If an offer doesn't arrive, it can be very disappointing, but it's still a useful opportunity to learn for the future. Interviewers are often willing to give applicants feedback, which can help them find out what wasn't quite right about their application or interview. Getting honest feedback and reflecting on their own performance allows teens to figure out how to improve and be successful next time.

▷ **Try again**
Seeing rejection as a chance to learn helps a person to build resilience.

Speaking up

As teens get older, opportunities to speak up at school or college, on special occasions, and on behalf of important causes come up. Sharing thoughts and opinions in front of others can feel daunting, but these moments build confidence—and forge great memories, too.

Big moments

Whether it is giving a speech at a club you belong to, accepting a prize for an achievement, or graduating from college, life is full of big moments for teens to present their best selves to the world.

▽ **Different occasions**
The occasion will determine the kind of speech and the approach the speaker should take.

△ When speaking to classmates, it's good to use a conversational tone.

△ Giving a speech in support of a cause at a rally requires clear ideas and a loud voice.

△ For debates, it's important to make notes and think quickly to persuade the audience.

△ Bringing objects and projects to show and explain can help when speaking in front of a club.

△ Wedding speeches typically include some jokes, but also personal stories about the couple.

△ People protesting tend to chant short, memorable lines that often rhyme.

△ Speaking at a group outing requires being clear about the plans and making instructions easy to understand.

△ When accepting a prize, speakers tend to be humble, humorous, and brief.

△ Graduation speeches are usually inspirational and reflect on the time spent in education.

Public speaking

Almost everybody speaks in public from time to time. How long a person speaks for will depend on the occasion. It might be necessary to speak for just a minute or two, but a presentation to an audience or a speech on behalf of a cause might take a lot more thought and preparation.

Public speaking tips

- Think about what you want to say in advance and write clear, easy-to-read notes that you can check if necessary.

- Be sure that the audience understands every word. Speak more slowly than you normally would, even if you feel silly, and pause after important points to allow them to sink in.

- Try to stand tall and maintain eye contact with those listening. In some instances, moving around and using gestures is a great way to engage people.

▽ **Being prepared**
When giving a presentation or speech to an audience that contains classmates, family, or friends, there are some key aspects to consider beforehand.

Think about your audience—is it family, your peers, a prospective employer, or your religious congregation? How formally should you speak? What topics will interest them?

What do you want the audience to know? If they remember one thing of what you say, what do you want it to be? Be sure to emphasize this point.

Are you trying to persuade people of something? Perhaps you've had a new idea? Or are you presenting information about an important cause that you care about?

Think about the structure—is there a beginning, middle, and end? Do you want to include an anecdote or a joke at the beginning to engage the audience?

Be creative—could you use a poster or a video, or pass around handouts or photographs?

Will the audience ask you questions? Do you need to think about what kinds of questions they might ask?

Conquering nerves

It's natural for someone to be apprehensive before a big moment, especially if they haven't had much experience with speaking in front of a group of people. Practice and preparation can help boost confidence on the day, as can positive thinking and a good night's sleep beforehand.

Nerves and anticipation

- Try to be as prepared as possible—know your topic as well as you can.

- Practice what you want to say in front of a smaller group beforehand to get feedback and build your confidence.

- Be excited—it's an opportunity to share your ideas with an audience.

- Before starting, place your feet firmly on the floor, take a deep breath, count to three, and breathe out slowly.

◁ **Practice makes perfect**
To get a sense of the audience's perspective, it's useful to practice in front of a mirror.

Digital life

The Internet

From chatting with friends and shopping online to checking the news and learning new skills, the Internet plays a major role in everyday life. It can also provide a way to relax, and a place to hang out with friends and communicate with the wider world.

Always changing

The Internet allows people to stay in touch and gives them access to up-to-date knowledge. It's also a built-in feature of many new inventions and accessories, known as "smart" devices, which learn the user's preferences over time.

Discover

- Find information on just about anything.
- Get advice for dealing with problems.
- Navigate around new places.
- Meet people with similar interests.

Learn

- Research and study for school.
- Find new hobbies and interests.
- Watch how-to tutorials.
- Participate in long-distance learning.
- Gain new digital skills.

Play

- Play video games online with people all around the world.
- Try out augmented and virtual reality.
- Discover new music.

Plan

- Organize and arrange events.
- Check the weather.
- Keep to-do lists and measure progress on projects.
- Track fitness.

Digital opportunities

Although the Internet can seem complicated or confusing sometimes, there are many incredible advantages to living life digitally. The Internet provides an exciting introduction to navigating the wider world, and is a space in which you can express yourself, strengthen friendships, relax, have fun, and learn.

Create

- Build websites.
- Write blogs.
- Film vlogs (video logs).
- Share art, music, and writing.

Making the most of the Internet

- With videos, quizzes, educational games, and interactive websites, the Internet is a great way to supplement your teen's education.
- The Internet can provide a great opportunity to spend time and learn together with your teen. Try asking them about what sites they like to visit and what digital skills they think are most useful.
- There are age-appropriate sites for tweens and teens. Find ones you approve of and point them toward these.
- If they're using a tablet or smartphone, it's a good idea to turn off app notifications to reduce distractions.

Communicate

- Talk to old friends and make new ones.
- Share photos and videos.
- Fundraise and crowdfund.
- Participate in news debates.
- Campaign and protest.

Social media

With billions of users worldwide, social media platforms are an exciting way for teens to stay in touch and connect, to entertain themselves, to organize and plan events, and to learn about the world around them.

Using social media

Understanding how social media platforms work and knowing what they can do enables teens to stay safe and get the most from them. The primary purpose of a social media platform is to offer its users an easy, instant way of connecting with family and friends, and others around the world. Many sites also offer the ability to share ideas, images, and videos, and to react to and comment on content that everyone can see, generating further debate and interest.

> "The Internet is becoming the town square for the global village of tomorrow."
> **Bill Gates, cofounder of Microsoft**

▽ **What can social media do?**
New uses for social media are being developed all the time. Here are some of the main ways people use it, but there are many more.

Interact

There are many ways for people to interact on social media. Users can talk through private messages or in a way that others can see. Users can connect with people of similar interests and organize to meet up in the real world if they want to.

Share media

Many users share content, such as images, videos, and music, through social media, whether they made it themselves or someone else did. The user's friends can then comment on the content or share it. If something is popular, it can quickly be shared hundreds of thousands of times, known as "going viral."

Arrange events

Social media allows users to organize events, often at short notice. These events could be anything from a birthday party to a homework club, or even a political demonstration. In this way, it functions like a digital message board that's tailored to each user's life.

Discover and debate news

News organizations post snippets of their stories on social media. Users can then share, comment on, and debate these stories, drawing them to the attention of others and thereby spreading news and debate more widely than traditional media might.

Checking in

"Checking in" on a social media site lets a person tell others where they are and what they're doing at that moment. But there are risks, as doing so reveals a person's location to a potentially enormous number of people.

A "check-in" could make burglars aware that a home is empty or allow a stalker to work out a person's routine. To reduce the risks, privacy settings should be changed, so that only close connections can see where a person has checked in, and the home address should never be revealed.

△ **Pros and cons**
Checking in at the premises of a business—a restaurant or shop, for example—might also mean that a person receives a discount or can leave a review. But businesses may not always be transparent about what information they're collecting or how they will use it in the future.

Taking a break

Maintaining a profile and keeping up with what everyone else is doing can take up a lot of time, so it's worth taking a break every now and then. If a teen wants to stop using social media, they have three options (always check the terms and conditions of the particular site first):

- Not logging in to the site will keep their account active, and they will continue to receive notifications.

- Deactivating the account will remove the user's profile from the site, but their information, including photographs and comments, is still there if they choose to reactivate it.

- Shutting down the account permanently means all information is deleted and they will no longer receive notifications.

> **TEEN HINTS**
>
> ### Comparing profiles
>
> Social media allows people to connect and communicate with each other, but seeing the lives of friends and celebrities, and how much attention they receive online, can lead some to make comparisons. These comparisons may cause teens to feel sad, lonely, or envious of other people, and as if they are missing out. Remember that people on social media present an edited version of themselves, which only reveals the best bits of their lives, and that they have times when they feel bored, lonely, or grumpy, too.

Social media and advertising

Most social media platforms are free, and so they earn money from placing ads on their sites. Advertising on social media is often tailored to the user, based on what they have revealed on the platform about their preferences and interests.

User inputs information

A user on social media shares information on their personal profile—such as their interests, photographs, and opinions.

Advertisers pay to advertise

Advertisers are drawn by the numbers of people who use the platform, and pay to advertise to them on it.

Direct ads appear

The ads target the users—for example, if a teen expresses a preference for a particular band, they will see ads for the band's concerts and merchandise.

Digital self

The Internet is a liberating space for teens—they can control how they present themselves, as well as socialize and explore the wider world. But it's also vast, so it's essential teens learn to be aware of how they are perceived online.

SEE ALSO

❮ 130–131 Social media

Making judgments	134–135 ❯
Digital habits	136–137 ❯
Cyberbullying	138–139 ❯

Selfies

Self-portraits taken with a smartphone, more commonly called "selfies," allow young people to have control over their online image. Through a selfie, teens can shape how they want to be seen, express their mood, and share important experiences with their online community, who can then comment on and "like" the selfie. Unfortunately, negative comments can be made online as easily as positive ones, which can influence a teen's self-esteem and become a real problem if the teen relies on selfies and other people's opinions to boost their self-worth.

▷ **Selfie esteem**
Selfies can be an effective way for teens to increase their confidence, test out new identities, and let their friends know what they're doing.

ALERT!

Dangerous selfies

Selfies of people in precarious positions have become widespread on social media. Across the world, creating daredevil selfies is putting people's lives at risk. With teens more prone to risk-taking due to the changes that are taking place in their brains, it is important that they don't buy in to this dangerous trend, in which people have been injured and died. Instead, a person should be aware and ensure that they're safe before taking a selfie.

Think before posting

While posting a photo or comment on social media may feel like the most natural thing in the world, it is important to pause and think about what a post is saying or showing.

Although the comment or picture might only be intended for a specific person or group, the person writing the post needs to remember that it can actually be seen by a wider community of people. It will remain online beyond the moment, years into the future, as a part of their digital history.

▷ **Consider the consequences**
It's a good idea before posting to think about whether or not it would be embarrassing or awkward if a family member, teacher, or future employer saw the post.

Oversharing

Social media can be a useful tool for teens to establish friendships, and share memories and thoughts. But sometimes these shared thoughts can cross the line into "too much information." Most people have read a post or viewed an image uploaded online by a friend, and cringed at the intimate details that have been shared with the world. Being too honest, or "oversharing," can have consequences. All information posted online remains online, and if inappropriate or hurtful comments are made, relationships can be damaged as a result.

Avatars

In video games, avatars are three-dimensional electronic images that represent the player in the game and interact with other elements of the game. Based on the gaming avatars, two-dimensional avatars are increasingly used on social media platforms, so that users have a visual representation of themselves without needing to use a photograph. Using an avatar instead of a photograph gives people more control over their digital footprints and the information that they are sharing with people.

△ **Unintentional clues**
Photos can give away clues to a person's identity, such as their hobbies and places they like to go.

△ **Unique but anonymous**
Teens can still show their personality through an avatar without revealing any personal information.

Digital footprints

A person's online activities leave a trail, commonly called a "digital footprint." It's a record of everything that they do on digital devices. Sometimes users intentionally leave their information online, such as through social media, but it's possible to unintentionally do this, too. Data about a person and their Internet usage and activity may be collected by websites without a person knowing. It is increasingly common for employers and universities to "cyber vet" people to make sure that their online history doesn't have any objectionable or potentially embarrassing content.

Making judgments

The Internet is full of content—ads, news, opinions, photos, and stories—produced by and shared on many different sources. It can be hard to know what and who to trust, so approaching information with a critical eye is the best way to separate fact from fiction.

SEE ALSO

❮ **130–131** Social media

❮ **132–133** Digital self

Staying safe online   **140–141** ❯

Understanding the news   **160–161** ❯

False information

False information can be shared in articles by journalists who haven't properly checked the facts, or spread by people or organizations who want others to believe inaccurate information to suit their own agenda. It's a big problem because people can start to believe things that aren't true or can claim that something is fake just because they disagree with it.

△ **Checking multiple sources**
Teens can watch out for fake news by seeing if the story is being reported on the radio, on TV, or in newspapers.

Questions to ask

- Are other sites reporting this story? What is their response to it?
- Who put this information there and why?
- Is there any evidence to support what's being said here?
- Does the site have an editorial bias? Some sites have a particular political or cultural outlook that affects what news they report and how.

What to look out for

All sorts of content appears on the Internet, so it's always essential to be on guard for false and inaccurate information, or for sites that contain malware that can cause harm to electronic devices.

Clickbait

These links play on people's curiosity to get them to click. They usually have outrageous headlines and promise to shock the reader, but typically lead to inaccurate and false content. They may also direct users to sites with viruses—malicious software that can damage computers.

Sponsored posts

Blogs and social media sites often feature "sponsored posts," where a company pays to promote a product. The site or blogger is supposed to announce that the post is an advertisement. The reviews of the product are typically favorable and encourage people to buy the product.

Pop-up ads

These ads appear on certain websites. They normally open in a new window. It's possible to download software to block pop-up ads. It's best not to click on them, as more might appear, or they might start to download unwanted files onto the computer.

Edited images

From merging separate images to adding special effects, editing photos can be a fun way to create something new. But edited images are problematic when they present unattainable standards of beauty or body shape as normal, crop out essential information, or are used as "evidence" to claim falsely that something has happened.

△ **Judging the risks**
Always think critically about the source of the images and the motives that source may have.

Product placement

Look out for product recommendations in user-generated content. Make-up tutorials by vloggers, for example, rarely make it clear that the vlogger is sponsored by the product manufacturers and benefitting financially from promoting it.

Echo chambers

Search engines and social media platforms are set up in a way that means people generally only see one side of the story and rarely encounter anything that disagrees with them. This means that people can end up in a bubble, often known as an "echo chamber." As a test, it's worth looking at a friend's search engine results and social media platforms to see how each person receives ads and news that is tailored to them. Teens can limit the risk of ending up in an echo chamber by seeking out information that challenges their opinion, which can strengthen their own views, as they have to work harder to think about and defend them.

TEEN HINTS

Using search engines effectively

Knowing how to find the most relevant search results when looking for information on the Internet will help ensure you are pointed toward a broad range of trustworthy content. When searching for information online:

- try out more than one search engine as their results might vary
- look for website addresses that end in .com, .gov, or .org
- don't trust the top results—scroll down to check out more options
- ignore search results that say "sponsored," "ad," or "promoted," as someone has paid for these to be at the top of the list
- be precise—use at least two keywords in the search
- be sure to spell the keywords correctly.

Online peer pressure

As in real life, teens can be pressured by others online to behave in ways that make them feel uncomfortable. Online challenges and dares are when people share a photo or video of themselves doing something unusual and nominate others to do the same. Safe challenges might raise money for charity or ask a funny question. These don't humiliate or harm anyone, but other dares may cause teens to feel uncomfortable or involve dangerous risks.

▷ **No pressure**
Making judgments isn't just about working out what's true and what isn't. It also includes making decisions about how to act.

Digital habits

The digital world enables teens to stay connected with friends beyond face-to-face contact. It is an extension of their real-world contact, allowing teens to be sociable and engage in activities with their friends even when they're away from them.

SEE ALSO

❮ 76–77 Sleep
❮ 130–131 Social media
❮ 134–135 Making judgments
Staying safe online 140–141 ❯

Digital respect

A person's virtual self is an extension of their real self. Just as many teens decorate their bedrooms to reflect their interests and personalities, so, too, do they embellish their social media profiles. Therefore, just as a person's behavior in the real world is a reflection of their values, such as showing respect to others and expecting respect in return, so it is in the digital world. The same rules apply: think before speaking, and think before posting.

▷ **Think before posting**
Just because posting online is easy to do, doesn't mean it doesn't need great care and thought.

PARENT TIPS
Model good behavior

- Teens can pick up habits from those around them, so model good behavior, such as putting down your phone when talking to people or at the dinner table.

- Engage with your teen about their digital profile just as you do with their day-to-day life, but respect their desire for autonomy.

- Discuss appropriate and inappropriate content with your teen.

- Turn off your phone before bedtime.

Netiquette

Good etiquette shows good manners and respect, and good Internet etiquette—or netiquette—shows the same. It is important to consider and follow this code of conduct to make the digital world safe and unthreatening. Unfortunately, some people abuse the Internet, behave badly, or target the online community for personal gain.

△ **Spam**
Unsolicited ads or messages—spam—are a nuisance and are sometimes used for phishing or spreading malware.

△ **Illegal downloads**
File sharing and streaming enables users to access copyrighted material without the copyright owner's consent. This is illegal.

△ **Abusive language**
The faceless anonymity that the Internet gives allows some users to act abusively and aggressively in ways they wouldn't face-to-face. Some forms of abusive language are illegal.

Helping others connect

The Internet can bring people together, but it is often seen as the realm of the young rather than a resource for all generations. Even so it can have many benefits for older people, who may feel disconnected from friends and family and be less able to get out and about. With online communities specific to them, video calls, and online groceries, there are many benefits to be gained.

△ **Sharing knowledge**
Teens can help others and teach them how to use the various digital resources available to them.

Staying healthy

Sitting in a comfortable position reduces the risks of developing any aches and pains associated with technology. If persistent pain is experienced, it's best to see a doctor.

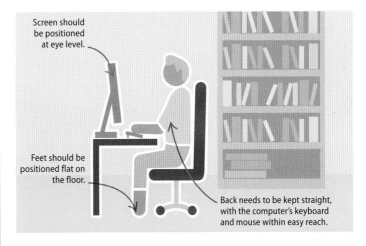

Screen should be positioned at eye level.

Feet should be positioned flat on the floor.

Back needs to be kept straight, with the computer's keyboard and mouse within easy reach.

△ **Sitting well**
Taking care to sit well and position screens correctly can help people reduce the risks associated with prolonged technology use.

Positive habits

How a teen uses digital media is more important than the amount of time they spend on it. Today, the digital world is as much a part of a teen's education as it is their social life. While passive TV-watching and listening to music allow a person to relax and unwind, digital media allows for so much more, such as interactivity, communication, and creating content. These are all valuable aspects of the digital world, but it's also important for teens to make sure they're not prioritizing their digital life over being with friends and family in person.

GOOD TO KNOW

Sleep

The blue light emitted by a smartphone can trick the brain into thinking it is daytime, causing a person to feel awake even when they should be sleepy. To combat this, experts recommend a person has gadget-free time before sleep, or that they reduce the blue light emitted by their device. In some smartphones, this is an built-in setting. For others, apps are available.

▷ **Missing out**
While a teen might feel that they're missing out on something if they're not online, they may instead be missing out on real-world experiences happening around them.

Cyberbullying

Digital communication and online profiles are easy and fast ways to share information with lots of people, but they can also be used to upset and hurt people.

What is cyberbullying?

Threatening or embarrassing someone through technology is a type of bullying. With many people carrying electronic devices 24/7, cyberbullying can occur at any time of day, no matter where the bully or bullied person is—making it very difficult for a person to avoid once they've been targeted.

Due to the ease with which information can be shared on the Internet, some types of cyberbullying can quickly reach a very wide audience, exacerbating the hurt and humiliation of victims. And, once something has been posted online, removing it completely can sometimes be impossible, causing harm to the bullied person long after the actual act first happened.

▷ **Electronic intimidation**
With the tap of a finger, personal, embarrassing, or cruel messages can be shared with the world, making cyberbullying both hurtful and dangerous.

Types of cyberbullying

Cyberbullying is invasive, cruel, and difficult to deal with. As cyberbullies often remain anonymous, tracing the source and stopping the cyberbullying can sometimes be extremely difficult. There are many types of cyberbullying, all of which can be carried out via email, text messages, or social media.

Hurtful, intimidating, and threatening messages may be sent.

Unwanted attention can turn into sexual harassment or stalking.

Embarrassing photos or hurtful posts could be posted or shared to humiliate a person.

Identity theft of a social media profile can occur if someone hacks into another person's online accounts.

A person can be impersonated through the use of fake profiles.

Personal or defamatory information about another person can be posted or shared.

PARENT TIPS

Signs of cyberbullying

Many of the signs are similar to those of regular bullying, but may be intensified by electronic devices.

- The way a teen uses their devices might change, such as suddenly not using them, being secretive when using them, or being online obsessively.

- A teen's behavior might change. They might become sad or withdrawn, lash out, or be reluctant to do things they usually enjoy.

- There may be unexplained physical symptoms, such as headaches, upset stomach, or decreased appetite.

- They refuse to talk about what they're doing online or who they're talking to.

Prevention

Cyberbullying is fairly common among children and teens, but there are ways to reduce the risk and limit its impact. Keeping passwords and personal information private is good practice in general, as is being cautious over what a person posts online—both images and text. A person should also always check their security options and privacy settings on any social media platforms.

△ **Active steps**
There are many sources of information and advice to help teens and parents prevent and deal with cyberbullying if it happens to them or someone they know.

Taking action

If cyberbullying is affecting you or someone you know, there are things you can do.

- Tell an adult you can trust.

- Keep a diary of what the bullies do, including dates and descriptions, or screenshots as evidence.

- Don't retaliate—bullies seek attention, so they will lose interest if there is no response.

- Contact service providers about bullying coming from within their network. Some have report buttons specifically dedicated to cyberbullying reports.

- Block anyone who makes you feel uncomfortable.

Recognizing cyberbullying

A person might be a cyberbully without realizing it. While somebody may share a comment or picture "as a joke" or simply to get a lot of likes, it's important that they consider their post carefully from all angles to ensure it isn't personally offensive to an individual. Whether it's due to not thinking or actively being mean—and even if it's in response to another cyberbully—posting or sending victimizing comments or messages about other people is cyberbullying.

△ **Don't get involved**
Cyberbullying is not acceptable. Many countries have passed laws that identify cyberbullying as a crime.

Online hate

Unfortunately, there are many forms of hate, including misogyny (disliking or being prejudiced against women), racism, and homophobia, as well as many ways of showing that hate, such as body shaming and insulting people. Much of this hate can find its way onto the Internet and public websites. Whether the hate is explicitly worded or insinuated through its exclusion of certain people, online hate is a worldwide problem that can easily filter into an individual's online browsing, and should always be reported to the appropriate service provider.

Trolling

There is a thin line between cyberbullying and trolling. Cyberbullying repeatedly targets a specific victim to intimidate them in some way, while the intent behind trolling is to provoke reactions. Trolling is as ugly as its name suggests, and usually takes the form of inflammatory and offensive comments. While it may feel like a personal attack for the person or people that it affects, trolling is about annoying as many people as possible into responding and voicing their annoyance. The best way to deal with attention-seeking trolling is to deny it the attention that it seeks.

Staying safe online

Children, teens, and adults must take steps to protect their identities, personal details, and images online. While Internet filters can help, the best way to stay safe is for everyone to work together.

Being prepared

Staying safe online bears many of the same rules as staying safe in the real world. Both involve knowing the potential dangers, talking them through before they occur, and having a plan of action for teens to follow if and when problems occur.

△ **In it together**

For teens and parents, one of the most important steps to ensuring safety online is discussing security measures together.

Open communication

Teens need strong digital skills to empower them to make safe choices online on their own. By communicating effectively, parents can help prepare their teen to deal with any problems.

- Ask your teen questions to get them to open up about their digital activities. Try asking about favorite websites, whether someone has helped them online, and who they like to follow.

- Discuss potential dangers, and work together to research and put in place strategies to reduce the risk. The conversation should adapt as teens gain maturity.

- It's easy to become complacent, but don't stop discussing Internet safety. It's relevant at every age.

- If you feel the need to block inappropriate content using Internet filters, it's best to discuss them with your teen first rather than to use them secretly. It's also important to note that Internet filters are not completely reliable.

Taking care

Not all content is appropriate for sharing online, even if other users request it. When using the Internet, teens should take care to follow two basic rules:

Don't share personal information

Never give out personal information—such as full name, contact details, home address, school name, or bank details—to unknown entities online.

Be careful with pictures

Photographs and videos should be guarded with care. If teens are asked for images or videos of themselves, they need to say no, walk away, and tell a trusted adult.

Webcams

Webcams are fantastic for video-calling friends and family, but there are also risks. A hacker can gain access to a computer through many different means. They might gain information from the computer's user or install malware that gives them access without a password. Once a hacker has done this, they can control the webcam and take images whenever they choose without the owner knowing. And it isn't just hackers that teens need to be wary of. Anyone can record a private video chat, which can later be shared online.

▷ **Reduce the risk**
It's critical to install firewalls and antivirus software to protect webcams from hacking.

Sexting

Sexting is when a person sends an image of themselves nude, partially nude, or in a sexually explicit pose to someone else. It comes with many risks, even if the sender and recipient are in a healthy relationship. If the relationship ends, or if a phone falls into the wrong hands, sexts can quickly be shared with a wide network of people. It's also illegal in some states if the person in the image and/or the person receiving it are under the age of 18 years old.

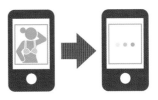

△ **Always risky**
Once a sext has been sent, the sender can no longer control who is able to see the image.

Stranger danger

As social media reflects elements of a person's real life, so, too, the potential dangers of sharing information with a stranger can affect a person's real life, even from a single online exchange. It is important that teens are cautious about revealing any information to any strangers who may go on to make contact and seek them out in person.

▽ **Being aware**
Tweens and teens should never share photos or videos online without their parents being aware.

ALERT!
Grooming

Grooming is when a person seeks to gain the trust of a child or teen with the intention of sexually exploiting or blackmailing them once embarrassing photographs or videos have been obtained. Online grooming allows the groomer to pretend to be someone that they're not in order to earn trust.

If a young person is being groomed, their behavior may change. Signs may include:

- being guarded about what they are doing online and being secretive about who they are speaking to

- wanting to spend more time online

- having new and expensive things that they're unable to explain

- having an older boyfriend or girlfriend. Many teens don't realize that they've been groomed, and believe the groomer to be a true boyfriend or girlfriend.

To reduce the risk of grooming, teens should always block strangers online and refuse to share any information or pictures. If a person suspects anything, it's best to talk it over, save any evidence, and report it to the police.

Privacy

With people inputting, storing, and accessing more and more of their personal information on digital devices and the Internet, it is crucial to keep this digital data secure and private. Breaches of privacy can lead to fraud and identity theft.

Privacy

A person's online privacy relates to the level of control that they have over their personal data, in terms of what information is available online, where it's stored, and how it's accessed. It can be managed, to control who or what sees an individual's personal information, using the privacy settings in an Internet browser.

△ **Taking steps**
Increasing online security helps to minimize the threat to people's privacy when they carry out personal tasks online.

Passwords

Passwords are the key to a wealth of personal information. They should be complex, difficult to guess, and never written down. The perfect password is eight or more characters long, with a combination of upper- and lowercase letters, numbers, and symbols. The same password should not be used across multiple websites. They should never be shared, even with friends.

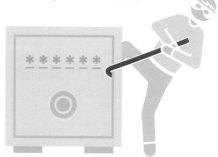

△ **Password rules**
A password should be unique and changed every six months.

Security check marks

Security check marks indicate that it is safe to input personal details into a website. They are recognized logos that suggest a level of quality and show that a site is trustworthy. These images or logos are typically displayed by online shopping sites to show that they have met various security and privacy requirements.

◁ **Safe to use**
Security check marks, which differ from country to country, appear in the search bar of a browser.

Online fraud

From deceiving people to pay for something that they never receive to identity theft, there are three main types of online fraudsters:

Phishing

People pretend to be a financial institution in order to get someone to give them their bank details.

Advance-fee fraudsters

Fraudsters send emails that offer huge sums of money in return for use of the victim's bank details.

Confidence fraudsters

These people get someone to give them money by pretending to be someone else.

Hacking and malware

Hackers look for weak spots in a device's security in order to access other people's digital information for personal gain. To do so, they may use malware (short for malicious software). Malware is any type of computer program that damages a device or gains access to sensitive information. Often known as a "virus," malware is designed to spread between devices, infecting each one and collecting or destroying data.

Types of malware

Knowing the different types of hacking can help people to be careful.

- A trojan horse is a harmless-looking file that unleashes a program that takes over a computer and potentially its networks.

- Keylogging is a way of monitoring the keys that are used on a computer in order to learn passwords and security data.

- Backdoor programs download malware that grants access to a computer, bypassing its security measures.

- A sniffer is a tracking tool that monitors data to and from a computer in order to obtain passwords and security data.

Protecting against malware

There are programs that protect against malware, but they must be kept up to date in order to be effective. Firewalls are a type of program that stop unauthorized access from unknown users, while antivirus software detects malware and any emails, ads, or messages that contain malware. It then blocks them to keep the computer and its information safe.

△ **Stay alert**
To reduce the risk of device damage and being hacked, teens should never click on suspicious links, visit unknown websites, or open attachments from strangers.

Distressing content

Because the Internet is largely unregulated, it can be easy to come into contact with distressing content. Some teens may search out upsetting material out of curiosity, while others stumble upon it unintentionally. Some teens are more affected by what they see than others. Explaining that unpleasant, sad, and illegal things happen, and that people can insult and exploit each other in all areas of life, can be difficult for parents, but it helps teens to put confusing and upsetting content into context.

▷ **Different responses**
Everyone reacts in their own way to upsetting online content. Talking about it can help.

Illegal content

Illegal content is content that breaks a country's laws. It is extremely offensive material that is placed online, and can include sites that encourage violence, criminal behavior, or dangerous behavior, such as creating weapons, taking or making drugs, or carrying out fraudulent or terrorist acts; highly graphic sexual acts that would be likely to offend a "reasonable adult"; and child abuse material.

Prohibited and illegal content can be found almost anywhere online, so it's sometimes hard to avoid and can be seen by accident. People should not look up illegal content online, even if they intend to report and remove it.

Gaming

Although the cause of much controversy, video games can help players develop and improve key life skills, including collaboration and problem-solving. When people balance the time spent gaming with other activities, gaming can be a fun and beneficial hobby.

SEE ALSO

❮ 74–75 Exercise
❮ 130–131 Social media
❮ 134–135 Making judgments
Friendships 188–189 ❯

Types of games

Tens of thousands of new video games are released every year. Whether they are played on phones, computers, or consoles, most video games can be categorized into six genres: sports, action, puzzles, role-playing, simulation, and strategy. Research shows that each type of game can help individuals to develop and improve different areas of cognitive thinking and abilities that can be applied in the real world. For parents, gaming with their teens can demystify it, enabling them to see for themselves what their teens get out of it.

"The obvious objective of video games is to entertain people by surprising them with new experiences."
Shigeru Miyamoto, creator of the "Super Mario" series

Sports games
Video games of sports mimic the real world in the rules, teams, and players they feature. These games are great for group-play, and can encourage involvement in the sport in the real world, too.

Action games
Often featuring exaggerated and energetic battles, action games test and improve players' hand-eye coordination, spatial awareness, and reaction time—improving a person's speed and ability to learn in general due to the fast-paced action.

Role-playing games (RPG)
RPGs allow players to control a character and their story, improving players' problem-solving skills as the characters encounter different challenges. Many RPGs are "open world" games, in which players can freely roam rather than following a strict linear story.

Puzzle games
Especially suited to occasional and smartphone players, puzzle games include problem-solving, pattern recognition, and word completion, often using a timer or limited chances.

Achieving balance

When a person is absorbed in playing a video game, it can be very easy for hours to roll by. However, prolonged periods of screen time are unhealthy, for the body and mind, and other aspects of life—such as seeing friends, doing homework, exercising, or sleeping—can end up being neglected. No matter what the game type, gaming is a sedentary, often solitary, pastime. To stay healthy, it's a good idea to fit in time for physical exercise, and to play video games as a family activity to make it sociable.

△ **Screen time**
Prolonged amounts of screen time are linked to obesity.

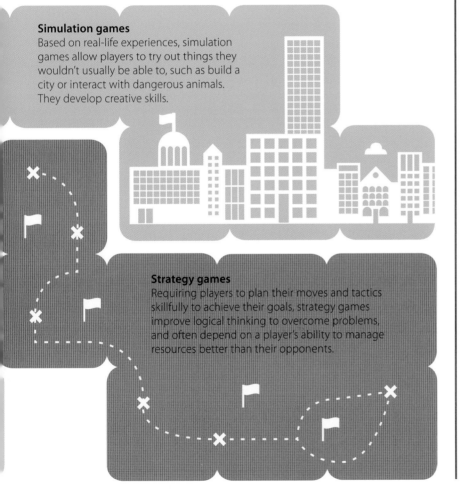

Simulation games
Based on real-life experiences, simulation games allow players to try out things they wouldn't usually be able to, such as build a city or interact with dangerous animals. They develop creative skills.

Strategy games
Requiring players to plan their moves and tactics skillfully to achieve their goals, strategy games improve logical thinking to overcome problems, and often depend on a player's ability to manage resources better than their opponents.

Playing online

Many games have an online option, which allows users to play and communicate with others around the world. This can be a fun way for teens to socialize with friends, but it can also open up contact with strangers. Basic security awareness—such as using an avatar to play and not using or giving out personal details, including name, address, and pictures—will keep online gaming safe. If other players become abusive or inappropriate, it's possible to report and block them.

Wider world

Safer streets

Staying safe in the streets and making them safe for others is all about courtesy and common sense. Being sociable and considerate creates a safe community. When everyone thinks about each other and works together, a place can be both safer and more pleasant.

Making streets safer

Streets, like parks, are public spaces that can shape a community. People use them to walk or drive to school, go for a jog, shop at different stores, or use public transportation. Streets belong to everyone in a community, which is why it's important to keep them safe and clean. When out and about, there are some useful pieces of advice to follow that can help teens stay safe.

PARENT TIPS

Setting boundaries

Set boundaries for when teens go out on their own—for example, where they can and can't go, or what time they have to be back. Explain why you're setting these rules, and try to be flexible on occasion.

▽ **Top tips**
There are all sorts of things to pay attention to when in public.

Sit near the driver or families if traveling alone on the bus.

Keep valuables out of sight and ensure bags or purses are zipped up.

Teens should tell parents and friends where they are going and when they expect to arrive and get back.

Technology in the streets

Technology is a great way for teens and parents to stay in touch, but here are some useful tips for using it in public.

Take off headphones and don't look at any devices when crossing the street.

Keep valuables out of sight as much as possible. It's also a good idea to set the phone's ringtone to vibrate to avoid attracting attention.

If confronted by someone who tries to take something, don't struggle or fight—personal safety should always come first.

Antisocial behavior

In society, it's always good to be considerate of other people. If friends are acting badly, being a good influence and calling them out on bad behavior can make the streets safer for everyone.

Things to avoid

- Drunken or threatening behavior
- Vandalism, graffiti, and littering
- Being unreasonably noisy
- Hanging out in large groups in the street
- Harassing people or causing distress
- Carrying weapons

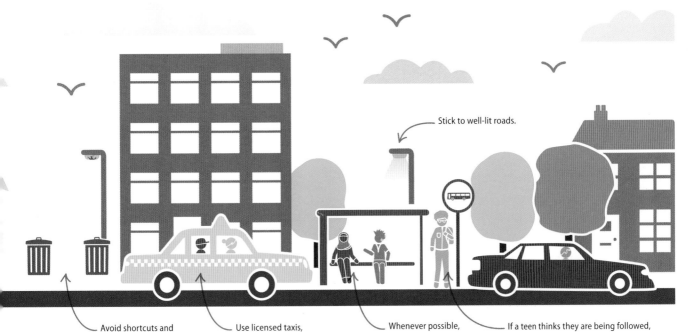

Stick to well-lit roads.

Avoid shortcuts and dark alleyways or parks.

Use licensed taxis, and sit in the back.

Whenever possible, use bus stops on busy roads.

If a teen thinks they are being followed, they should cross the street or go to a place with lots of people around.

Bullying

A bully is someone who behaves in an aggressive way toward another person. Bullying is intended to be emotionally or physically hurtful. It's very common, but that doesn't make it okay. Nobody should have to tolerate bullying of any kind.

SEE ALSO

❮ 90–91 Resilience

❮ 94–95 Anxiety and depression

❮ 138–139 Cyberbullying

Dealing with conflict   178–179 ❯

Types of bullying

Bullying can happen anywhere, such as on the way to school, at home, or online. Whenever and wherever it happens, bullies behave this way to enhance their own sense of importance, security, or popularity. They use different tactics to dominate other people and to make them feel intimidated and scared.

MYTH BUSTER

No age limit

Bullying doesn't just happen to children and teens. Unfortunately, not everyone grows out of bullying. It happens to adults as well.

▽ **Types of bullying**
Some types are obvious to spot. Others might be hidden, harder to identify, or disguised as something else.

△ **Exclusion**
Leaving people out of activities and making them feel alone.

△ **Joining in**
A person doesn't have to initiate the act in order to participate in bullying.

△ **Verbal bullying**
Name-calling, taunting, and making verbal threats.

△ **Body shaming**
Using hurtful and upsetting words regarding a person's appearance, body size, or shape.

△ **Physical bullying**
Harming a person using violence or force, or making mean or rude gestures.

△ **Sexual bullying**
Making sexual jokes, gestures, or comments, and spreading rumors about someone.

△ **Cyberbullying**
Bullying or trolling someone online or via texts or messages.

△ **Standing by**
Seeing someone being bullied and not saying anything at the time or afterward.

Tackling bullying

Bullying can seem like a difficult situation to resolve, but it's important to take action, as everybody will suffer if it continues.

If you're being bullied

- Try not to react to the bully in the way they anticipate or get angry, as they may lose interest.
- Block bullies online or on your phone and keep any abusive messages as a record.
- Tell a trusted adult what is happening, or contact a support group if you feel you can't talk to your parents or teacher.

If you're trying to help someone who is being bullied

- Don't watch or join in with the bullying, as this may encourage the bullies.
- Stand up for the person as long as you feel it is safe to do so.
- Advise the person being bullied to tell, or help them to tell, an adult they trust. Tell an adult yourself if they are unable to.

If you're the bully

- Apologize to the people you have bullied and try to make amends.
- Ask a trusted adult to help you resolve any difficult feelings or situations you might be struggling with.
- Forgive yourself, learn from your behavior, and move on.

If you're the parent of a bully

- Bullies often resort to bullying because they feel insecure, fearful, or unable to cope. Sometimes they're being bullied themselves. Try to find out why they've behaved in this way.
- Encourage your teen to apologize and to try to make amends.
- Help your teen to see that how they behaved is not who they are as a person.

Impact of bullying

Being bullied can affect every aspect of a young person's life. It can disrupt their ability to sleep, enjoy activities, or study, and have an impact on their physical health. Their mental health might suffer as bullying can lead to low self-esteem, anxiety, feelings of anger or aggression, and depression.

PARENT TIPS
Seeing the signs

It can be hard to know if your teen is being bullied, as they may not want to tell you. The following signs may indicate a problem:

- sudden reluctance to do activities they previously enjoyed
- unexplained changes in behavior, such as becoming withdrawn or preoccupied
- coming home with bruises or without certain belongings
- anxiety about going to school or complaining about feeling too ill to go to school when they are well

Getting help

A teen may find it difficult to admit they are being bullied, but acknowledging the problem is the first step toward resolving it. It's important for a teen to call on their friends for emotional support, and to talk to a trusted adult who can take action to improve the situation.

△ **Opening up**
If a young person feels in physical danger or if the situation has spun out of control, telling the school, or even the police, might be appropriate.

Discrimination

Sometimes people make assumptions about others based on who they are, or on the way they look or act. These assumptions, which are usually false, are known as prejudices. When a person treats someone unfairly because of a prejudice, it is called discrimination.

What is discrimination?

Discrimation can include insulting a person, bullying them, or denying them opportunities, or instead favoring others for opportunities. Sometimes discrimination can be easy to spot, such as when someone is excluded from a group of friends, but it is often disguised or excused as something else.

Discrimination isn't always deliberate, but it is still hurtful if it causes someone to feel excluded or judged.

SEE ALSO

❮ **18–19** Thinking independently

❮ **134–135** Making judgments

Equality **154–155** ❯

Understanding the news **160–161** ❯

GOOD TO KNOW

If it happens to you

- Is there something about you, or who you are with, that has caused someone to treat you in this way?

- Talk to a parent, teacher, or tutor, as discrimination should be taken seriously.

- Feel positive about your identity, and don't let discrimination discourage you from reaching your full potential.

Types of discrimination

There are many different types of discrimination. Most types are directed at people who belong to certain groups, or who have particular backgrounds or lifestyles. Some people can be victims of more than one type of discrimination at a time.

Ableism happens when the needs of people who are in some way disabled fail to be accommodated by society.

Ageism refers to assumptions about a person because of their age. It works in both directions, young and old.

Class discrimination occurs when someone is treated unfairly because of where they grew up and whether they are rich or poor.

Heterosexism is the assumption that everyone is straight (heterosexual).

LGBTQ+ discrimination limits the opportunities of people because of their sexuality or gender.

Racism is the unfair treatment of a person or group because of their skin color, nationality, citizenship, or ethnicity.

Religious discrimination occurs when someone is poorly treated because of their beliefs or religion.

Sexism is the unfair treatment of another person because of their sex, and is usually directed toward women.

Stereotypes

Stereotypes are oversimplified ideas that are often widely held about a person or group of people. They stop people from seeing the real individual and can be very damaging. Sometimes people don't see how prevalent stereotypes are in society, particularly in the media—even when they're part of the group being stereotyped.

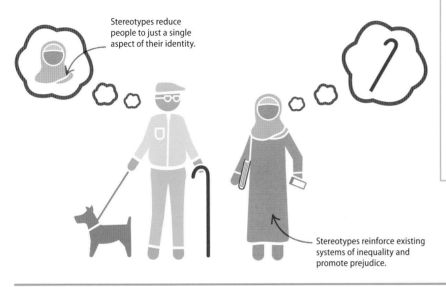

Stereotypes reduce people to just a single aspect of their identity.

Stereotypes reinforce existing systems of inequality and promote prejudice.

Breaking the cycle

Learning about each other and the things we have in common, as well as actively seeking out as many perspectives as possible on an issue, helps everyone to avoid discriminating against others.

▽ **Positive solutions**
Individuals or organizations often exclude or disadvantage disabled people without realizing they are doing it. Talking to people about their needs makes society more inclusive.

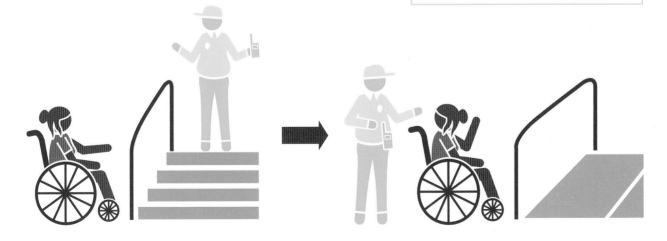

Equality

Equality is the idea that everyone is entitled to the same rights, status, and opportunities. This means that no person or group of people should be treated less favorably than everyone else.

Equality and equal rights

Equality is achieved through ensuring that everybody is given the human rights to which they are entitled. Making sure that people are treated with equal respect is an important part of achieving equality. As long as people are treated unfavorably because of stereotypes, prejudice, or discrimination, equality will continue to be an issue that needs addressing.

▽ **In it together**
Everyone is different, which is something to be celebrated.

Equality, equity, liberation

Equality is only the first step toward removing the barriers to opportunities that people might face. In order to enjoy equality, people's differences should be acknowledged.

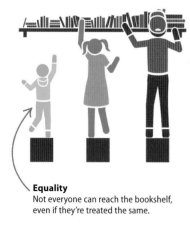

Equality
Not everyone can reach the bookshelf, even if they're treated the same.

Equity
Giving a leg up to those who need it most allows everyone to reach the bookshelf.

Liberation
The simple act of lowering the bookshelf means everyone can participate equally, without any additional support.

Gender equality

Gender equality occurs when men and women have the same opportunities and rights. Equal opportunities and rights mean that every individual, regardless of their gender, is free to realize their full potential.

The idea that there are certain toys, roles, and activities that belong just to boys or just to girls places limitations upon everyone and can keep young people from achieving their goals and ambitions. Unfortunately, because these assumptions are so widespread, they're often accepted and even encouraged by people without them questioning it. But this is changing—more and more people now acknowledge that a person's gender should not dictate their interests or dreams.

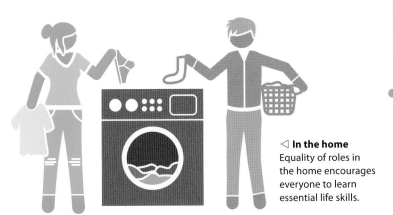

◁ **In the home**
Equality of roles in the home encourages everyone to learn essential life skills.

PARENT TIPS

Gender equality at home

- Teens of either gender should have the freedom to express themselves and their emotions honestly.
- Make sure that rules are based on maturity, rather than gender.
- Both genders should participate equally in the household, part of which involves sharing chores.

△ **Gender equality in play**
Gender equality can be encouraged from a young age by letting boys and girls play any type of role, with any type of toy, free from gender stereotypes.

Tackling inequality

Inequality can seem like too big of an issue for one person to tackle on their own, but there are things a person can do to make the world a fairer place.

Take responsibility for day-to-day words and actions.

Understand that there is no "one-size-fits-all" solution to a problem.

Talk to lots of people from all types of backgrounds to make sure their needs are being met.

Stand up for people's rights to live without encountering barriers, whenever it's safe to do so.

Report bullying and abusive comments or behavior to a parent, teacher, or the police.

Write to politicians to tell them about changes they should make.

GOOD TO KNOW

Explaining privilege

Privilege refers to any unasked for or unearned advantages given to one group of people over another. These advantages might be based on ability, age, education, family income, race, or sex. You can be privileged in some ways but not others, such as being born into a stable, comfortable family, but with a physical disability. It can feel awkward to talk about your own privilege, but that discomfort can help you to be more aware of inequality and to do something about it.

Religion

As teens begin to form their own opinions, practice more independent thought, and develop their own moral code, they may start to explore different religious ideas, beliefs, and values.

SEE ALSO
❮ 16–17 Identity
❮ 18–19 Thinking independently
❮ 22–23 Self-expression
❮ 152–153 Discrimination

Young people and religion

Whether a person is brought up practicing a specific religion or not, it's normal for teens to question what they believe as they explore who they are and how they fit in the world. Some teens may investigate different ways to practice religion, or approach it differently from the traditions of their elders. Some may consider new aspects of spirituality, or lose their faith.

▷ **Questions and answers**
It is natural and healthy for teens to explore and educate themselves about the many different belief systems around the world.

Faith systems

There are thousands of faith-based belief systems around the world. Some are organized, some have huge followings, and others are comparatively small.

Buddhism

This 2,500-year-old religion originated in Asia. It is unlike most other religions in that it's not based on worshipping a god or gods. Instead, its 500 million followers aim to reach "enlightenment"—true wisdom about the meaning of life—by following the teachings of the religion's founder, Gautama Buddha.

Hinduism

The 1 billion followers of this 4,000-year-old religion have extremely varied traditions and worship different deities that represent different attributes of the supreme spirit, Brahman. Hindus believe that a person's soul is reincarnated and governed by karma—actions in this life and previous lives influence future ones.

Christianity

This monotheistic religion (belief in one god) is about 2,000 years old, with 2.2 billion followers. Christianity is based on the belief that Jesus Christ, son of God, was sent to Earth to save humanity from its sins. Christians believe in the teachings and the resurrection of Jesus, detailed in the Bible, Christianity's sacred book.

Islam

Islam's 1.6 billion Muslims believe in one god, Allah, who revealed teachings to the prophet Muhammad near Mecca, 1,400 years ago. These form the Qur'an, Islam's holy text. Muslims live by the five "Pillars of Islam": prayer, helping the needy, declaration of faith, fasting, and pilgrimage to Mecca.

Family strain

Religion and belief are very personal things, and an important part of a person's sense of self. It is natural for emotions to run high during religious discussions, and if a teen is experimenting with different religious ideas. What's important is for parents to respect their teen's individuality, and to provide a secure and open-minded environment in which a teen can explore their own spiritual identity or opinions.

TEEN HINTS

Conflict with parents

Both parents and teens can feel frustrated when their views differ. Understanding and respect on both sides is key. Ask your parents questions about their views and beliefs, and how they came to those beliefs. At the same time, be willing to answer any questions they ask you. You can agree to disagree, but it is important to show respect for each other's values and beliefs.

ALERT!

Extremism

An extremist is someone who holds extreme political or religious opinions, often advocating illegal or violent actions to support their cause. Extremists exploit a person's internal confusion by focusing exclusively on one aspect of their identity, such as their religion, and distorting it into something negative. Vulnerable individuals, such as teens undergoing their own process of self-discovery, are particularly susceptible to being swayed by extremist views through exposure to radical propaganda.

Other belief systems

For as long as there have been religions, there have been people with different worldviews.

Judaism

Originating 3,500 years ago, the teachings of this religion, compiled in the Jewish sacred text, the Torah, formed the basis for both Christianity and Islam. The 14 million Jews around the world believe that they share a special bond—a covenant—with God, passed on by the prophet Abraham.

Agnosticism

Agnostics question belief and certainty. They are sceptical of both religious and atheistic beliefs. They don't deny the existence of a god or gods, nor any supernatural beings—but they do deny that anyone can know for sure if such entities do or don't exist.

Sikhism

Founded by Guru Nanak in India's Punjab region in the 1400s, Sikhism shares aspects of Hinduism and Islam. Its 24 million followers believe in only one god and live life by three basic rules— pray, work, and give—and believe that being close to God is as much about a person's actions as it is about their belief.

Atheism

There are approximately 1 billion people in the world who are non-religious, and about half of those identify as atheist. Atheism means "without god," and atheists believe that the universe can be explained without a god, and that decent moral codes have social origins.

Citizenship

A citizen is an inhabitant of a country in which they were born or where they live. Each country has its own rules and beliefs about the roles of citizens and what it means to be a good citizen. It is important for teens to explore their role in society.

Understanding citizenship

Every individual is a member of a country, usually the country in which they live or were born. Citizens are granted certain freedoms and privileges, such as access to education and healthcare, specific to their country's law. In return, a citizen has obligations to their country, including paying taxes and abiding by laws. A citizen is part of a community, and active citizenship supports and adds to society and country.

▷ **Give and take**
Being a citizen grants individuals certain rights, and expects certain commitments and duties in return.

Citizenship values

A good citizen thinks and acts to uphold the law, is informed about issues relating to the community, and supports the values of good citizenship:

Responsibility

Citizens have personal and public responsibilities. To carry these out, a person's first responsibility is to learn, so that they can act in an informed and educated way.

Respect

Good citizens, first and foremost, have respect for themselves. They show respect for other people, the country's laws, and the environment in which they live.

Tolerance

Showing respect, awareness, and appreciation for the differences, as well as the common likenesses, between individuals and groups of people is part of citizenship.

Honesty

Honesty is the cornerstone of good citizenship, as it facilitates moral behavior. Good citizens are honest with themselves, as well as with others.

Compassion

A sense of compassion encourages citizens to care about the well-being of other people and living things, and motivates them to act against suffering and injustice.

Courage

A good citizen shows strength of mind in the face of adversity. This courage means that they do not lose sight of what is good and right, and that they will fight for it.

Citizen actions

Active citizens appreciate their freedoms and take their responsibilities seriously. Many aspects of citizenship produce a sense of pride and belonging. Singing a country's national anthem in public, for instance, inspires a sense of unity among citizens, and celebrating national holidays is also a way for citizens to honor the events and people that shaped their country.

◁ **Voting**
Voting is both a right and a responsibility in democratic societies for people above a certain age. Voting works on the principle of "one person, one vote," with the resulting government representing the views and beliefs of the majority of voters.

Citizen rights

A country's Bill of Rights is a formal declaration of legal and civil rights—such as the rights to vote and worship freely, the right to a fair trial, and freedom of speech. These rights and freedoms are granted to all citizens, but can be taken away if a person breaks their part of the citizenship deal, such as by committing a crime.

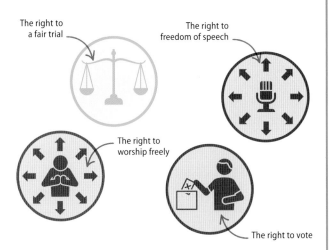

The right to a fair trial

The right to freedom of speech

The right to worship freely

The right to vote

GOOD TO KNOW

Universal Declaration of Human Rights

In 1948, the United Nations (UN) adopted the Universal Declaration of Human Rights, which aims to secure basic citizenship rights—such as the right to life, liberty, and security—for every individual in the world. Despite international support of the declaration, there is still neglect and abuse of human rights in many countries around the world.

Laws of a country

Most laws are based on the basic rule of "doing the right thing," and all citizens must abide by these laws. Some countries' laws follow religious law, too.

Each country has lots of citizens, and they all need to get along and behave in respectful ways in order for society to function. Laws spell out what behavior is acceptable. Some laws are the same across the world—for example, in every country, murder is considered a crime. Most countries constantly scrutinize their laws to ensure they are fair and appropriate to and for all citizens.

▽ **The scope of the law**
Laws strive to ensure fairness and order across all aspects of society. In many countries, dropping litter is an offense.

Understanding the news

As teens start to take more interest in the world around them, they discover how to find news and learn to digest it. Seeking out various points of view on a news item helps a teen to have a balanced understanding of issues and politics.

SEE ALSO

❮ 18–19 Thinking independently

❮ 82–83 Positive mental health

❮ 134–135 Making judgments

❮ 158–159 Citizenship

News media

Some news sources are more reliable than others. News items should be provided in a transparent and accountable way—this means they are examined critically, without any bias, and that the provider is responsible for what they report. The facts should be verified and the people they source the details from should be trustworthy. It's important to find out where news comes from before digesting its content.

△ **Newspapers**
A traditional medium of news, newspaper journalism follows a strict code of ethics to promote transparency.

△ **News websites and apps**
Websites and apps allow people to get news on demand. Some websites and apps are reliable, but a lack of regulation means many spread false information.

△ **Social media**
The lack of regulation on social media means that news released there is often misleading, unreliable, and without accountability.

△ **Television**
Traditionally a widely viewed news source, TV news has strict guidelines to ensure the news is properly sourced and verified.

Critical analysis

It's important to be critical about the news, rather than accepting everything as fact. Some news companies may focus heavily on negative news, or sensationalize stories and events in order to attract interest. Others may be biased toward a particular ideal or owned by people with an agenda. A company's owner might support a particular political party, for example, and want to influence voters in an election. All of this can lead to stereotyping and a narrow, selective presentation of events.

▷ **Seeking answers**
Questioning news outlets about their sponsorships, agendas, and transparency ensures they are held accountable for the content they broadcast.

Ask yourself

- Who put this information here, and why?
- Does the author have an agenda?
- Is it a sponsored news item? Or is the information sourced independently?
- Is there a balanced outline of viewpoints, with reliable evidence to support each argument?
- Are they asking questions and looking at detail, or making generalized statements?

Social media bubbles

Social media is designed to identify a person's interests and tailor the content they see according to their "likes" and what they share. This can be really useful in filtering out things they aren't interested in, but also means that the news that appears on their social media platforms only offers a narrow point of view. When people simply absorb this news without seeking other perspectives, they don't get the full story. This creates a "bubble" effect that stops people from seeing viewpoints that differ from their own.

TEEN HINTS
Keep an open mind

Try to look for news and opinion from a variety of sources and many different opinions, including those that you don't like or agree with. Taking measures to be an active news consumer will help you to form your own informed thoughts and opinions on important matters.

Escaping overexposure

It can sometimes feel like there's no escape—especially when the news focuses on alarming events. It's natural to feel angry, sad, or anxious about it all. Taking time away from the media can help teens to digest the news and properly understand their reactions to it.

▽ **Taking time out**
Going for a walk, playing with a pet, and speaking to friends are all great ways to relax.

PARENT TIPS
Disturbing news

It can be exciting when teens takes an active interest in current affairs, but it's also important to help them digest the news they consume. Ask their opinions on different viewpoints, including difficult topics. When there are particularly distressing news items, remind them that it's possible to be informed about what is happening without knowing every detail.

Social conscience

Many people seek out ways to help a particular cause they've seen on the news. Getting involved can introduce a teen to like-minded people, which can be energizing and inspiring, as can talking to and debating with people who have rival views.

Attend a rally or protest

Volunteer for a charity

Organize a fundraising campaign

Sign a petition

Attend a talk to find out more

Write to politicians

Alcohol

Alcohol is a legal, socially acceptable drug. For many people, drinking alcohol is a pleasant experience, usually with friends or family. However, as with any drug, there are risks, so it's important to do so responsibly.

SEE ALSO

❮ **18–19** Thinking independently

❮ **148–149** Safer streets

Building trust **176–177** ❯

Peer pressure **192–193** ❯

What is alcohol?

Alcohol is created by a chemical process called fermentation, which breaks down the sugars found in fruits, vegetables, or grains. Alcoholic beverages include beer, wine, and spirits. In moderate amounts, it reduces anxiety and social inhibition, and tends to make people feel more relaxed.

Most countries have an age restriction on when people can buy or drink alcohol. This is because the effects of alcohol can be more harmful for children and teens than they are for adults, as their brains are still developing.

TEEN HINTS

Deciding to drink

Don't feel under pressure to drink alcohol because your friends are, or because it seems like everyone on TV or on social media is doing it.

Alcohol is not the solution if you're feeling anxious or worried about something.

◁ **Party time**
Some people enjoy having a drink when celebrating a special occasion.

Intoxication

In low doses, alcohol encourages feelings of sociability and talkativeness. However, binge drinking—drinking a large amount in a short time period—can lead to intoxication, or drunkenness. Drunkenness happens when the liver is unable to remove the alcohol and its toxins from the body quickly enough to keep up with consumption, causing the level of alcohol in the blood to rise quickly.

It's usually possible to tell if a person is drunk—their speech may slur, their balance may become impaired, they may seem more clumsy, and their skin may redden. Alcohol also affects a person's ability to form new memories, and to make decisions and judgments, making them more likely to take risks or engage in dangerous behavior.

◁ **Being drunk**
Some people get drunk more easily than others. As drinking alcohol can compromise a person's ability to make judgments, it's important to be in a safe space with trusted people.

GOOD TO KNOW

Hangovers

After a period of drinking, a person is likely to experience some unpleasant side effects, collectively known as a hangover. Scientists aren't sure exactly what causes hangovers. The toxins that alcohol leaves in the bloodstream, lowered levels of vitamins and minerals in the body, and the fact that alcohol causes dehydration are all contributing factors. It's not possible to cure a hangover, but drinking lots of water and taking painkillers can ease the symptoms. Even if you take these steps, a hangover can last for up to 24 hours and have several symptoms, including:

• a headache and muscle aches

• a dry mouth and a sensation of thirst

• nausea, vomiting, and stomach pain

• low mood and anxiety

• sensitivity to light and sound

Responsible drinking

Practicing responsible drinking helps teens and adults to stay safe.

Keep an eye on how much you drink and know what your limit is.

If you're going out with friends, help each other to stay safe.

Eat beforehand. Having a full stomach delays how quickly alcohol is absorbed into the bloodstream.

Drink soft drinks or water between alcoholic drinks.

Never accept drinks from strangers. They may have "spiked" your drink by adding drugs or a shot to it.

Never drink and drive. Alcohol impairs a person's coordination and judgment.

Make sure you watch your drink at all times, in case someone tampers with it.

Say no if you feel you've had enough. Everyone has different limits, so don't try to keep up with friends.

Long-term effects of drinking excessively

Regularly drinking alcohol in large quantities can have a long-term, negative impact on a person's mental and physical health, so it's important to drink in moderation.

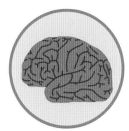

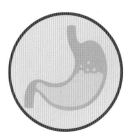

△ **Brain**
Alcohol can cause anxiety, depression, low mood, and sleeplessness.

△ **Mouth**
The effects of alcohol range from bad breath to mouth cancer.

△ **Heart**
Alcohol increases blood pressure, heart rate, and the risk of having a stroke.

△ **Liver**
Heavy drinkers are susceptible to liver damage.

△ **Stomach**
Regularly drinking large amounts can cause diarrhea and heartburn.

Smoking

Smoking cigarettes releases nicotine into the bloodstream. This chemical alters brain chemistry, causing relaxation, but in the long term it's highly addictive. Smoking releases other harmful substances into the body that damage organs and overall health.

SEE ALSO

❰ **60–61** Keeping clean

Drug use and abuse   **166–167** ❱

Building trust   **176–177** ❱

Peer pressure   **192–193** ❱

Teen smokers

Some teens start smoking because they feel pressured to do so by their friends, while others smoke to feel independent, even though they know the risks. Teen smokers have poorer fitness than nonsmokers due to the build-up of tobacco residue, or "tar," which reduces heart and lung function, as well as causing tooth and gum decay. Smokers also have a higher risk of cancer and are more likely to develop type 2 diabetes. One in two people who smoke will die from a smoking-related disease.

Saying "no"
No one should feel pressured to try smoking if they don't want to.

◁ **Teen smokers**
Most people who start smoking as teens are surprised by how addictive it is.

MYTH BUSTER

The truth about smoking

It doesn't look cool. It also comes with bad breath, stinky hair, and a reduced sense of taste.

It won't help you fit in. Never feel that you have to do something dangerous to fit in with people you call friends.

You won't just be able to have one or two. Research suggests that the brains of young people are more vulnerable to nicotine addiction than adults, so even one or two is enough to develop an addiction.

Nicotine addiction

It's difficult for smokers to stop smoking, even if they want to quit, because cigarettes contain nicotine, an addictive chemical. Nicotine alters the balance of two hormones, dopamine and norepinephrine, in the brain. These hormones produce feelings of pleasure and reduce anxiety and stress. When a smoker does quit, nicotine cravings can cause stress, depression, and irritability.

▽ **Cigarettes**
Nicotine causes addiction, but it's not the most harmful chemical in cigarettes. The smoke from just one cigarette contains more than 4,000 harmful chemicals, including carbon monoxide and tar.

GOOD TO KNOW

E-cigarettes

E-cigarettes (also known as vapes) are designed to be used by people who want to give up smoking. They contain nicotine, but are much safer because there's no smoke or tar. However, they are not completely harmless, and are just as addictive as regular cigarettes.

Passive smoking

Passive, or second-hand, smoking occurs when a person inhales smoke in the air, emitted from a burning cigarette or exhaled smoke. Prolonged exposure of nonsmokers to second-hand smoke increases their risk of cancer, heart and lung disease, respiratory problems, and premature death.

▷ **Second-hand smoke**
There is no known safe level of exposure to second-hand smoke, and it's especially harmful to young children.

Stopping smoking

After smoking a cigarette, a person's body will start the process of recovery from the harmful effects within 20 minutes. If a teen wants to quit, there is a variety of methods, from nicotine patches and gum, to hypnotherapy.

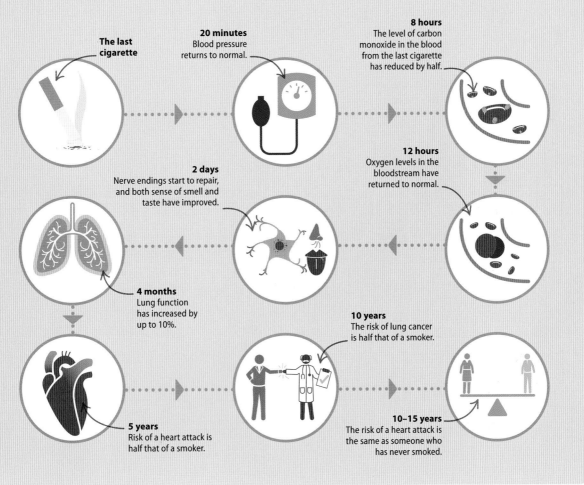

The last cigarette

20 minutes
Blood pressure returns to normal.

8 hours
The level of carbon monoxide in the blood from the last cigarette has reduced by half.

12 hours
Oxygen levels in the bloodstream have returned to normal.

2 days
Nerve endings start to repair, and both sense of smell and taste have improved.

4 months
Lung function has increased by up to 10%.

10 years
The risk of lung cancer is half that of a smoker.

5 years
Risk of a heart attack is half that of a smoker.

10–15 years
The risk of a heart attack is the same as someone who has never smoked.

Drug use and abuse

Drugs are chemical substances taken by people for various reasons. They affect the body and brain, and may have a short- or long-term impact on a person's mental state and physical well-being.

SEE ALSO

❰ 18–19 Thinking independently
❰ 94–95 Anxiety and depression
Types of drugs   **168–169 ❱**
Peer pressure   **192–193 ❱**

Why people use drugs

People have been experimenting with drugs for medicinal, spiritual, or recreational purposes for thousands of years. People who use drugs recreationally—for the purpose of getting "high"—tend to use them as a form of escapism, or because it makes them feel good; but it can be easy to lose control and depend on those drugs.

Most countries have laws about the manufacture, sale, and misuse of drugs. If teens are caught with drugs or selling drugs, they could end up with a criminal record, which can make other areas of their life more difficult.

TEEN HINTS

Making the decision

Some people first try drugs because they are curious about the effects. Others use drugs because they feel under pressure from their friends, or they worry about being judged if they don't join in.

If you are thinking about experimenting with drugs, your decision should be informed by the risks and based only on what you think is best for you—not what your peers think you should do.

◁ **Peer pressure**
A teen shouldn't take drugs just because their friends do. It's a personal choice.

Risks and dangers

Drugs may invoke pleasurable feelings in the short term, but they can have harmful effects, both when they are being taken and in the long term.

▽ **At risk**
There is a wide variety of risks associated with taking drugs. Here are just some.

Addiction	Poor mental and physical health	Bad decision-making
Broken relationships	Impact on studies	Criminal charges

Seeing the signs

Drug use is problematic when a teen starts to need the drug in order to feel "normal." Addiction is when the cravings for the drug become so intense that a person feels they can't exist even a day without it. The following signs could indicate that a young person is developing a dependency on drugs.

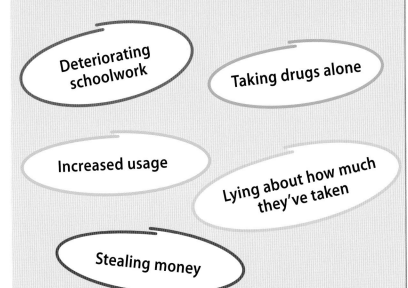

Deteriorating schoolwork

Taking drugs alone

Increased usage

Lying about how much they've taken

Stealing money

Talking about drugs

It can be worrying to know or suspect your teen is thinking about taking, or already taking, drugs. Talking about drugs is important, whether your teen is just curious, already using drugs casually, or you are concerned they are becoming dependent.

- Try to understand why your teen is using or wants to use drugs and discuss these reasons with them.

- Let them know you love them unconditionally.

- Listen to your teen and talk to them in a calm, nonjudgmental manner.

- Know where to find additional support if you feel out of your depth.

- Be informed about drugs to avoid giving your teen false or misleading information.

Getting help

It takes courage for someone to recognize and admit that they are dependent on drugs, but acknowledging the problem is the first step to recovery.

There are several treatment options available for those who want to stop taking drugs. A doctor can direct drug users to specialist counselors who can help make the transition to a drug-free life easier and more likely to last. Support groups provide safe spaces among other users where a person can discuss and reflect on their relationship with drugs.

Drug withdrawal

Drug withdrawal describes the symptoms (both emotional and physical) experienced when someone who has taken a drug or drugs for a prolonged period stops taking them abruptly. Withdrawal is caused by decreased levels of the drug in the body's blood or tissues. Different drugs have different timelines of withdrawal symptoms. The symptoms of withdrawal can be life-threatening, so professional supervision is essential when stopping usage.

▷ **Get the right help**
Coming off drugs can be hard, but there is guidance and support for those who need it.

Types of drugs

There are many different types of drugs, as well as many street names associated with each of them. All drug use carries risks, and teens should be aware of the effects and risks before making a decision about whether or not to take drugs.

SEE ALSO

❬ 18–19 Thinking independently
❬ 94–95 Anxiety and depression
❬ 166–167 Drug use and abuse
Peer pressure   192–193 ❭

Categories

Some drugs have hallucinogenic effects, which means that they cause people to see things that are not real, while others affect a person's mood and behavior. Other types of drugs have a depressant effect, which means they slow down the body and its functions. Stimulants are drugs that have the opposite effect—they speed up the body, giving the user more energy and alertness. Certain drugs combine some or all of these characteristics.

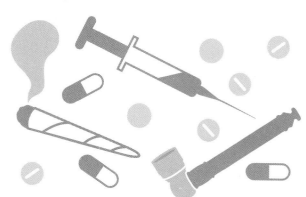

Drug	Form	Use	Effects	Risks
Anabolic steroids	Liquid, tablet	Swallowed	The effects of this stimulant include increased muscle mass, and the ability to complete more strenuous exercise sessions and recover more quickly.	Risks include acne; hair loss; interrupted physical development; high blood pressure; risk of heart attack, stroke, liver failure; menstrual problems; mood swings; paranoia; and violent behavior.
Cannabis	Dried herbs or soft brown lumps	Drunk, eaten, smoked	Cannabis can act as a depressant and stimulant, as well as a hallucinogen. It can cause relaxation, giggliness, and talkativeness, and affects a person's sense of time.	Users may experience anxiety, paranoia, poor concentration, and mental health problems.
Cocaine/Crack	White powder (cocaine), lumps or "rocks" (crack)	Snorted up the nose, injected, smoked	This highly addictive stimulant leads users to feel alert, confident, and often aggressive.	Risks include breathing problems, chest pains, heart failure, mental health problems, overdose, seizures, and infections as a result of injecting.
Crystal meth	Crystals, pills, powder	Injected, smoked, snorted, swallowed	Crystal meth is very addictive. This stimulant induces feelings of elation, and alertness.	Using crystal meth can lead to infections as a result of injecting. Brain damage is possible. People can overdose, leading to organ damage, unconsciousness, or death.
Heroin	Brownish powder, white powder	Injected, smoked	This highly addictive depressant can cause users to experience feelings of well-being and relaxation.	Users are at risk of dizziness, vomiting, infections as a result of injecting, overdose, coma, or death.

Drug	Form	Use	Effects	Risks
Ketamine	Liquid, pills, white powder	Injected, snorted, swallowed	This depressant drug is an anaesthetic that causes users to experience feelings of disconnectedness and relaxation, as well as hallucinations and paralysis.	There is a risk of abdominal pain, bladder problems, increased heart rate, liver damage, and infection as a result of injecting. It is linked to depression with frequent use.
LSD (acid)	Small absorbant squares of paper known as "tabs", liquid	Swallowed	This hallucinogenic drug is very powerful. It causes a "trip," a period of time in which a user's perception of sounds, color, objects, time, and movement is altered.	Bad trips can occur, with frightening or unpredictable hallucinations. LSD should not be taken if the user is in a bad mood or feeling anxious or depressed. It can exacerbate existing mental health problems. There is a risk of flashbacks weeks, months, and years after taking LSD.
Magic mushrooms	Dried mushrooms of different colors	Brewed as a tea, eaten	This hallucinogen causes altered perception of colors, sounds, objects, and time, and feelings of relaxation or fright.	Users may eat poisonous mushrooms by mistake. Some people experience sickness and confusion, flashbacks, or feelings of terror afterward.
MDMA/Ecstasy	White powder (MDMA), pills (ecstasy); MDMA is the active ingredient in ecstasy pills	Powder is rubbed on gums; ecstasy pills are swallowed	MDMA is a stimulant that makes users feel chatty, energized, elated, and loving. Users experience colors, feelings, and sounds more intensely.	Users can dehydrate and overheat, or drink too much water, which can also be dangerous. It can cause confusion, anxiety, and panic. Ecstasy pills often contain other unknown drugs, which can lead to unexpected reactions. Taking MDMA or ecstasy has been linked to kidney, liver, and heart problems, and death.
Poppers	Liquid	Inhaled, sniffed	Poppers can be both a stimulant and a depressant. They cause "head rushes" and feelings of faintness, sickness, or lowered sexual inhibition.	Users might feel disorientated or sick, or become unconsciousness, or have reduced blood pressure. Users may engage in risky sexual behavior. The liquid can burn the skin.
Solvents	Aerosols, gases, glues	Inhaled, sniffed	Solvents can work as depressants and hallucinogens, leading users to experience feelings of drunkenness, slow reactions, and hallucinations.	Users might experience confusion, disorientation, unconsciousness, mood swings, poor judgment, or vomiting, and higher risk of death.
Tranquilizers	Injections, pills	Injected, swallowed	Tranquilizers can be depressants and hallucinogens. They slow the user's reactions and cause hallucinations and feelings of calmness and relaxation. They are highly addictive.	Users are at risk of anxiety, depression, headaches, memory loss, seizures, and vomiting.

Families

Different families

Families come in all shapes and sizes. Every family is unique, no matter what structure it is categorized under. Whether there are one or two parents, multiple kids or one kid, everyone in the family unit has an important role.

One of a kind

In modern society, there is a large range of family structures, some of which are shown here. Each family has its own special setup, which includes how individuals in the family show love and care for each other, what their values are, and how they set boundaries for the family to operate within. All these elements help a family to build a strong foundation together.

TEEN HINTS

Family structures

Sometimes a family structure can change—due to a death, separation, divorce, or new marriage, for example. Finding your way in a new family structure can be hard, especially when what was your "normal" has been unexpectedly altered. But change often brings the opportunity to form relationships with new people. These people will never replace the people in your old family structure, but will help you to form, and be a part of developing, a new family structure.

▷ **Small families**
Sometimes called a "micro-family," this family includes two adults and one child.

▷ **Foster families**
Sometimes, due to issues in their own family, children may need to leave their biological parents to join a foster family temporarily. Foster parents are specially trained carers.

△ **Stepparent families**
When one of a child's parents finds a new partner, that partner becomes the child's stepparent and their children become stepsiblings. The adult assumes the role of a parent, but is not biologically related to the child.

△ ▷ **LGBTQ parent families**
Families with lesbian and gay parents are also called "same-sex families." This is a large and varied group.

▷ **Extended families**
When extended family—such as grandparents, aunts, and uncles—live under one roof, childcare may be shared and close family bonds develop.

▽ Young carers
Some children care for another family member in their household. That family member may be ill, a younger sibling, or disabled in some way.

◁ Single dad families
There are many reasons why a family may have one parent, including separation and divorce, or the death of a parent.

▽ Donors and surrogates
Donors give either their eggs or sperm to help other people conceive. A female surrogate carries an embryo that has been implanted into her uterus for a couple unable to conceive.

▽ Adoptive families
Due to issues in their own family, some children may go to live with a family that doesn't include their biological parents.

△ Single mom families
A family can have a single parent for different reasons, including separation and divorce, or the death of a parent.

△ Families without children
Couples who don't have children are simply a family of two adults. Sometimes adults choose not to have children, and sometimes they are unable to have children.

△ Young parent families
Teen parents are closer in age to their children than parents in other family units. Young families often benefit from extended family support.

▷ Nuclear families
This traditional family structure is found in most societies. They tend to have two to three children.

Parent-teen relationships

The family dynamic evolves as a teen matures, and can test the parent-teen relationship. With both sides feeling mixed emotions, this time can be challenging.

Changing relationships

Puberty brings lots of emotions for teens, and is a time of readjustment for the whole family. Parents have a huge influence on a young child's values and interests, and so it can often feel hard for them to separate from their teen, who wants to develop their own identity and to have new freedoms. This may lead to conflict, as both parents and teens need time to figure out how to adapt the relationship.

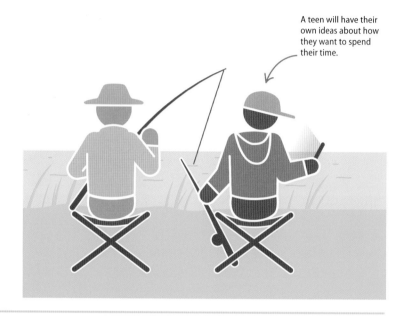

A teen will have their own ideas about how they want to spend their time.

▷ **Different interests**
Both parents and teens are likely to feel confused at times about their relationship. Working out a new dynamic can take time, and both sides might experience some feelings of frustration.

Routine and expectations

As teens get older, it is important for them to take on responsibilities. This highlights the valuable contribution each family member makes to a home, and teaches teens about what it's like to be an adult. Setting clear rules about routine and home life helps teens to know what's expected of them—even if they do complain or resist. Expectations go both ways, however, and so constant communication and flexibility when necessary will help avoid conflict.

PARENT TIPS

Creating structure

- Ensure that teens know how much their contribution to completing chores is valued. Encouragement is more effective than criticism.

- Regularly discuss with your teen what you expect them to do within a clear time frame, and what you'll do in return.

- Model what you are asking for to show what you expect. More clarity will mean fewer arguments.

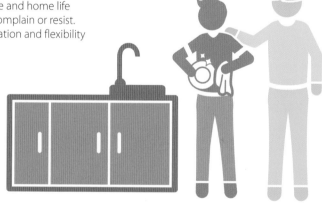

△ **Household chores**
Acknowledge the instances when your teen does something right, and particularly when they do something without being asked.

Staying connected

It is important for parents and teens to overcome life's many distractions in order to spend quality time together. For parents, maintaining a close relationship with a teen who is preprogrammed to separate from them can be tricky, but it helps to be present and willing. Talking about the things that are going well is as helpful as discussing areas of conflict.

◁ **Be inventive**
A chat during a commute can count as quality time.

Building a strong relationship

- Build in regular time together to do something that you both like. Put difficult issues to one side so you can enjoy each other's company.

- By asking questions and showing interest in your teen, you can improve their self-esteem and make them feel valued. When your teen is speaking, give them your full attention.

- Make clear that your teen can come to you with problems. Be open, not judgmental, and ready to listen. If the timing isn't right, explain this and schedule a time to talk.

- Talk to your adult friends about their teens to help you keep perspective and clarify in your head what you are prepared to accept.

Encountering problems

Most parent-teen relationships encounter difficulties at some point, but there are practical steps that both sides can take.

▽ **Resolving relationship issues**
If teens or parents feel they can't cope with a situation themselves, it may be worth seeking help outside the family.

	Situation	Advice
For teens	You feel unsupported when your parents disagree with a decision you've made.	Give your parents time to digest your decision. Explain to them how much time you have taken to think things through. They might not agree with every decision you make, but they'll still love you.
	You feel anxious about opening up to a parent about something personal.	Choose a good time to talk to your parents, when they're not distracted, and decide in advance what to say. Ask them to help you think about something but to keep an open mind, and to let you finish talking before sharing their opinion.
	You feel worried that you haven't met your parents' expectations.	Your parents want the best for you and may not realize how their comments and expectations affect you. Explain to them how they make you feel.
For parents	You feel concerned that your teen is rebelling.	Remember, every teen rebels a bit. Let them know you understand this. Speak to your teen in case worry or angst is the underlying cause of such behavior.
	You feel irritated when your teen compares your parenting style to that of their friends' parents.	Acknowledge that parenting styles vary between families. Explain to your teen the reasons why your household has certain rules and expectations.
	You feel distant or isolated from your teen.	Stay calm when your teen is distant. Maintain interest in what your teen is doing, and make yourself available so they know you're there when they want to talk.

Building trust

Feelings of trust are built and nurtured over time. A parent who feels they can trust their teen will be confident about allowing them more independence and privacy.

The advantages of being trustworthy

Trustworthiness is a great attribute to have in life. Looking to the future, a person who is reliable and honest is attractive to employers and more likely to be offered new and exciting opportunities. Friends are also more likely to support someone that they feel they can count on.

At home, too, trust is a great attribute for family members to feel for each other. With the basis of trust established and with parents confident in their child's ability to show good judgment, a teen may gain more freedom.

△ **Healthy relationships**
Trust is a big factor in building positive, secure relationships that can endure challenging times.

Trust

Trust is given by one person to another because of what they do. By showing that they are able to behave sensibly, take care of themselves, follow the rules, and contribute to shared family tasks, teens can build their parents' trust in them. Similarly, parents earn trust by supporting their teen.

Honest conversations about problems or misunderstandings are also important for positive family relationships. Bad choices can cause trust to be lost. Everyone makes mistakes, but how a person deals with it is what matters. A genuine apology is the best way to start repairing a relationship after a betrayal of trust.

▽ **When things go wrong**
Admitting mistakes and not making excuses demonstrates an ability to take responsibility.

TEEN HINTS
Taking responsibility

- Your parents want to keep you safe. Reassure them with honesty—explain who you are with and where you are going, give them a way to stay in contact, and let them know if your plans change.

- Be reliable and keep your promises. Little things are important, such as being on time.

- Following family rules demonstrates responsibility. If you want to change how chores are organized, discuss this with your parents to develop a new routine.

- If family time is requested, such as at mealtimes, make sure you are there, so that when you want to be separate, this will be respected, too.

△ **Extra effort**
Showing you can help with household tasks will build your parents' trust in you.

Encouraging independence

- Set achievable goals, and reward your teen by giving a bit more independence every time they succeed.

- Understand what your teen hopes to gain. By knowing this, you can focus on building independence in these areas.

- Acknowledge when things go well, and reflect with your teen when they don't. Accept responsibility if you didn't make the right call.

- Teens may want input into family decisions. Show you value their contribution by asking for their opinion.

- As teens grow, let them make their own choices, but if things go wrong, they should face the consequences.

Independence

All teens strive to become more independent. To feel in charge of their lives and able to make decisions makes them less likely to push boundaries and feel held back. Naturally, many parents feel apprehensive about this, but it is important to allow teens opportunities, and to celebrate their successes, too.

Through small, incremental steps toward an agreed goal, teens can be guided in developing independence. Setbacks are inevitable, but discussions about what might help next time will ensure realistic expectations.

▽ **It takes time**
Teens gain independence as they get older, perhaps with a part-time job or by learning to drive.

Privacy

Everyone wants and needs some level of privacy. For teens, wanting to be private is all part of growing up. Teen privacy could mean having a lock on a bedroom door or having time alone each day away from family life. Every teen and family has different boundaries, but clear rules relating to personal space will help avoid unnecessary problems.

If parents are concerned about their teen's well-being, they may feel the need to invade their privacy—for example, by reading their text messages. However, this should not be done without permission—invading someone's privacy may violate their trust and damage the relationship.

Privacy and secrecy

A teen's desire for privacy does not mean that they have something to hide or that they are avoiding the family. A teen needs time alone during adolescence to develop their identity and figure out who they are.

▷ **Teen bedrooms**
A messy teen bedroom can be irritating for parents, but acknowledging that it is a teen's personal space allows them to feel that their privacy is respected.

Dealing with conflict

Gaining a deeper understanding of their own and others' boundaries is a vital aspect of growing up for teens, but this can lead to family arguments. It is natural for people in close relationships to argue, but both teens and parents can learn techniques to defuse conflict.

SEE ALSO

❮ **174–175** Parent-teen relationships

❮ **176–177** Building trust

Difficult events **180–181** ❯

Siblings **182–183** ❯

Arguments

Arguments occur when people feel that they or their needs have been misunderstood, or that they have not been heard. Often, people find themselves in a heated argument over something trivial, but with an underlying issue that is difficult to talk about. As teens explore and experiment with ideas and values other than those of their parents, they are also generally less willing to accept a parent's opinion as the last word on a subject.

▽ **Sticking points**
During adolescence, teens and parents may find that they disagree about all sorts of issues.

PARENT TIPS

Avoiding escalation

- Decide whether this is an argument you want to have. Often, teens just want to get something off their chest, and your best response is to listen and show understanding for their frustration. Also, by letting some things go, your teen will recognize that when you do take a stand, you mean it.

- Avoid arguing in the heat of the moment. Let your teen know that you value their opinion, but that both of you need to be calmer and may need more time to think the issue through.

- Try not to raise your voice. Shouting can be interpreted as a loss of control, and your teen will either shout back or shut down.

appearance

friends

chores

respect

bad habits

politics

rules

homework

Resolving arguments

Listening is key to resolving arguments. To settle a dispute, everyone needs to air their views and have space to reflect on both what others have said and what they hope to achieve. This can be done through empathy, negotiation, and compromise. If a dispute continues, it's time to accept that different opinions need to be respected even if they are not agreed with.

1. Empathizing

Empathy is the ability to understand how somebody else might feel—to see things from somebody else's point of view. To consider how an action might upset someone can help you see their side. If, by empathizing, you realize that you've made a mistake or misunderstood, don't be afraid to say so.

2. Negotiating

Make clear what it is you are hoping to achieve, but always listen to the other side and let them finish talking. Making eye contact will show the person that you are interested in what they are saying. Clarify anything that you do not understand, and set the goal of trying to agree on one or two points.

3. Compromising

To achieve a resolution, both sides need to make concessions to allow everyone to achieve something. Listening and being open to changing your mind is a good skill to have. It will help you navigate relationships with others even when there are difficult issues to resolve.

"Holding onto anger is like grasping a **hot coal** with the intent of throwing it at someone else: you are the one who gets **burned**."
The Buddha

Saying sorry

Following an argument, apologies by everyone involved for their part in the dispute is the best way to move on. It's also important to say sorry if hurtful things were said in the heat of the moment. It can be difficult to take responsibility for an argument, but apologizing shows that a person can admit when they are wrong, and helps the other person feel valued. It also helps an individual to recognize what is important—valuing a relationship over holding a grudge.

Difficult events

Every family experiences upsetting events and faces difficult challenges. These tough moments affect every family member. It can take time to accept new situations and to adjust to them.

SEE ALSO

❮ 172–173 Different families

❮ 174–175 Parent-teen relationships

❮ 178–179 Dealing with conflict

Siblings   182–183 ❯

Sharing big news

No one is ever really sure how to share big, perhaps upsetting, news. From sad news like a death in the family to exciting news of a new job, it's natural to feel uncertain. But discussing things as a family can help to ensure that everyone—teens and parents alike—feel included, important, and acknowledged.

▽ **Sensitive subjects**
Big news can be unsettling, especially for teens who are already coping with the changes of puberty.

PARENT TIPS

Sharing big news

- Choose what you're going to say in advance, keeping your message as clear as possible.

- Make it clear that it is okay to be upset.

- Allow questions, and give honest answers.

- Be reassuring about the impact this news will have on the family.

TEEN HINTS

Telling your parents something

- Decide in advance how much you want to tell your parents—but be as honest as you can be.

- Choose an appropriate time and place.

- You may not get the reaction you were expecting, so try to see your news from their perspective.

- If necessary, think about what actions should be taken after breaking the news.

Moving to a new place

Moving can be an adventure, but it can also feel like a loss of things and people that a teen knows and cares about. Parents can prepare teens for a move by explaining why it's necessary, the practicalities of the moving process, and the changes that will be involved, such as going to a new school. Discussing plans will help make the transition as smooth as possible, as will outlining a way to maintain current friendships. Helping to look at houses and schools in the new area, and with packing, can allow teens to feel part of these big decisions.

▽ **New adventures**
Moving can be daunting for parents and teens alike. Being aware of each other's feelings about the move can help to soothe uncertainty.

Separation and divorce

Most parents start their relationships full of hope for a long future together and a shared desire to build a strong and healthy family. Over time, relationships can change, and this may mean that parents feel that their only solution is to separate. How a teen copes is unique to the individual, but many hold on to a desire for their parents to stay together and to work out their problems.

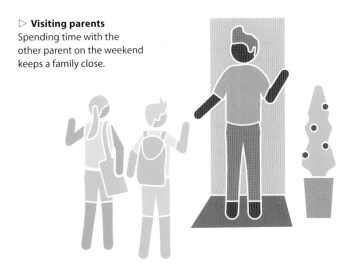

▷ **Visiting parents**
Spending time with the other parent on the weekend keeps a family close.

Supporting your teen

- Be clear about the fact that they are not a part of, or the reason for, the breakup, and that their relationship will continue with each parent.

- Refrain from sharing too much with your teen, or expecting them to handle information about your relationship.

- It's normal for teens to feel confused and angry when parents separate. Give them time to understand and adjust.

- Avoid complaining about your former partner, and don't expect your teen to take sides. Respect the fact that they need to maintain a positive relationship with the other parent.

- Expect difficult behavior and speak to your teen's school so they can inform you of any behavioral changes.

- Try to spend quality time with your teen, and with extended family, too. At the same time, be consistent with discipline and keep routines going.

Family illness and bereavement

The feelings that a person has when someone is sick, or after they have died, are often difficult to understand and deal with. Whether it be due to old age, long-term illness, or sudden death, losing a loved one is devastating, and no one can ever really be prepared. Everyone's experience of grief is unique, with different feelings and different ways of coping. It is important that everyone is given the space to talk (or not to talk) about what they are going through without pressure or judgment.

Coping with bereavement

- Talking about your feelings can help you to organize your thinking and to understand the situation fully.

- Allow yourself to feel whatever it is that you are feeling. You might feel numb, disbelief, frustrated, angry, lonely, depressed, or anxious, and you may have regrets. It is normal to go through a range of emotions.

- Grief can be very tiring, so it's important to take care of yourself.

- Continue the hobbies and traditions that remind you of the person.

- Writing down how you feel can help you to express what the person meant to you.

◁ **Sharing memories**
Some people need to be with others when grieving. Other people prefer to be left alone.

Siblings

Just as parent-teen relationships change and are tested throughout puberty, so too are teens' relationships with their brothers and sisters—but in different ways.

SEE ALSO	
❰ **174–175**	Parent-teen relationships
❰ **176–177**	Building trust
❰ **178–179**	Dealing with conflict
❰ **180–181**	Difficult events

Having siblings

Siblings play different roles in each others' lives—they are friends one minute, adversaries the next. This role-play and role-switching allows teens to test relationship boundaries. Having arguments allows teens to learn how to resolve conflict, while heated discussions teach siblings how to debate, compromise, and respect different opinions—even if they don't agree with them. When they confide in each other, they learn the value of friendship and a trusting relationship.

△ **Hanging out together**
Sibling relationships can form the template for future relationships, and also help to shape valuable social skills.

Birth order

Brothers and sisters share a family, and yet can be opposites in personality and behavior. Where a sibling sits in the birth order can influence and shape their character traits.

Oldest child

The first-born leads the way. This can put pressure on them, but it also allows them to explore who they are without comparison to another sibling in their early years.

Middle child

The middle child often has to be flexible to the needs of others. They tend to be peacemakers.

Youngest child

The baby of the house may have to fight to be heard, but they typically have more freedom and less responsibility.

Resolving arguments

When arguments occur, it can be hard for siblings not to lash out, but learning to resolve difficult situations is a very useful skill to have.

It can be hard for parents not to get involved, but giving teens the time and space to work things out themselves will help them to develop essential relationship skills. Parents shouldn't take sides, but instead praise efforts at resolution. However, if things turn violent, intervention may be necessary to separate siblings until they calm down.

TEEN HINTS

Keeping the peace

- Remember that the issue you are arguing about is separate from the person you are arguing with. This might help you to see your sibling's point of view.

- You can disagree with someone without being disagreeable. Take a deep breath, stay calm, and think things through before you speak.

- Keep your distance if things become heated, and reconvene once everyone is calm.

- If you feel out of your depth or overwhelmed, emotionally or physically, ask a parent to step in.

Sibling conflict

Conflict usually occurs when people are frustrated or feel that they are not being heard. Each family has a unique dynamic, but here are some common problems.

Rivalry

Sharing parents with a sibling can be hard for a teen. They might feel their sibling gets more attention, and that they need to compete with them. Parents need to be alert to any perceived inequalities.

Favoritism

Sometimes, a teen may feel excluded or as if the parent prefers their sibling. This favoritism can be real without the parent realizing. To ward off perceived bias, parents need to ensure no one is left feeling excluded.

Problem behavior

Setting firm family rules will help parents and siblings alike to know what is acceptable. When a teen breaks the rules, parents should try to understand the feelings underlying the behavior.

Interfering

At a time when teens want more privacy, invasion into their personal space and belongings can cause disagreements. Parents can help by setting clear rules about space and privacy.

Blended families

A blended family is when two adults bring together their children from previous relationships into the same home. Households can be thrown into disarray while everyone makes space for the new arrivals and reassesses their place in the family dynamic.

A family unit of step-parent, biological parent, step-siblings, and half-siblings can be tricky for everyone to navigate and feel at home with. Small steps and allowing time for everyone to adjust are the keys to household harmony.

▷ **Being friends, too**
Seeing step-siblings as friends can help to resolve conflicts. Enjoying this friendship can be rewarding.

Expanding families

- Try to do things together as a new family, giving everybody a chance to choose activities that everyone can enjoy.

- In a blended family, have one-on-one time with your biological children. Keeping that bond strong is important for children to accept the changes—they can often feel a huge loss of a parent as the relationship dynamics inevitably change.

- Be clear about who disciplines who in the step-family. Too much change can cause confusion and possibly anger.

Relationships

Communication skills

People communicate and interact with each other in different ways. Verbal communication involves speech and nonverbal involves body language. Communication depends on many factors, such as tone, volume, and vocabulary, as well as expression and movement.

SEE ALSO

❮ 22–23 Self-expression

❮ 84–85 Emotions

❮ 124–125 Speaking up

Interactions   190–191 ❯

The importance of communication

Good communication skills can be learned and will help a person in many aspects of life, such as building friendships and during job interviews. They can also help people to feel more connected, which is important for their happiness and well-being. People communicate with each other to share information and socialize, which is why communication skills are often called social skills.

▷ **Handy gestures**
Facial expressions, gesticulations, and body posture all give subtle clues to what a person is thinking and saying.

Verbal communication skills

Verbal speech is a direct way of communicating, while nonverbal methods are more subtle messages that add to what a person is saying. Choice of vocabulary and tone of voice affect the verbal communication and how it is received—and perceived—by the listener. Tailoring what is said and how it is said to the intended listener is also important, be it a peer, person in authority, or friend.

> "Good words are worth much, and cost little."
> **George Herbert, poet**

Politeness

Simple good manners, such as saying "please" and "thank you," show respect for, and consideration of, the other person.

Compliments

Expressing genuine admiration or praise for someone—be it their appearance, achievements, or personal qualities—cements the connection between two people. Compliments suggest approval, which is something that most people seek in social encounters.

Apologizing

When saying "sorry," it is important to mean it. While it can be hard for a person to admit that they're wrong, resolving conflict and bad feelings is a good skill to have. Often, it can lead to the other person apologizing for their part in the conflict, too.

Listening

Good communication requires both sides to listen well and to speak well. To listen well is to think about what the other person is saying and show attentiveness through nodding, making listening noises like "uh-huh," and asking questions about what's been said. This can be especially difficult if a person is nervous and thinking about what they are going to say next instead of actually listening.

▷ **Active listening**
Being still, sitting face-to-face, and displaying positive body language show that a person is fully engaged and listening.

TEEN HINTS

Effective communication

Good communication can be learned and developed.

- Maintaining eye contact shows interest in what the other person is saying, and confidence in yourself.

- Asking the other person's opinion shows attentiveness to the conversation and draws the other person into revealing more.

- Mirroring the other person's body language and tone suggests a connection and builds rapport.

Nonverbal communication skills

Sometimes, a person doesn't even need to speak for a message to be conveyed loud and clear. At other times, the things we write (such as in text messages or on social media) may not be understood as the person who wrote it intended. This is usually because facial expressions and tone of voice, which would be clear face-to-face, are not part of the message. Body posture, facial expressions, and hand movement all add to what is being said—as well as giving clues to feelings a person might prefer to keep to themselves.

▽ **Reading body language**
Paying attention to body language will give silent clues as to how a person is feeling in any given moment.

An interested person will face the person talking, and may react with their facial expressions as they listen.

When one person is attracted to another, they may lock their gaze on them, stand near them, or silently try to catch their attention.

An annoyed person may seek to look away or avoid the eye contact of the person who annoyed them.

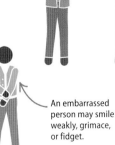

An angry person may flare their nostrils and sometimes even make a fist with their hands.

Smiling, laughing, and matching the posture of others are signs of friendly body language.

A bored person may roll their eyes, look away, or fidget.

An embarrassed person may smile weakly, grimace, or fidget.

Friendships

Friendships teach people to be sensitive to each other's thoughts, feelings, and well-being. They also provide support systems and a sense of belonging.

SEE ALSO

❮ 88–89 Introversion and extroversion
❮ 130–131 Social media
Peer pressure   192–193 ❯
Healthy relationships   198–199 ❯

Making friends

Individuals can have many different friendships that start in many different ways. A teen might be friends with one person because they sit next to each other in class, and another person because they have the same interests or sense of humor. Certain connections can take time to evolve into a friendship, especially if it takes someone a while to build trust in others. However they begin, friendships should contribute to a teen's well-being.

▽ **Making memories**
A friendship can last a summer or an entire lifetime. However long it is, a good friendship adds something positive to a teen's life.

Friendships can be easy and tough. Both are important in a teen's development and understanding of how relationships work.

Playing a sport together and sharing a passion for it can establish lifelong friendships.

Some friendships can be more difficult than others.

Sharing hobbies is a typical way for teens to spend time together.

Different friends play different roles. Teens may have different friends for different activities, such as hanging out or studying.

Friends support each other through good times and bad.

PARENT TIPS

Feeling left out

Parents can feel left out when a teen's friendships start to become more important to them than before. Encouraging teens to bring friends home can help parents to still feel involved and in the know about their teen's friends. Keeping in touch by phone when teens are out with friends can help alleviate any worries.

Laughing together can ignite a new friendship or strengthen an existing one.

Discovering new places with a friend brings excitement to the friendship.

A friend can give a person confidence to try new things and offer encouragement in new activities.

Dealing with difficulties

When arguments or other problems arise between friends, it can feel like the end of the world. However, part of growing up is learning how to manage friendships when they become tricky.

Jealousy

Lots of things can make people jealous, such as when friends get better grades at school or develop a new friendship with someone else. Jealousy can make people unkind to others. Often, just talking about these feelings can help.

Isolation and feeling left out

When friendships begin to drift apart, a teen might feel excluded and not recognize what is happening. Friendships can often be repaired by letting others know that their behavior is hurtful. If they continue to be negative, it might be better to invest in friendships that are more welcoming.

Oversharing

Revealing intimate details about life experiences and sharing secrets can create powerful bonds. Occasionally, someone who seems like a friend will exploit this closeness and use the information told in confidence to spread rumors. If a teen knows a friend is prone to gossip and not worthy of trust, then that friend is probably not someone to confide in.

Toxic relationships

Some young people come to realize that they're friends with someone who they dislike or who is a rival in some way. They may feel that they need to keep this person close, but severing ties can release them from an unhealthy relationship, especially if it's causing emotional or psychological harm.

Interactions

At home and at school, in their social lives and hobbies, teens interact with many different people for many different reasons. All of these interactions are important to their own social development.

Different people, different roles

As well as family and friends, teens naturally cross paths with many different people. From their doctor to their bus driver, their friend's brother to the cashier at the store, these interactions can be important elements in people's lives. It is through these moments that teens learn how to relate to different people. For example, the way a person speaks to their close friends is very different from the information they share with, and the way they speak to, a teacher—and yet both are essential relationships within the teen's life.

△ **Connecting online**
Online social platforms allow people to interact with real-world friends and online connections, too.

Making acquaintances

Acquaintances can be just as valuable as friendships in a person's life, with many people contributing through different day-to-day interactions. This creates a sense of belonging in a community and helps to hold a society together.

◁ **Peers**
Strong friendships provide support and close emotional bonds.

▽ **Public transportation**
People end up in each other's personal space on public transportation. Being courteous to others can help relieve the tension, but teens should seek help if someone makes them feel uncomfortable.

△ **Doing charity work**
Charity work gives people a chance to meet new people and introduce the public to different ideas.

▷ **Playing sports**
Sports attract people from all different backgrounds. Sports also teach people how to communicate.

Being receptive

Staying open-minded to different people is an important part of developing relationship skills and growing up. It's quite normal for a person to gravitate more toward others who think similarly and share the same values and viewpoints. However, mixing with people who challenge those values with opposing viewpoints and opinions can open a person's mind to new ways of thinking—a key element of developing independent thought.

△ **Young and old**
Connecting with different generations allows young people and old to see the world from each other's point of view.

△ **Family**
Some family members live near each other, while others may live farther apart.

△ **Staying in touch**
Social media has made encountering people with similar interests much easier.

△ **In places of work**
Being polite and maintaining eye contact with other people in a workplace makes it a nice place to be.

◁ **Neighbors**
Even a casual acquaintance with neighbors can make home life more pleasant.

▷ **At the library**
Observing common etiquette with other people in public spaces makes being there more enjoyable.

△ **Visiting the doctor**
Communicating honestly with a doctor is the most efficient way of getting the best care.

GOOD TO KNOW

Online receptiveness

The Internet allows people to interact with others outside their real-life circle of friends and acquaintances. Websites with the sole purpose of connecting people with specific interests allow a person to form new acquaintances through posting thoughts and sharing articles online. Through these connections, in addition to friends, a person becomes exposed to new information and ideas.

Peer pressure

During adolescence, friends play bigger roles in teens' lives.
They can influence and inspire them—just as during adulthood.
The opposite can also be true: in emotional situations, peer pressure
can make some teens do things they're uncomfortable with.

Understanding peer pressure

When a person feels influenced by their friends or peers to
behave in a certain way and/or adopt a particular type of
behavior, dress, or attitude in order to fit in, this is peer pressure.
Feeling accepted is a strong driving force for people of all ages,
and so learning how to deal with peer pressure—both positive
and negative—is an important life skill.

△ **One in a million**
Many people—both adults and teens—find speaking against
the majority, or acting differently from their peers, stressful.

Negative peer pressure

Peer pressure is usually perceived as something negative, such as
when a person feels compelled by their peers—whether friends or
not—to do something that they don't want to do. The teen years
are a time when many people experiment and push boundaries,
often because they want to impress their friends.

▽ **Under pressure**
Some teens may put pressure on others to take risks
with them, and ridicule anyone who challenges them.
There are different situations in which this might occur.

Looking a certain way

When a person thinks they look good,
it makes them feel good, and the
views of others can either reinforce
that feeling or knock it down. Building
self-confidence help teens to feel
assured—in themselves, in their
individuality, and in how they
look—and not to care so much
about what their peers think,
especially when their peers give
them negative feedback.

Bragging on social media

Social media gives teens forums for
sharing their thoughts and lives with a
wide network of people. It can be easy
to brag to attract comments and
interest from others, but it's important
to remember that the reaction they get
from their peers might not be the one
they were hoping for. Teens should be
careful about what they post online, as
such reactions can breed negativity
that spirals out of control.

Risk-taking

While taking risks is part of growing up,
individuals must make their own
decisions about danger, as they will be
the ones to suffer any consequences. It
can be tempting to take chances to fit
in, but having the confidence to say "no"
puts a teen in charge of their actions,
and shows inner strength.

Positive peer pressure

While negative peer pressure makes a person feel unhappy, unwell, or uncomfortable, positive peer pressure boosts a person's feelings of wellness and happiness. When individuals align themselves with positive people, the supportive atmosphere can lead to healthy choices. When friends join a club or sports team, or work hard to achieve good marks, for example, it can have a positive effect on everyone in that group.

People are constantly influenced by peers, but the decision to act or not is, ultimately, up to the individual.

Pressure points

Teens, and adults, too, give in to peer pressure for many complex reasons, but common to most people is a desire to be liked and to fit in. They may also feel concerned that they will be made fun of if they don't participate, or are curious to try something that others are doing.

▽ **Joining in**
Doing what everyone else is doing can help a person feel like they fit in, but it's not worth it if the activity is dangerous.

Science of peer pressure

Teens can find it difficult to control risky behavior, especially when their friends are around, or in situations that are emotionally charged. This is because the teen brain is still maturing and learning the skills to control impulsive behavior, to think ahead, and to resist pressure from others.

While teens are able to make accurate evaluations of risks when given time and space, heat-of-the-moment situations push them to pay more attention to the immediate rewards and external factors such as peer pressure, and less attention to the possible risks.

Tips for dealing with peer pressure

While joining in with friends provides people with a sense of belonging, resisting the urge to fit in can show great strength of character.

Having friends helps build self-confidence, but it's important to have self-confidence on your own terms, too, to help you resist negative peer pressure.

Don't apologize for being yourself and for standing up to peer pressure. Be clear, as uncertainty can lead to further pressure.

Be assertive, but brief and to the point. Say "no" and mean it. You might even walk away to show you won't compromise.

If you're feeling unsure, think about what the consequences will be if you give in. This will help you weigh up your possible actions.

Listen to other people's reasons before acting. Consider the different options available, rather than joining in straight away.

Dating

Dating is when a person spends time with someone who they're romantically or sexually interested in. Different people are ready for dating at different times of their lives, and some people never want to go on a date at all.

Why people date

People date for lots of reasons. They may be attracted to the person that they're dating, they might really enjoy talking to them, or they may simply find dating fun. Many people go on dates because they want to be in a long-term relationship, and dating is a way to find out more about a person and whether they are compatible.

Some people go on dates because they think that they should be, and not because they want to. Others date because they feel lonely or because someone popular asks them out. These are bad reasons for dating, and are unfair to the other person.

TEEN HINTS

Peer pressure

Different people feel ready to date at different times. Sometimes, teens get pressured into dating, even when they don't really want to or don't think it's a good idea. It's important only to date when you feel ready, and when it is with somebody you are genuinely interested in.

Types of date

People date in many different ways. There's no right or wrong way to date, as long as everyone is enjoying themselves and being honest.

Paired dating

When two people are romantically or sexually interested in each other, they often like to spend time together, alone. On these dates, both know that they are more than friends. The date is a time when they can have personal conversations, and be physically intimate if that's what they both want.

Group dating

Many teens find that group dating is a fun way to spend time with their "date" without the pressure of being one-on-one. In a group date, two people in the group are romantically or sexually interested in each other and are spending time together within a group of other friends.

Cross-cultural

Individuals in cross-cultural or cross-religious relationships need to be open-minded and accepting. Some experience pressure from their families to break up due to worry over the compromises that they might need to make in their own culture or religion to accommodate their partner's beliefs.

Getting involved

Many parents feel anxious at the idea of their teens dating, but it is perfectly normal for teens to want to date as they grow up. It's difficult to gauge how much involvement is needed from parents—it really depends on the teen, as well as their age and maturity level.

- Teens have no lessons on dating. Speak to your teen about personal values and respecting each other, and how they apply to dating.

- Provide guidance before your teen starts dating, and continue to be available to offer help and advice on the relationship.

- Set some dating rules early on, such as where your teen can and can't go, and then trust your teen to be able to figure out how they want to proceed with these rules in place.

- Respect your teen's privacy.

Healthy dating

Dating is a process of getting to know another person better and, if both people want to, being in a long-term relationship. While it can be tempting for a person to spend every single second with the one that they're dating, it is important to strike a balance to ensure that each individual has their own time, as well as quality time with their boyfriend or girlfriend. This helps to build the foundations for a healthy relationship.

◁ **Caring couple**
People who are dating often support each other through hard times. How the individuals in the relationship respond to these difficulties will often determine how healthy the relationship is.

Age gaps
Older people have more life experience than younger people, including being sexually intimate with others. When two people of different ages date, these facts can give the older person more power in the relationship and can lead to mismatched expectations.

Online dating
Dating apps are a way of meeting new and like-minded people. Some are tailored for specific identities, such as religion and sexuality. If someone wants to meet an online "date" in person, it's important to meet in a public place, and only share personal details once they know the other person well.

Long distance
Whether by choice or design, some couples find themselves living in different parts of the world. To maintain a long-distance relationship, it is important to get the level of communication right—too much can become a chore, while too little can be seen as a lack of interest.

Rejection

Everyone goes through rejection at some point, perhaps in a friendship, a relationship, or a job. Rejection hurts and can stir up a variety of emotions, but how a person handles the experience will affect how long those feelings last.

SEE ALSO

❮ **186–187** Communication skills

❮ **194–195** Dating

Unhealthy relationships   **200–201** ❯

Breakups   **202–203** ❯

Unrequited interest

When a person is romantically or sexually interested in someone who doesn't feel the same way in return, it can cause the person to feel hurt. This can lead to feelings of not being good enough when, in reality, those two people just aren't a good match. Brain scans show that rejection and physical pain are dealt with by the same areas of the brain, which helps to explain why rejection can feel so painful.

△ **Facing rejection**
It's difficult, but the feelings of pain and rejection do pass with time.

GOOD TO KNOW

How it feels

Rejection affects people in different ways. It can be felt mildly or deeply and it can hurt emotionally or physically—it all depends on how much an individual cared for the rejector. Even if the individual doesn't have strong feelings toward the other, rejection can still be hurtful if it affects a person's confidence.

Avoiding negativity

Individuals react to rejection in various ways. Some become self-critical, which can lead to feelings of low self-esteem and other negative emotions. Acknowledging and experiencing these feelings are part of the process of moving on. If the negative feelings remain, the person may need to set goals to act on and push themselves to move on.

PARENT TIPS

How to help

If your teen is hurting from a rejection, you have to follow their lead. While you want to try to make it all better, your attention may actually make them feel worse. Make sure that they know you're there for them, but don't overwhelm them with sympathy and advice. Invite your teen to do some of their favorite activities with you—but don't feel hurt if they say no.

Don't fixate

Focusing on the person who rejected you will make you feel worse, and won't help you deal with the situation. Keep your mind and body active, such as by playing music or sports.

Limit time alone

Isolating yourself can make you lose perspective and feed negative emotions. Hang out with family and friends who care about and love you—and remember, they want to spend time with you.

Redirect anger

While it is natural to feel angry when rejected, it's never okay to act on that anger by shouting at or hurting others. Doing something physical will help, such as exercise or dancing.

Moving forward

While feelings of rejection are unpleasant, they are temporary. An individual can take active steps to help them get over their rejection and stay productive. For a teen who is struggling with rejection, making the decision to do things that will enable them to move on will help them to feel more in control of the situation and their feelings.

Look after yourself

Feelings of rejection can make you feel drained both emotionally and physically. Eating healthfully, sleeping well, and staying physically active will keep your body healthy, and help kick-start your mind into recovering from the setback.

Talk things through

Discussing a problem with others helps you to reflect on what went wrong and to gain perspective when things feel overwhelming. Some people find counseling helpful, preferring to confide in someone they don't know.

Engage in physical activity

Keeping active is a great way of distracting yourself from any negative thoughts and feelings prompted by a rejection. It can feel good to be working toward a goal. Activity also makes the body release endorphins, its natural mood elevator.

Meet new people

People have a natural desire to be liked, and so they tend to emphasize their positive qualities when they meet new people. Attending an event or engaging in a hobby where you'll meet new people will make you see yourself in a new light.

Learn something new

Taking up a new hobby or learning a new skill encourages you to stop focusing on the rejection. It transforms negative feelings into positive experiences that remind you of all the skills, and the value, you have.

Make plans

Having a diary full of plans and arrangements helps you to find the fun in your life again. Engage in activities with others or on your own—it doesn't matter. Throw yourself into whatever excites you, be it meeting up with friends, sports, or studying.

Healthy relationships

Teens form relationships with different people. They range from friendships and teacher-student connections to family and romantic relationships. Every relationship is different, but they should all involve some basic qualities to make them worthwhile and positive.

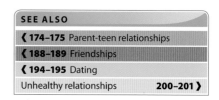
What is a healthy relationship?

Understanding what makes a relationship healthy or unhealthy can be a tricky thing to establish. In short, a healthy relationship is built on respect, equality, trust, and safety. All of these elements are needed, and they need to be present on both sides.

Stronger together

In a healthy relationship, these traits exist without condition, exception, or pressure. Each person should feel that they can respond or act in a way that they feel comfortable with. People can show each trait to somone by the things they do and say, and the kindness and affection they show each other.

> Your diary was open, so I closed it. I didn't read it, but wanted to let you know.

> Let's figure out which movie to watch together.

> I'm glad you told me that. I won't talk to anyone else about it.

> I'm feeling angry—can we talk about this?

respect

equality

trust

safety

▷ **Healthy traits**
Collectively, the different traits, bonded together, make a relationship strong and lasting. Each individual trait is important to a relationship's health.

What makes a healthy relationship?

Whether a person is going to the movies with a friend or sharing a meal on a date, the same principles of respect, equality, trust, and safety apply to the relationship.

1. Supporting each other

In the best possible relationships, people feel supported by the other person and offer support back. This support can be emotional, social, psychological, academic, creative, or professional. Some relationships offer one or the other, while others—such as romantic interests—offer a mixture. When both people are guided by what is best for each other, they can thrive and shine, both in the relationship and in their personal endeavors.

2. Spending time together

Spending time together is an important part of a healthy relationship. Whether that time is spent online or in person, at school or at work, with others or just as a pair, it shows that an individual cares for another person, and that the feeling is reciprocated. Regardless of whether two people are in a romantic relationship or are platonic friends at school, the time that they spend together should make them feel good about themselves, the other person, and the relationship itself.

3. Maintaining healthy boundaries

Everyone is entitled to privacy, and setting boundaries is one way to maintain a healthy relationship. The boundaries may relate to personal space preferences or how much time is spent together. When two people set boundaries, it helps the individuals to know what they both want and expect from the relationship—especially when the two people are romantically involved. Boundaries should be set by both people together.

4. Communicating openly

Communication in a healthy relationship draws on respect, equality, safety, and trust. It puts them into language, including choice of vocabulary, tone of voice, body language, and listening. In a strong relationship, both people feel able to talk about any worries and frustrations. This openness helps show respect for both people's feelings and opinions, equality in being able to talk on equal terms, trust in the other person to listen, and safety to voice any concerns.

Unhealthy relationships

When someone's behavior toward another person doesn't exhibit respect, equality, safety, and trust, something is wrong with that relationship. Sometimes, the "unhealthy" behavior is one-sided. In other couples, both people behave badly.

SEE ALSO

❮ **86–87** Confidence and self-esteem

❮ **94–95** Anxiety and depression

❮ **198–199** Healthy relationships

Breakups **202–203** ❯

What is an unhealthy relationship?

Unhealthy relationships don't have the crucial elements of respect, equality, trust, and safety that make a relationship strong. In an unhealthy relationship, these elements are either not there or they are false. A relationship can also be unhealthy if these things come with conditions, exceptions, or pressures. These behaviors and attitudes make the relationship unhealthy and have a negative impact on the other person in that relationship.

GOOD TO KNOW

Controlling communication

If a friend or partner wants to monitor or check your text messages, emails, or social media, then there's a problem in the relationship, as the crucial elements of respect, equality, trust, and safety are not present. No one has the right to control your communication or limit the people you communicate with.

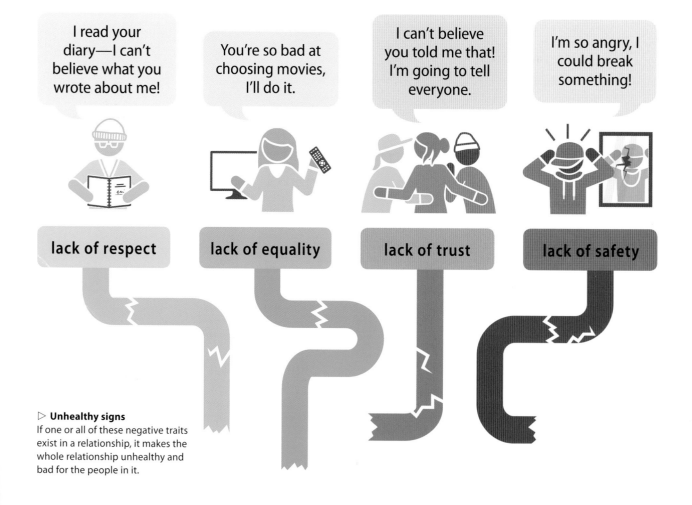

I read your diary—I can't believe what you wrote about me!

You're so bad at choosing movies, I'll do it.

I can't believe you told me that! I'm going to tell everyone.

I'm so angry, I could break something!

lack of respect

lack of equality

lack of trust

lack of safety

▷ **Unhealthy signs**
If one or all of these negative traits exist in a relationship, it makes the whole relationship unhealthy and bad for the people in it.

Signs of an unhealthy relationship

An unhealthy relationship doesn't usually start out that way. It often begins with a small insult that's in the gray area of what's appropriate and becomes more abusive, and sometimes violent, over time. It is only usually once both people are invested in the relationship that the abuse, be it physical or emotional, becomes apparent. Pay attention to early warning signs.

Isolation from loved ones

Discouraging a person from seeing loved ones is a way of controlling them. It isolates them from their support network.

Emotionally demanding

Needing a lot of comfort and demanding attention can be emotional abuse and denies a person private time.

Guilt trips

An abuser makes a person feel like they've done something wrong in order to justify their abuse and to have an excuse to punish the person.

Short fuses

Anger can be emotionally manipulative, especially if the abuser blames the other person for that anger. Sometimes, it can become physical abuse.

Why people stay

It is very easy to say, "I would never allow myself to be treated that way," but there are lots of reasons that can make it hard for someone to walk away from a bad relationship. Sometimes, the people in the relationship just don't recognize that it's unhealthy, even if it seems obvious from the outside. At other times, people stay because they think it will get better.

TEEN HINTS

Supporting a friend

If a friend is in an unhealthy relationship, you may notice they become withdrawn from their friends over time. They may show signs of depression, low self-esteem, and fearfulness. Even if your friend denies there's a problem, they need to know that you will be there for them. Try to be understanding, and seek help if you're worried for your friend's safety.

Seeking help

Leaving an unhealthy or abusive relationship can be incredibly hard, but it is not impossible. Finding a network of emotional and practical support is critical to the process.

PARENT TIPS

How to help

If your teen is in an abusive relationship, intervening may seem like the only option, but it could push your teen away from you, as they struggle for autonomy, and back to the abuser.

- Ensure your teen knows that you will always support them, without judgment, no matter what.

- Seek support from your community and your teen's community about whether or not to intervene.

Breakups

Different relationships end for different reasons. It's natural to look for someone or something to blame—but sometimes, things just don't work out. For both the person doing the breaking up and the person being broken up with, ending a relationship is difficult.

SEE ALSO
❰ **194–195** Dating
❰ **196–197** Rejection
❰ **198–199** Healthy relationships
❰ **200–201** Unhealthy relationships

Why relationships end

The end of a romantic or sexual relationship does not mean that it was a failed relationship. Sometimes, people change and grow apart. At other times, a relationship turns bad, and ending it is the best thing to do. There are times when ending a relationship is a mutual decision, but usually, one person chooses to end it.

▽ **Breakup reasons**
While the breakup details are unique to each relationship, there are some common causes for relationships coming to an end.

△ The people in the relationship may not be connecting in some way, emotionally or physically.

△ If one person in the couple moves away, it can be hard to make a long-distance relationship work.

△ One person may meet someone else who they're more interested in, or may "cheat" on their partner.

△ Neither person in the couple takes the relationship or their partner seriously.

Breaking up with someone

Kindness and honesty are important in a relationship—and this is true when ending a relationship, too. If one person in a couple has lost interest in the other, then explaining this is the kindest thing to do. Breaking up face-to-face, in person, is best, or by video or audio chat if distance or lack of transportation makes that impossible.

Feigning interest is dishonest and unfair to everyone involved, and will only lead to more pain further down the line. It's also kinder to tell someone that the relationship is over rather than hoping that they get the message by avoiding them or talking to them less and less.

△ **Splitting up**
Walking away from a relationship can be difficult for both people in a couple.

ALERT!

Safety concerns

If you're worried about being harmed, emotionally or physically, then you need to consider your safety over being kind to the other person. Call on your friends and family as a support system, so that you know you will be safe. Ending an unhealthy or abusive relationship by text message is the best choice instead of in person. It's also a good idea to block the person online—not out of meanness, but so that you can recover and move on.

Coping with a breakup

Whether a person made the decision to end a relationship or not, it's normal for them to feel a range of emotions after a breakup, from confusion and sadness to anger, denial, and disbelief. There are active steps teens can take to cope with the emotions caused by a breakup. These steps won't necessarily happen naturally, and so teens may need to push themselves through each stage.

PARENT TIPS

How to help

If your teen is going through a breakup, it's natural for them to feel sad—whether they want it to end or not. They may want to be closer to you and the family, or they may want distance and time alone. Follow your teen's lead on this. Let them know that you're there to talk if they want to.

Acknowledgment
A person needs to recognize and accept their feelings before they can move on.

Distraction
Seeing friends and keeping busy helps a person to overcome breakup emotions.

Acceptance
Over time, a person will grow to accept that the relationship is over.

Moving on
As a person accepts the breakup, they become able to look to the future.

Learning from a breakup

It's not possible to change the past, but people can learn from it. It's helpful to think back on the positives and negatives of a relationship.

Think about your last relationship—the good and the bad. What can you bring to a new relationship that you learned from this one?

What did you like about yourself when you were in the relationship? Build on this belief for the future—strong individuals form strong couples.

If thinking about the relationship brings back painful memories, acknowledge them, and then think of ways to avoid this in the future.

Staying friends

Remaining friends with the person on the other side of a breakup can be extremely difficult, particularly if one person did not want the relationship to end. Continuing to lean on the person who ended the relationship can send the other backward in the process—and so most people cut all contact with their exes. However, those who succeed in staying friends often benefit from strong, lifelong friendships.

△ **Moving on**
Ensuring that both people have enough time and space to recover and move on is the key to staying friends in the future.

Sexuality

Sexuality

Sexuality is more than just having sex. It is the complex interaction of a person's desires, preferences, experiences, and beliefs throughout their life.

What is sexuality?

Because everyone's innate self and experience of being in the world are different, everyone's sexuality is different. Exploring sexuality can mean thinking about things that aren't obviously about sex, like the rules in society and culture that influence how people behave. Sexuality is a marker of a person's identity, just like their gender, hair, eye or skin color, culture, or religion.

Understanding sexuality

As much as people might want to, it can be hard to tell what factors affect their sexuality or why they feel a certain way. Some people don't question or even think about their sexuality, while others find that their understanding and relationship with their sexuality evolves over time. It can be confusing, particularly for teens who become increasingly aware of their sexuality during adolescence, but exploring sexuality and the ideas connected to it can help teens to better understand this important aspect of themselves.

▷ **Influences**
The factors affecting sexuality overlap and interlink. There are far more factors than this image shows.

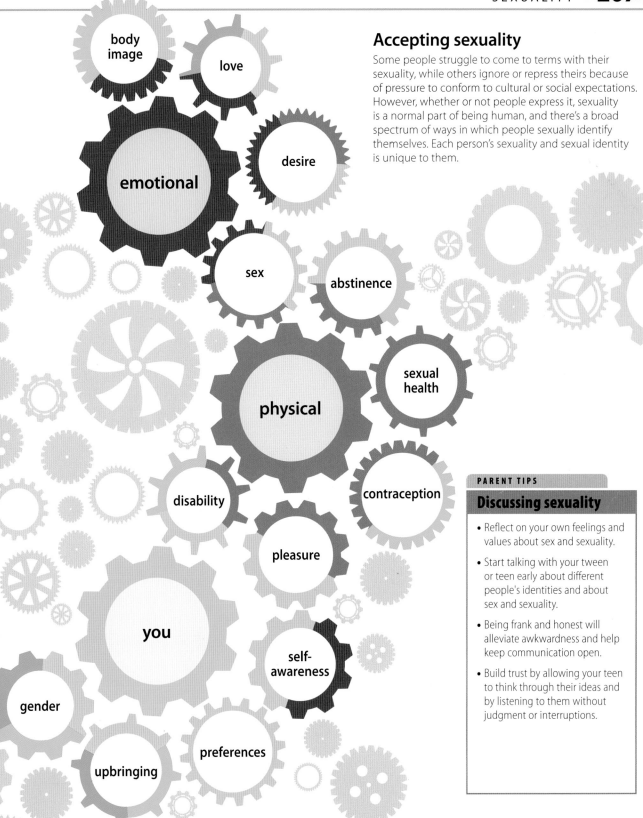

body
image

love

desire

emotional

sex

abstinence

sexual
health

physical

disability

contraception

pleasure

you

self-
awareness

gender

upbringing

preferences

Accepting sexuality

Some people struggle to come to terms with their sexuality, while others ignore or repress theirs because of pressure to conform to cultural or social expectations. However, whether or not people express it, sexuality is a normal part of being human, and there's a broad spectrum of ways in which people sexually identify themselves. Each person's sexuality and sexual identity is unique to them.

PARENT TIPS

Discussing sexuality

- Reflect on your own feelings and values about sex and sexuality.

- Start talking with your tween or teen early about different people's identities and about sex and sexuality.

- Being frank and honest will alleviate awkwardness and help keep communication open.

- Build trust by allowing your teen to think through their ideas and by listening to them without judgment or interruptions.

Different sexual identities

A person's sexual identity describes the gender(s) of the people who they want to be romantic or sexual with. Sexual identity is just one part of who a person is, and they should not be defined by it.

Useful terms

There are many different words that are used when people talk about sexual identity. If a person doesn't see themselves represented in the list below, it is because of the limitations of such definitions, not because that teen cannot be who they are.

Straight
A person is described as straight, or heterosexual, if they want to be romantic and sexual with people of a different sex.

Gay
This term descibes someone who prefers to be romantic and sexual with people of the same sex. They are sometimes referred to as homosexual.

Bisexual
A person who is bisexual, or bi, wants to be romantic and sexual with people of the same sex and of a different sex. They are sometimes called pansexual.

Asexual
An asexual person isn't interested in sexual contact with anyone. They may or may not be interested in romantic connections.

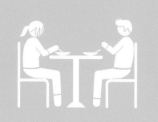

Aromantic
Someone who is aromantic isn't interested in romantic connections with anyone. They may or may not be interested in sexual contact.

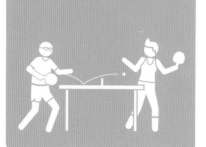

Queer
This term is used to describe a wide range of sexual identities other than straight.

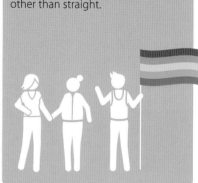

△ **Choosing a label**
Romantic and sexual preferences can change over time. Some people discover the label that was once right for them needs to be reevaluated.

Discovering an identity

It can take time for teens to discover their sexual identity. For some, it's easy to find a term that perfectly suits their romantic and sexual attractions. Others might prefer to wait or to experiment first. Most people are teens when they develop an understanding of their romantic and sexual feelings, but some know from the time they are children, and others, not until they are adults.

PARENT TIPS
Be supportive

Parents commonly assume that their child's interests or values as a teenager are "just a phase." However, it can be damaging to treat an experience as if it is insignificant. Some teens will feel rejected and react defensively. Take your teen seriously, ask questions if they want to talk, and listen carefully to them. Find out about different sexual identities, and be prepared to challenge your own expectations and stereotypes.

◁ **Safe space**
Get to know the person your teen is dating by including them in family dinners and other events.

Heterosexism

Heterosexism is the common assumption that someone's sexual identity is straight. For LGBTQ+ individuals it can be exhausting to correct the same assumptions repeatedly.

ALERT!
Homophobia

Homophobia literally means the fear of people who are gay. People with homophobic views believe that being gay is morally and/or ethically wrong. They may deliberately ignore people who are gay, or be actively cruel toward them, through bullying, discrimination, or showing disrespect. Societies across the world are gradually becoming more accepting of people of different sexual identities.

△ **Nosy relatives**
When a relative asks a teenage boy if he has a girlfriend yet, they are assuming that he wants a girlfriend.

△ **Difficult doctors**
When a doctor presses a sexually active teenage girl to use contraception to avoid pregnancy, the doctor is assuming she is sexually active with a person who could get her pregnant.

Attraction

Attraction is about wanting to be closer to someone else. It might be emotional, intellectual, romantic, or sexual, and can evoke passionate feelings that are both exciting and confusing.

Different kinds of attraction

When people talk about attraction, they're usually referring to romantic and sexual attraction, but there are many ways in which a person can feel attracted to another. Emotional and intellectual attraction is based on feeling supported, or having things in common, and provides the basis for most friendships. Loving relationships between partners are built upon romantic attraction, while sexual attraction involves feeling physically drawn to somebody.

◁ **Attraction**
Sometimes people may not be able to tell what type of attraction they're feeling.

Crushes

Crushes are similar to the romantic love that couples feel for each other. They allow people to process feelings of attraction, and to discover what features they find attractive in a person. When a teen starts to have a crush on someone, it can be hard to know what to do with those feelings. Teens might find they think about their crush all the time, or feel excited or nervous when they see them.

Sometimes telling a crush is the right thing to do, but there are times when it isn't appropriate. It can be difficult to tell if the other person feels the same way. If the other person isn't interested, it's important to respect their wishes and try to move on.

◁ **Overwhelming feelings**
Crushes can feel like they are taking over a person's life, but they tend to last only for a few months.

Lack of feelings

Some teens are left wondering what's going on when their friends start developing crushes. If they don't have a crush on someone, it can be hard to understand the intensity of a friend's crush. Romantic and sexual attraction may happen as teens get older or when they meet the right person, or they might never experience it. When or whether a teen feels this type of attraction has no bearing on the way that person cares about and loves other people.

△ **Other interests**
If a person is not interested in romance or sex, that's okay, too.

△ **Attraction and love**
All sorts of reasons attract people to one another.

TEEN HINTS

When someone has a crush on you

When you first realize that someone is attracted to you, it can bring a whole range of responses. Maybe you're excited because you feel the same way. You might be uncomfortable or unsure what to feel or say. Or you might feel awkward because you don't feel the same way. You might even worry that the friendship will change. Whatever your feelings are, they are completely valid. Just because someone likes you doesn't mean that you have to like them or act a certain way. Just be yourself and be honest about how you feel.

△ **When someone acts inappropriately**
If you've told someone you're not interested and they don't listen, that's not romantic and it's not acceptable behavior. A trusted adult can help you decide what to do.

Coming out

The term "coming out" is used when a person shares their sexual or gender identity with others. For the person who is coming out, it can be both daunting and rewarding to be honest and open about who they are and how they really feel.

Everyone comes out about something

Coming out is usually understood as a person telling friends and family that they identify as LGBTQ+. But in a broader sense, it means revealing something to another person. It is usually something important to a person's identity, for example, their religious or political beliefs, or an event from their past. Sharing this information can make people feel vulnerable, and, because of this, many individuals take a long time to decide when and how to come out. For LGBTQ+ people, coming out ultimately allows them to embrace how they feel.

Ways of coming out

Everybody comes out in different ways. Many people come out to someone less critical to their life before telling family and friends. Others prefer to tell their parents and closest friends first. Some tell the people in their lives one by one, while others choose to come out to everyone at the same time. It's possible for a person to be out to some people but not others—for example, out at school but not at home, or vice versa.

It can be useful to find out how family or friends feel about different sexualities in advance, to try to find out what reaction to expect. Some people may be more surprised than others, or take longer to absorb such new information. Whoever they are, the first person to know should always be someone trusted who will respond with kindness and acceptance.

> **PARENT TIPS**
>
> ### If your teen comes out to you
>
> - Discuss people who are LGBTQ+ openly and positively, so your teen knows you will be okay if they come out to you.
>
> - It may be a shock at first, but try to stay calm and praise them for sharing. Your teen is still the same person.
>
> - Teens may not be able to explain fully their own feelings at first. Be patient and allow them time to figure things out.
>
> - There are many organizations that provide support for both parents of LGBTQ+ teens and LGBTQ+ teens themselves.

▷ **Everyone is different**
Sometimes people come out in conversations, letters, or emails; others choose to come out with a party.

△ **No rush**
Deciding who to come out to, and when, should be based on whether a teen feels ready.

Making the decision

Coming out to friends and family is a big and brave step to take. Most people choose to share their gender or sexual identity when they feel loved and supported. Confiding in supportive people is normally a positive experience for most LGBTQ+ individuals, as it can lead to more honest, open relationships and create a network of support.

Not everyone who identifies as LGBTQ+ has to come out, however. The decision to do so is completely personal. If someone prefers not to come out, perhaps because they face homophobia at home, in the workplace, or at school, that decision should be respected.

A lifelong experience

Most people think of coming out as something that happens once—when someone first tells their family or friends that they are LGBTQ+. In reality, most people who identify as LGBTQ+ often keep coming out throughout their lives—for example, to new friends or partners. Identifying out loud as LGBTQ+ can be intimidating, but telling new people does get easier with practice.

◁ **It gets better**
Having the support of friends and family makes coming out to others easier.

Tough situations

People who identify as LGBTQ+ are likely at some point to encounter someone who is rude, or who gossips about them in order to be hurtful. This is usually because that person is ignorant or scared, but knowing that doesn't make it any easier. If you need to walk away to ensure your physical safety, then do that. It's not worth ending up in a confrontation or getting hurt.

▷ **Take care**
Choosing whether to ignore upsetting behavior or argue back can be a tough choice in the moment.

Supporting a friend or family member

Accepting someone's sexual or gender identity allows an existing relationship to grow. At an unsettling time, an anxious teen needs the love and support of those closest to them.

▷ **Love and care**
A teen sharing their sexual or gender identity is likely to feel vulnerable, and will need support.

How to help

- Listen carefully to their experiences and show interest, but let them tell you more in their own time.
- Ask them what you can do to help and support them.
- Find out who else knows and if they want you to keep it private.
- Help them find supportive communities, online and in person.
- Be an ally by standing up for LGBTQ+ people if you hear others talking or behaving negatively about people with diverse sexual and gender identities.

12

Sex

Masturbation

Masturbation is often a person's first sexual experience. It's a common form of sexual activity that involves touching the genitals. It carries no risk of pregnancy or sexually transmitted diseases (STDs). It's up to a teen whether they want to masturbate or not—some people like it and others don't.

SEE ALSO	
❮ 34–35 Female sex organs	
❮ 54–55 The penis	
Orgasms	226–227 ❯
Pornography	242–243 ❯

What is masturbation?

Masturbation is touching or rubbing of the genitals and other parts of the body for sexual pleasure. It often, but not always, ends in orgasm. An orgasm is the climax of sexual arousal. It feels pleasurable and usually includes a release of fluid from the penis and sometimes from the vagina (known as ejaculation).

People start masturbating at different ages, and some never start at all. It all comes down to personal preference—it appeals to some people, but not to others. It's a way for people to learn about their bodies and discover what they like.

▷ **Curious feelings**
Many teens masturbate for the first time because they are curious about sex and how it feels.

A normal activity

Masturbation is a natural part of human sexuality. It can be done alone or with a partner. No one should feel pressured to masturbate if it doesn't appeal to them.

As a part of foreplay or sex, some people in relationships engage in "mutual masturbation," in which they masturbate with or for each other. People in a couple may also continue to masturbate by themselves.

Masturbation has benefits, including improving an individual's body image, acting as a stress reliever, and providing sexual pleasure for people who choose not to have a sexual relationship with other people.

MYTH BUSTER

The truth about masturbation

It isn't something to be ashamed of. Masturbation is normal, natural, and commonplace. It's not something to feel bad or guilty about doing.

It won't harm you. Masturbation is not emotionally, physically, or mentally harmful.

Masturbation won't affect a person's ability to have children. It has no impact on a person's fertility.

◁ **Opportunity to experiment**
Masturbation is a way for people to experiment and find out what feels good for them.

Frequently or not at all

How often a person masturbates is up to them. It might be as frequent as several times a day, or not at all. There are no health risks involved in masturbation. The frequency with which a teen masturbates is only a problem if it begins to interfere with their daily life, or if they masturbate around other people.

▷ **Healthy balance**
Teens should find a healthy balance and ensure that masturbation doesn't cause them to miss out on other aspects of life.

Privacy

Masturbation is generally a private activity—there is no need for a teen to tell anyone about it if they don't want to. Getting caught, or catching someone masturbating, can be embarrassing, but the best idea is to laugh it off and not make a big deal of it.

Masturbation should also never be done in public. No one should feel that masturbation is something to be ashamed of, but it's best to recognize it's a personal act and not everybody feels comfortable with it.

△ **Peace and quiet**
Although masturbation is normal and natural, it should be done privately.

Having fantasies

Some people like to fantasize about things they find sexual to help them become aroused or to experience an orgasm. They may also use material such as pornography or romance novels while they masturbate. Having fantasies is normal and can help people explore what they like and who they are attracted to.

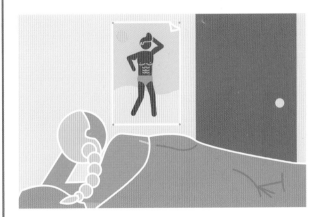

△ **Desire and dreams**
Some people think about a person they are attracted to or imagine a sexual situation when they masturbate.

Virginity

Someone is a virgin if they haven't had sex with another person before. The first time a person has sex, they are said to "lose their virginity."

What does it mean?

Virginity can mean different things to different people, because sex has different meanings for different people.

- People decide to first have sex at different stages in their lives and relationships. It's an important and personal decision.

- Some people define losing their virginity as the first time they have vaginal sex.

- Others define it as the first time they have oral or anal sex.

- Whether or not someone is a virgin has no bearing on their value as a person, whatever their age.

△ **Different for everyone**
You can't tell by looking at people whether they've had sex or they are still virgins.

Deciding to have sex

When someone feels ready, and trusts and feels comfortable with their partner, the experience is more likely to be enjoyable. Once both partners decide that they want to have sex, they can plan for it by choosing when and where to have sex, and arranging contraception in order to prevent sexually transmitted diseases (STDs) and pregnancy.

It's important to remember that most countries have a legal age to protect people from making the decision to have sex at an age when they may be too young. This age doesn't indicate the age that a person ought to first have sex—instead, many people wait until they're older and feel ready.

△ **Making the decision**
The most important thing about deciding to have sex is making sure that neither person feels under any pressure.

TEEN HINTS

Talking to your parents

- When talking to your parents about sex, tell them the truth, and ask them to respect your decision.

- If they advise you not to lose your virginity, ask for their reasons. They may suggest something you haven't thought about.

- To begin a conversation about virginity, you might want to ask your parents how they would feel if you decided to have sex.

PARENT TIPS

Talking to your teen

- Make starting a conversation easier by letting them know you're open to talking about sex.

- Whether you agree with their decision or not, ensure your teen feels heard and understood. Explain that you want to be certain they've made an informed choice, free from pressure.

- Give them advice on the practicalities of safer sex, and the importance of using contraception to avoid STDs and pregnancy.

The first time

For many people, having sex for the first time is an exciting, strange, and nerve-wracking experience. Feeling relaxed and making sure that both partners are emotionally ready and physically aroused will help to make the experience a good one, but if one partner wants to stop at any point, the other must respect that decision.

△ **Unrealistic portrayal**
Unlike in films, having sex for the first time is sometimes a bit embarrassing and awkward.

GOOD TO KNOW

What to expect

- Sex might feel odd or uncomfortable at first, but it really shouldn't be painful.

- If it's painful for a young woman, it's most likely because she isn't fully aroused and the vagina isn't lubricated enough. This may be due to nerves or not enough foreplay.

- For females, bleeding during the first time is not the result of the hymen breaking, but instead due to a lack of vaginal lubrication and tears in the vaginal wall.

- Young men shouldn't feel anxious about sex lasting a long time or making their partner orgasm. It's normal for people not to orgasm the first time they have sex, and nerves may mean that it doesn't last for very long or that it is difficult to get, or to keep, an erection.

- Safer sex practices are essential to avoid sexually transmitted diseases (STDs) and pregnancy. It is possible to contract an STD or get pregnant the first time you have sex.

GOOD TO KNOW

Virginity and stigma

People who haven't had sex are sometimes portrayed in the media as naive or sexually repressed, while people who have had sex often are shown to be promiscuous or prone to taking risks. Additionally, old ideas and misconceptions still exist that suggest women are uninterested in sex or should remain chaste, while men are keen to have sex and should be sexually experienced.

All of these ideas can make women feel as if they shouldn't want or enjoy sex, and men feel embarrassed about being virgins.

Remember, feeling sexual and wanting to have sex is a natural part of growing up, but many people choose to wait to have sex until they are confident they feel ready. Losing your virginity should happen at a time and in a situation in which you feel comfortable, no matter what age you are.

Talking to others

It's natural to want to talk about a decision as big as having sex for the first time, or to want to ask someone else for advice before or after it happens. Some teens will want to tell everyone they know that they've had sex for the first time. Others may only want to tell someone they feel really close to.

▽ **Confiding about sex**
Talking about it can provide advice and support, but it's important to make clear that the conversation is private.

Consent

Consent is an important part of any healthy sexual relationship. It means that at a certain time, someone agrees that they want to engage in a specific type of foreplay or sex. Consent is only given if the person wants to give it and is able to give it.

SEE ALSO

❰ **198–199** Healthy relationships

❰ **200–201** Unhealthy relationships

❰ **218–219** Virginity

Sex **224–225** ❱

What counts as consent

In order for consent to be given, the person consenting must agree by choice, and have the freedom and capacity to make that choice. It may take some time for both partners to feel ready, and that should be respected. When both people consent to a sexual activity, it makes for a safe and satisfying experience, and helps to build a healthy relationship.

▷ **No pressure**
Consent is about choosing of your own free will, without any pressure.

TEEN HINTS

Being respectful

Whether you're beginning a sexual relationship with a new boyfriend or girlfriend or you're in a long-term sexual relationship already, it's important to discuss what you both enjoy and what you're happy with. Discussing what you want from sex or what feels good to you is healthy and respectful. Don't ever make your partner feel ashamed. Criticizing, body shaming, or making them feel self-conscious is disrespectful.

You should always check to make sure the other person is definitely happy having sex. If they don't want to have foreplay or sex, reassure them that that is completely fine and that you are still interested in them.

Asking for consent

It's important when checking for consent not to pressure a boyfriend or girlfriend into saying "yes." Even if they have consented to sex before, they may feel uncomfortable this time or in this situation. Be careful not to make them feel like they have to do anything—for example, don't start a sexual behavior before the other person has consented.

The easiest and surest way of asking for consent is to ask out loud if they are happy and comfortable with what's happening or about to happen. This eliminates any uncertainty, misinterpretation, or pressure. It also makes it easier for the partner to say "no" if they want to.

Giving consent

Sometimes consent can be communicated by encouraging words and noises during foreplay. But talking is the best way to give consent. Trusting a boyfriend or girlfriend means that both people in a couple feel comfortable and confident about having that type of chat.

▷ **Being clear**
Asking respectfully if the other person consents is the best way to make sure both people feel comfortable and ready.

△ **Building trust and knowledge**
As partners build trust in and knowledge of each other, they will learn what they like and enjoy.

When consent isn't given

When someone says "no" to foreplay or sex, then their "no" means "no." Consent has not been given. If a person wants to stop or do something else, that must be respected. If they don't consent to one act, that doesn't necessarily mean they want to end the sexual encounter, or that they have no interest in the partner. But if their partner forces them to do something they don't want to do, then that counts as sexual assault or rape.

> Nobody should think saying "no" is a game or "playing hard to get."

> If someone consents once, it doesn't mean they consent for that type of foreplay or sexual activity to happen again. A person might not be comfortable another time.

> Consent to one type of foreplay or sex does not mean that consent to any other type of sexual activity is given. Different people feel comfortable with different things, and enjoying one thing doesn't mean they want to do everything.

> Some signals and body language can be misinterpreted and don't count as consent. It's important for a partner to check that they understand what any sounds or signs really mean.

ALERT!

No consent

Laws about the age of consent vary from country to country. A situation in which someone cannot give consent is rape. A person cannot give consent if:

- they are under a certain age (in the U.S., 16 to 18 years old).

- they are asleep or unconscious, or they fall asleep or become unconscious during sex.

- if they are threatened or forced. This might happen in an abusive relationship or in a gang environment.

- if they are high on drugs or drunk.

- if they have a medical condition or learning disability that means they are unable to understand what they are being asked to consent to.

> Even when foreplay or sex is happening, either partner can change their mind and reverse their consent. If one feels awkward or uncomfortable and wants to stop, their partner should stop, and there should be no guilt or pressure.

> It's wrong to assume consent, and if someone has any doubts at all, they need to ask their partner whether what they want to do is okay.

GOOD TO KNOW

Acts without consent

Sexual assault involves any unwanted intimate touching or behavior. It includes a wide spectrum of offences, from groping and harrassment to rape. It is against the law.

Sexual abuse is a crime that involves a person forcing someone to engage in sexual activity. It can include pressuring someone to reveal their genitals or to be touched sexually. Sexual abusers are often in positions of responsibility (such as a family member, teacher, or caregiver). This can make it very difficult for the person being abused to tell a trusted person about it in order to get help, but speaking out is really important so that the abuse can be stopped.

Rape is any type of sex that happens without consent. Rape is an invasive and often very violent crime. It causes the victim physical pain and emotional trauma.

Female genital mutilation (FGM) is a criminal act in which the female genitals are deliberately removed or altered. It's often carried out in unsanitary conditions without anaesthetic. Some cultures and religions believe that practicing FGM allows them to control a girl's sexuality. In fact, FGM is a type of abuse. It causes serious psychological and physical trauma (including infections and constant pain). Girls whose families originate from FGM-practicing communities are most at risk.

Intimacy

Being emotionally and physically close to someone is a loving and exciting experience. Intimacy is a warm, affectionate type of closeness. It's a natural part of romantic relationships and can develop into something sexual.

Kissing

When two people kiss, it brings them close into one another's personal space. As well as the sensation of lips touching, kissing awakens a person's senses of smell and taste.

◁ **Making out**
A kiss can progress to tongues touching and exploring—sometimes called making out or French kissing.

Touching

As two people become more intimate with each other, the areas that they touch, and enjoying being touched, become more personal. From holding hands to caressing, these can be sweet or intense acts.

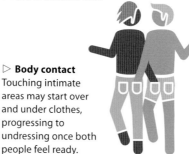

▷ **Body contact**
Touching intimate areas may start over and under clothes, progressing to undressing once both people feel ready.

PARENT TIPS

Parental concerns

It can be nerve-wracking to imagine your teen becoming intimate with a boyfriend or girlfriend.

- Teens who talk openly with their parents about sex and intimacy are more likely to delay sexual activity.

- If your teen wants to have sex, they probably will—regardless of efforts to dissuade them. Instead, try to emphasize consent, respect, having a personal connection with a partner, and contraceptive advice.

Foreplay

As the name suggests, foreplay often comes before sexual intercourse—but not always. It includes kissing and touching in ways that stimulate sexual arousal. It signifies a certain level of trust in the other person. Foreplay itself can be a satisfying end in itself rather than progressing to sex. As a step toward sex, it helps both partners become relaxed and feel ready.

TEEN HINTS

That's far enough

People feel ready for different types and levels of intimacy at different times. Don't put pressure on yourself, or on your boyfriend or girlfriend, to do anything that you're both not fully comfortable with. Understand and respect what is right for you and for your partner. Be sure that neither of you just goes along with anything because you feel pressured or awkward.

△ **Fondling**
Foreplay goes a step beyond kissing and touching, but doesn't necessarily lead to sex.

△ **Open and honest**
Both parties need to be completely comfortable with the level of intimacy.

Erogenous zones

There are certain parts of the body that are highly sensitive due to their number of nerve endings. These are known as erogenous zones, and they can be stimulated to make a person sexually aroused. Kissing, stroking, caressing, and massaging the erogenous zones can evoke sexual desire.

△ Mouth
Kissing sends a wave of sensory information to the brain. This triggers the release of desire-inducing chemicals, such as dopamine and oxytocin.

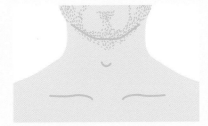

△ Neck
The back and nape of the neck can cause sexual arousal when lightly touched or kissed.

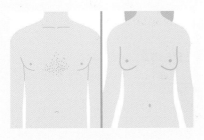

△ Breasts and nipples
Stimulation of the nipples can be arousing for both females and males. The nipples respond to arousal by becoming hard.

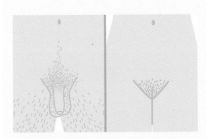

△ Genitals
Stimulation of the penis in males and the clitoris in females increases blood flow to these sensitive areas.

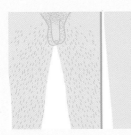

△ Inner thighs
Caressing the inner thighs can be a turn-on in itself. It can also create anticipatory pleasure, as it's so close to the genitals, and can stimulate blood flow to the genitals to increase arousal.

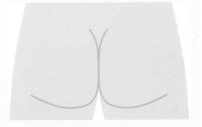

△ Bottom and anus
Squeezing or stroking the bottom can cause arousal in some people, as can stimulation of the anus itself.

Talking about pleasure

Intimacy is about sharing something personal with another person, and so sharing a kiss and other physical intimacy is a two-way street. Openness and communication will help individuals to understand and learn what they and their partners are comfortable with and find pleasurable. From sustained eye contact to sexual intercourse, everyone is different in how they're aroused and in the level of intimacy that they enjoy.

◁ Emotional intimacy
Emotional intimacy and physical intimacy are strongly linked. Each can amplify the other.

Sex

Sex means different things to different people. In general, it's an act of physical intimacy between two people that involves their genitals. It can be very pleasurable and can be an important element of any romantic relationship.

Sex and consent

Most countries have laws that relate to sex, to protect people's rights and to safeguard young or vulnerable people. It's against the law to make someone have sex if they don't want to and haven't given their consent. Most countries have a legal age of consent—the age at which the law says a person is able to consent to having sex. In the U.S., this is between 16 and 18 years of age.

GOOD TO KNOW

Getting consent

Talk to each other and listen carefully to ensure you're both comfortable and want to continue. It's a good sign if you can each tell the other when you like what they're doing. It's time to stop if someone expresses uncertainty or pain and pulls away.

Vaginal sex

Vaginal sex occurs when a male inserts his erect penis into a female's vagina. Once the penis is inside the vagina, it is withdrawn partially, then fully inserted again in a rhythm. This repeated motion is pleasurable and may stimulate one or both partners to orgasm.

Both the male and female should be aroused before vaginal sex—otherwise, it can be uncomfortable. Arousal ensures that the penis is erect and hard and that the vagina is lubricated.

When the male reaches orgasm, he will ejaculate (release semen) into the vagina, if the sex is unprotected. Some sperm from his semen could reach an egg and pregnancy might occur.

▽ **Vaginal sex**
Vaginal sex between males and females is often simply referred to as "sex." It is the only type of sex that can result in pregnancy.

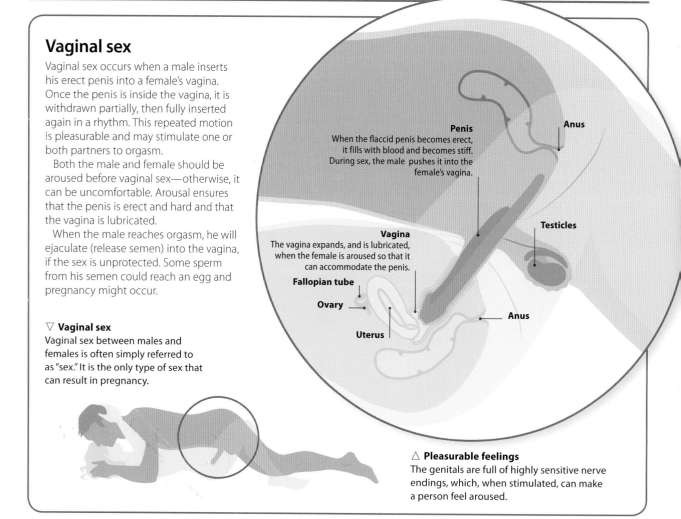

Penis
When the flaccid penis becomes erect, it fills with blood and becomes stiff. During sex, the male pushes it into the female's vagina.

Anus

Vagina
The vagina expands, and is lubricated, when the female is aroused so that it can accommodate the penis.

Testicles

Fallopian tube

Ovary

Anus

Uterus

△ **Pleasurable feelings**
The genitals are full of highly sensitive nerve endings, which, when stimulated, can make a person feel aroused.

Oral sex

When someone uses their mouth or tongue to stimulate their partner's genitals, the act is known as oral sex. This can be a type of sex, or a part of foreplay, for all kinds of partners. Not everyone finds oral sex pleasurable, or wants to do it. It depends on the preferences of both the person giving and the person receiving the stimulation. Some people enjoy it, and many partners experience orgasm during it.

Anal sex

Any sexual activity involving the anus is known as anal sex. This can be a type of sex, or a part of foreplay, for all kinds of partners. It's important to agree that it's what both partners want. Some people don't want to have anal sex, but some people enjoy it and experience orgasm during it. It's important not to have vaginal sex after anal sex without washing the penis or replacing a condom.

Open conversations

Talking about sex can be embarrassing for everyone, but it's better teens find out the facts from their parents rather than discovering incorrect information through friends or on the Internet. Some parents worry that talking about sex will encourage their teen to have sex, but there is no evidence to support this. In fact, open discussions are proven to reduce the occurrence of STDs and lower the rates of teen pregnancy.

▷ **Awkward conversations**
Talking about sex is often awkward, and both teens and parents may feel embarrassed, but it's best to acknowledge that and laugh it off, rather than let it prevent communication.

TEEN HINTS
Talking to your parents about sex

- Although a lot of teens probably talk to their friends about sex frequently, it's a good idea also to speak to your parents, who can make sure that you have the right information.

- Try asking them questions about relationships first.

- Think in advance about what you want to say—do you need advice about contraception? Are you just curious? Or do you want to know about something in particular?

- If you're concerned your parents will react negatively or will refuse to discuss the topic, it's probably best to speak to another trusted adult, such as a teacher or school counselor.

PARENT TIPS
Talking to your teen about sex

- It's best to speak to your teen about sex as early as possible, and certainly before they are sexually active. The amount of information you give can vary depending on how mature they are, but the younger the teen, the less likely they are to be defensive or feel awkward:

- Break down the topic into chunks to be discussed over time. Use what's on television or in the news to inspire a chat.

- If you don't want to talk about it in person, equip them with resources that are factually accurate in order to counteract any misinformation found online or through friends.

Orgasms

An orgasm is a climax of sexual activity. After a period of sexual arousal, partners might reach orgasm (separately or together), experiencing a rush of pleasurable feelings. A person generally feels a sense of sexual release and relaxation afterward.

SEE ALSO
❮ 216–217 Masturbation
❮ 222–223 Intimacy
❮ 224–225 Sex
Sexually transmitted diseases 234–237 ❯

Arousal

A person can become sexually aroused by being in a sexual situation with, or by fantasizing about, another person. What and who stimulates a person to feel aroused is unique to them. During sexual arousal, blood flow to the genitals increases, causing the penis to become erect and the clitoris to swell and become more sensitive. The millions of nerve endings send messages to the hypothalamus, which then releases more endorphins, the body's natural feel-good hormones.

△ **Building pleasure**
A period of arousal can last from a few minutes to several hours.

Orgasms

When arousal reaches a climax, known as an orgasm, a person experiences an intense rush of pleasure and release, followed by relaxation. During orgasm, the brain is flooded with oxytocin, a hormone that causes people to feel intimate with their partner, and dopamine, which creates feelings of pleasure. An orgasm is almost always accompanied by ejaculation (a release of fluid) in males, and occasionally in females.

△ **Intense pleasure**
An orgasm can feel like a release of control and can be accompanied by an explosion of pleasure.

Talking things through

Different people have things that they find pleasurable and other things that they don't find pleasurable at all. Talking this through with a sexual partner shouldn't be a cause for embarrassment. What each person finds sexual or pleasurable varies greatly, so it's important to chat about intimacy and what feels good.

▷ **Open and honest**
If something doesn't feel good, both people should be honest.

Faking orgasms

Some people fake orgasms due to the pressure they feel to be able to orgasm, or because they are worried about hurting their partner's feelings. However, lying about orgasms can negatively affect future sexual activity with that partner. It's always better to be honest.

Sexual arousal response cycle

The sexual arousal response cycle has four stages.

1. Excitement

When a person is sexually stimulated, blood flow to the genitals increases, muscles tense, and the heart rate rises. In males, the penis becomes erect and the testicles swell. In females, vaginal lubrication begins.

2. Plateau

Now the buttocks tighten, and breathing and heart rate remain rapid. In males, the head of the penis swells and the testicles pull toward the body. In females, the vagina and clitoris begin to contract rhythmically. This extends to the brink of an orgasm.

3. Orgasm

At this stage, oxytocin and dopamine are released into the brain, causing feelings of pleasure. Ejaculation usually occurs in males, and sometimes in females. Some people experience orgasms just in the sex organs, others over the whole body.

4. Resolution

After sex has finished, the body returns to functioning as normal, but there is often a feeling of relaxation or fatigue.

Male and female orgasms

Men and women experience orgasms in similar ways, although there are key differences in the length, ejaculation, and recovery period.

The male orgasm

- Hand and feet muscles begin to spasm.
- Rhythmic contractions at the base of the penis, 4–6 times per orgasm, result in the ejaculation of semen from the penis.
- While most males experience orgasm as a result of sex, it's important to remember that some partners require additional stimulation.
- About half of the erection is lost immediately, and it goes down altogether soon after.
- After males experience an orgasm, it is usually not possible for them to get an erection again for a while.

The female orgasm

- Muscle contractions occur in the vagina, pelvic floor, anus, and uterus, typically 6–10 times per orgasm.
- It may take a prolonged period of sexual stimulation before females experience an orgasm during sex.
- Although some females orgasm as a result of vaginal sex, for many others it requires a variety of forms of stimulation of the genitals in addition to, or instead of, vaginal sex.
- Females can have a succession of orgasms.

Male and female ejaculation

Ejaculation is a reflex action that accompanies an orgasm. It's the release of fluid from the genitals.

Male ejaculation

This is the release of semen from the penis during orgasm. Semen contains the sex cell, sperm, which is produced and stored in the testicles. The tubes that store and transport semen contract to squeeze the fluid toward the base of the penis. Then, muscles at the base of the penis contract and push the semen out of the penis. In some males, the semen spurts out; in others, it dribbles out. Both are normal.

Female ejaculation

This is the involuntary release of fluid during or before orgasm. Some researchers think the fluid includes some urine, but it's important not to worry about this—it is normal and natural. Whether a woman ejaculates or not, it doesn't affect the intensity of an orgasm. The amount of fluid involved also varies from person to person.

Sexual reproduction

The changes that happen to young people during puberty prepare their bodies to be capable of sexual reproduction when they are older.

What is sexual reproduction?

Sexual reproduction is the result of the fusion of two sex cells, the female egg and the male sperm, to produce an embryo. During sex, sperm is ejaculated out of a male's penis into a female's vagina, and travels up through the uterus. Although most males produce millions of sperm, just one is needed to fertilize the egg. The fused egg and sperm then start to divide and grow into a cluster of cells. Within 3–4 days, these cells leave the fallopian tube, enter the uterus, and attach to the lining of the uterus, where they develop into an embryo.

△ **Sperm**
This is the male sex cell. During orgasm, up to 250 million sperm can be ejaculated from the penis into the vagina in a fluid called semen.

△ **Egg**
This is the female sex cell. On average, one of the two ovaries releases an egg every 28 days. This is known as ovulation.

▽ **Fertilization**
Fertilization can happen if vaginal sex occurs, without contraception, when the female has released an egg.

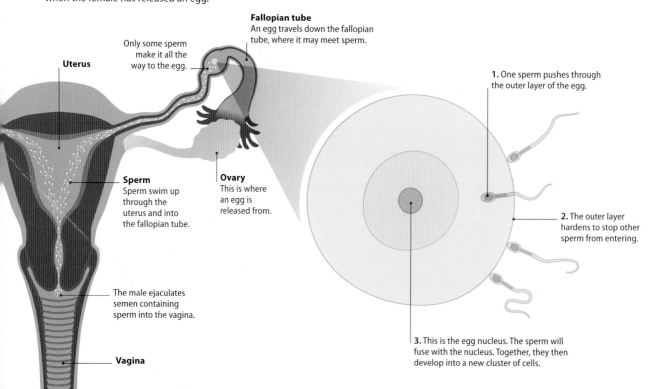

Fallopian tube
An egg travels down the fallopian tube, where it may meet sperm.

Only some sperm make it all the way to the egg.

Uterus

1. One sperm pushes through the outer layer of the egg.

Sperm
Sperm swim up through the uterus and into the fallopian tube.

Ovary
This is where an egg is released from.

2. The outer layer hardens to stop other sperm from entering.

The male ejaculates semen containing sperm into the vagina.

Vagina

3. This is the egg nucleus. The sperm will fuse with the nucleus. Together, they then develop into a new cluster of cells.

Assisted conception

Some couples who want to have children don't find it easy to become pregnant. Becoming pregnant is known as conception, and not conceiving is known as "infertility." Infertility can have many causes, and many different treatments, too. Some females don't produce eggs regularly, but this can often be treated by stimulating the ovaries with drugs. In other cases, the fallopian tubes may be blocked, which stops the sperm and egg from coming together, but this can be treated with delicate surgery, as can other problems in the uterus. Some males don't produce many sperm, and there are a variety of ways to treat this.

In vitro fertilization (IVF) is a medical method often used to help couples who can't conceive naturally. This involves collecting eggs from the ovaries and mixing them with sperm "in vitro" (in glassware or a laboratory dish). If fertilization occurs, the embryo can then be placed into the uterus, leading to a pregnancy.

Gestation

From fertilization to birth, pregnancy lasts for an average of 40 weeks. This is known as the gestation period.

12 weeks

12 weeks after conception, the placenta, which provides the fetus with oxygen and nutrients, is fully formed.

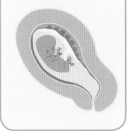

20 weeks

The fetus measures about 10 in (25 cm). It can hear voices from the outside world, and its sense of motion is developing.

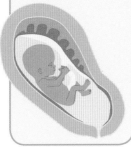

26 weeks

The lungs and brain are developing. The fetus has periods of being asleep and awake. It moves around a lot, and can respond to light, touch, and sound.

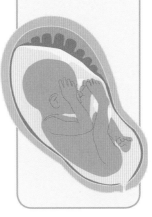

32–42 weeks

The baby usually turns to be head-down, ready for birth. During labor—the process of delivering a baby once it is fully developed—the muscles in the uterus and vagina contract to push the baby through to the outside world.

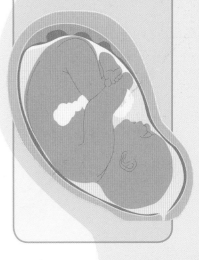

Safer sex

Safer sex means having sex in ways that reduce the risk of sexually transmitted disease (STDs), as well as pregnancy. The term "safer sex" covers many different options, including using barrier contraception, choosing sexual partners carefully, and avoiding certain sexual practices.

What is safer sex?

Safer sex means having sex in ways that minimize the risk of catching sexually transmitted diseases (STDs). Because no method of protection is 100 percent safe, it is called "safer sex," rather than "safe sex." Although safer sex can also reduce the risk of pregnancy, it is primarily focused on limiting the spread of STDs for everybody. STDs are bacterial, parasitic, or viral infections that are passed on during sexual contact with a person who already has that infection. Many types of STDs do not have any visible symptoms.

GOOD TO KNOW

Effectiveness

No method of protection is guaranteed to be completely safe. However, they may help to reduce the risk of STDs. The only way to be certain not to get an STD or get pregnant is not to have sex, known as "abstinence."

◁ **Being aware**
As STDs often don't have symptoms, people that are sexually active should know the risks and take precautions to help them stay healthy.

Unsafe sex

Unsafe sex is when partners do not adequately protect themselves against the risk of STDs. Sometimes this is intentional—for example, when a couple decides to have sex without using a condom—but at other times it can occur by accident—for instance, if a condom splits due to incorrect usage.

Regardless of the circumstances, acting quickly after unsafe sex is essential. The first step is to get checked out for STDs at a sexual health clinic, as treatment is more effective when it is received right away. As many STDs aren't immediately detectable, partners should be sure to use barrier contraceptives during sex until it is confirmed they do not have any type of infection.

GOOD TO KNOW

Emergency contraception

If a couple hasn't practiced safer sex or their contraception fails, but they are keen to avoid pregnancy, they can obtain emergency contraception from a sexual health clinic or pharmacy. This is often known as the "morning-after pill." Emergency contraception needs to be taken within 72–120 hours after unsafe sex in order to be effective.

◁ **Alleviating concerns**
The possible consequences of unsafe sex can lead to stress and worry for both partners, so it's best to always take precautions and to be prepared to act if something goes wrong.

Practicing safer sex

STDs can be transmitted via foreplay and during all types of sex. They may be spread through contact with the genitals or through exchanging bodily fluids (including blood, semen, and discharge from the vagina and anus). There are various ways to reduce the risk of catching or transmitting an STD. Here are just a few:

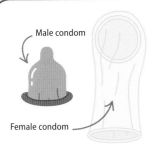

Male condom

Female condom

Using barrier contraceptives

Using a condom is probably the easiest way to protect against STDs. But remember that some STDs can still be transmitted by other parts of the body and bodily fluids coming into contact.

Having regular STD tests

Some STDs don't have any visible symptoms, so if a person is sexually active, they should get tested regularly just in case.

Avoiding certain sexual practices

Sex is the most common way an STD can be passed on, so sticking to low-risk activities, such as masturbation or foreplay, will reduce the risk of catching one.

Choosing sexual partners carefully

When a person refuses to have sex with a potential partner who is having sex with other people, or until they have had an STD test, they are practicing safer sex.

Avoiding alcohol and drugs

Drinking alcohol and taking drugs affects a person's ability to make judgments. A person may plan to stick to masturbation or foreplay, or use condoms, but end up engaging in unsafe sex if they are under the influence of alcohol or drugs.

Not having sex

Being abstinent is choosing not to have sex or engage in any type of sexual activity. When practiced properly, abstinence is the only method that is 100 percent effective against STDs. If a teen decides they don't want to have sex, others should respect their decision.

Contraception

Contraception is a range of methods that couples can use to reduce the chances of pregnancy. No method of contraception is 100 percent effective. Both people in a couple have joint responsibility for the correct use of contraception.

SEE ALSO
❰ **220–221** Consent
❰ **228–229** Sexual reproduction
❰ **230–231** Safer sex
Sexually transmitted diseases **234–237** ❱

Methods of contraception

There are two main types of contraception: barrier and hormonal. Barrier methods, including the male and female condom and the diaphragm, physically block sperm from reaching the egg. Hormonal methods, such as "the pill," act in different ways, including stopping the ovaries from releasing eggs, or preventing sperm from making it to the egg. All contraceptives can be obtained privately and anonymously from a sexual health clinic, and some types can be purchased from pharmacies.

△ **Advantages and disadvantages**
Researching the side effects, pros, and cons of each method can help teens make a decision.

Male condoms

During sex, a male condom is worn on an erect penis to provide a physical contraceptive barrier. It works by "catching" the semen so that it doesn't enter the sexual partner. Condoms also protect against sexually transmitted diseases (STDs), including HIV.

A condom should only ever be used once. Following vaginal intercourse, the male should withdraw his penis before he loses his erection. The condom should be tied and thrown in the trash (not down the toilet). If a condom tears, it should be discarded and a new one used instead, as even the smallest tear makes it ineffective.

ALERT!

Using male condoms safely

Condoms are easy to use and take effect immediately, but they need to be used properly.

- If contact occurs between the penis and vagina before a condom is used, pregnancy can still result.

- Oil-based lubricants damage the material that the condom is made from, making it likely to fail.

- Condoms have an expiration date, after which they shouldn't be used.

Using male condoms

To use a male condom correctly:

- The person needs to be aroused, because a male condom can only be used on an erect penis.

- The correct-sized condom must be used so that it fits comfortably and securely around the circumference of the erect penis without being too tight or too loose; otherwise, it can split or come off during sex.

△ To open the condom package, use fingers (not scissors) to tear down the side of the packaging.

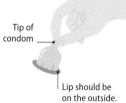

Tip of condom

Lip should be on the outside.

△ Check that the condom's lip is on the outside. Pinch the condom's tip to prevent an air pocket.

△ Keep the tip pinched and roll the condom down the entire length of the penis. It should roll easily.

Female barrier contraceptives

Female condoms and diaphragms are barrier contraceptives that work in a similar way to male condoms; they provide a temporary barrier between sperm and the uterus. They can be worn some time before sex and do not have to be removed immediately after sex.

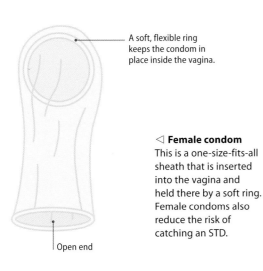

A soft, flexible ring keeps the condom in place inside the vagina.

◁ **Female condom**
This is a one-size-fits-all sheath that is inserted into the vagina and held there by a soft ring. Female condoms also reduce the risk of catching an STD.

Open end

◁ **Diaphragm**
This soft silicone cap is worn inside the vagina, and covers the cervix to prevent sperm from entering the uterus. Sizes vary and should fit the wearer. Diaphragms can be washed and reused.

Hormone-based contraceptives

These affect a female's hormone levels in order to stop the processes that may result in pregnancy. The most common type of hormone-based contraceptive is "the pill," but there are other methods including patches, rings, implants, and injections. There are many different types available. Some stop the ovaries releasing eggs, while others prevent sperm from reaching the egg.

Hormone-based contraceptives are very effective at stopping pregnancy—as long as they are taken regularly and on time—but all are ineffective against STDs.

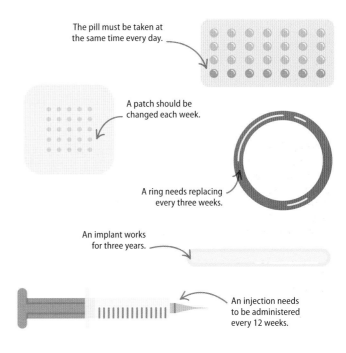

The pill must be taken at the same time every day.

A patch should be changed each week.

A ring needs replacing every three weeks.

An implant works for three years.

An injection needs to be administered every 12 weeks.

△ **Plenty of choice**
There are many different types of hormone-based contraceptives. These include pills, rings, patches, implants, and injections.

Emergency contraceptive pill

Sometimes called the "morning-after pill," the emergency contraceptive pill is designed to be used only after unprotected sex, or when contraception doesn't work properly—if a condom splits, for example. The pill needs to be taken within 72 or 120 hours (depending on the pill type), as its effectiveness reduces over time. Most types prevent pregnancy in a variety of ways: by stopping the release of an egg, by preventing sperm from fertilizing the egg, or by stopping the fertilized egg from implanting in the uterus.

▷ **Act fast**
The morning-after pill doesn't need to be taken in the morning, but it should be taken as soon as possible following unprotected sex. It can be obtained, often for free, from a sexual health clinic or pharmacy.

Bacterial and parasitic STDs

If someone has a sexually transmitted disease (STD), also known as a sexually transmitted infection (STI), it can be spread by vaginal, oral, or anal sex. STDs can have a variety of causes, among them bacterial and parasitic infections.

STD testing

Not all STDs cause symptoms, and it's possible to have one without knowing it. If a teen has had unprotected sex or is concerned they may have an STD, they should visit a doctor or sexual health clinic to be tested. This is sometimes called "getting screened." Clinics are confidential and available to everyone of all genders or ages.

For some tests, the results are instantaneous; others might take a few weeks to come through. If a teen tests positive for an STD, they will be given treatment, and should tell their partner and any previous partners.

GOOD TO KNOW

What to expect

An STD screening might involve a blood or urine test, a sample from the urethra or the vagina, or a genital examination. You'll also be asked some questions:

• Why do you think you might have an STD?

• When did you last have sex, and have you ever had unprotected sex?

• What symptoms do you have, if any?

Bacterial STDs

Bacteria are microscopic, single-celled organisms that exist in air and water, on objects, and in the body. Bacteria can benefit the human body—for example, by aiding digestion—but some types can cause harm.

	Causes	Symptoms	Diagnosis	Treatment
Chlamydia	Chlamydia can be caused by unprotected vaginal, anal, or oral sex, or sexual contact, including sharing sex toys.	Mostly there are no symptoms, but there could be pain when urinating; discharge from the vagina, penis, or rectum; pain in the abdomen; bleeding during or after sex; bleeding between periods; or pain and swelling in the testicles. If left untreated, chlamydia can cause potentially serious problems, including infertility.	Diagnosis is made by a urine test or by taking a swab from the affected area.	A course of antibiotics is the usual treatment.
Gonorrhea	Gonorrhea can be spread by unprotected vaginal, anal, or oral sex, or sharing sex toys.	Symptoms include pain or a burning sensation when urinating; discharge from the vagina or penis; pain or tenderness in the lower abdomen or testicles; pain during or after sex, and bleeding during or after sex or between periods; or heavy periods. Some people have no symptoms, however. It can cause serious long-term health problems if left untreated, including infertility.	A urine test or swab from the affected area can indicate gonorrhea.	Gonorrhea is usually treated with antibiotics.
Syphilis	It can be spread through unprotected vaginal, anal, or oral sex; sexual contact, including sharing sex toys, or skin-to-skin contact with syphilitic sore or rash.	Some people have no symptoms, but others may experience small painless sores or ulcers on the vagina, penis, around the anus, or in the mouth; blotchy red rash on the palms of the hands or soles of the feet; small skin growths; white patches in the mouth; tiredness; headaches; joint pains; a high temperature; and swollen glands in neck, groin, or armpits. Syphilis can spread to the brain or other parts of the body if it's not treated, causing serious, long-term problems.	A blood test is conducted.	Antibiotic injections are given to treat syphilis.

Parasitic STDs

Parasites are organisms that live on or in a host, which they use as a food source. They can cause disease in humans.

	Causes	Symptoms	Diagnosis	Treatment
Pubic lice	Pubic lice are transferred by close bodily contact, most commonly sexual contact. Lice crawl from hair to hair, but can't fly or jump.	It can take several weeks before symptoms appear. Symptoms include itching in infected areas; inflammation and irritation caused by scratching; black powder in underwear; or blue spots or small spots of blood appearing on the skin, caused by lice bites. Itching caused by pubic lice can lead to irritated skin or skin infections. If the eyelashes are infested, eye infections may occur.	Pubic lice are usually easy to diagnose. The doctor or nurse may use a magnifying glass to look for signs of the lice.	Pubic lice can be treated with cream, lotion, or shampoo at home, and by removing the hair from the infected area. The treatment varies depending on the infection.
Scabies	Tiny mites that burrow into the skin cause scabies. They are usually spread through long periods of skin or sexual contact.	One of the main symptoms is itching that gets worse at night, but can also lead to skin becoming inflamed and irritated, causing a secondary skin infection. Sometimes a skin rash is caused in areas where the mites have burrowed.	It can be diagnosed by looking for the mites' burrow marks, and by using ink to make the marks visible.	Scabies is treated with topical cream, which is applied to the whole body.
Trichomoniasis	Trichomoniasis is caused by a tiny parasite that mainly infects the vagina and urethra in females, and the urethra or occasionally head of the penis or prostate gland in males. It is usually spread by unprotected sex, or by sharing sex toys that aren't properly clean. It can also be passed through oral or anal sex, toilet seats, or by any naked contact.	Symptoms include abnormal vaginal discharge; thin, white discharge from the penis; soreness, inflammation, and itching around the vagina or the head of the penis; pain or discomfort when urinating, having sex, or ejaculating; or needing to urinate more frequently.	Trichomoniasis can be diagnosed by examining the genitals and with a laboratory test carried out on a swab taken from the genitals.	Most cases of trichomoniasis can be treated with an antibiotic, which is usually taken twice a day for five to seven days.
Vaginitis	It can be caused by infections, including thrush, bacterial infections, or parasitic infections; or by irritants.	Vaginitis is inflammation of the vagina that can cause itching, discomfort, and discharge. Symptoms include vaginal itching or unpleasant-smelling vaginal discharge; pain when urinating or having sex; and light bleeding, or spotting.	A doctor or nurse will examine or test based on symptoms.	Treatment depends on cause. Yeast infections are treated with antifungal medicines. Bacterial infections are treated with antibiotics.

Viral STDs

Sexually transmitted diseases (STDs), also known as sexually transmitted infections (STIs), can be spread by vaginal, oral, or anal sex. STDs can have a variety of causes, among them viral infections.

SEE ALSO

❰ **224–225** Sex

❰ **230–231** Safer sex

❰ **232–233** Contraception

❰ **234–235** Bacterial and parasitic STDs

Viral STDs

A virus is a microorganism that multiplies inside the cells of other living organisms, and can cause serious harm. Unlike bacteria and parasites, viruses can't survive away from a host cell. They need host cells inside which they multiply. Viruses can enter the body from the environment or through contact with other people.

	Causes	Symptoms	Diagnosis	Treatment
Genital herpes	Genital herpes is caused by the herpes simplex virus (HSV), which can be spread by skin contact. HSV remains dormant (inactive) most of the time. Some triggers, such as illness, stress, or alcohol, reactivate the virus, causing blisters to develop. It is highly contagious, especially when a person has sores.	Small, painful blisters, or sores usually develop, which may cause itching or tingling, or make it painful to urinate.	A doctor or nurse will diagnose genital herpes based on visible symptoms.	There is no cure for genital herpes, but the symptoms can usually be controlled using antiviral medicines.
Hepatitis B	This is an infection of the liver caused by a virus spread through bodily fluids. Most often spread by unprotected sex, hepatitis B can also be spread by blood and bodily fluids; for example, by a mother to her newborn baby, injecting drugs, unclean tattoo or body piercing equipment, or sharing infected toothbrushes or razors.	Symptoms can include painful sores around the genital and anal area, nose, and mouth (cold sores).	Hepatitis B can be serious, so it's important to get medical advice if there is a possibility of infection. Hepatitis B is diagnosed with a blood test.	There is a vaccine for hepatitis B for those most at risk. Treatment varies based on how long it's been since the person was first exposed to the virus. After six months, the infection is incurable, but medicines are available to keep the virus under control and reduce the risk of liver damage.
HPV (genital warts)	It is spread by skin-to-skin contact.	Small, fleshy growths, bumps, or skin changes can appear on or around the genital or anal area. It can lead to cancerous growths. Usually HPV is painless, but it may cause itching, redness, or occasionally bleeding.	Diagnosed with a simple examination by a doctor or nurse, possibly using a magnifying lens.	It's treated with creams or by freezing the warts (cryotherapy). Vaccinations are offered to females age 12–13 against HPV because it is the main cause of cancer of the cervix (neck of the womb).

HIV and AIDS

HIV stands for human immunodeficiency virus. It attacks the immune system and weakens the body's ability to fight infection and disease. HIV is most often spread by unprotected sex, but can also be transferred by sharing contaminated needles, or by some types of bodily fluid being transferred between an infected person and another. This is because HIV can be passed via breast milk, blood, semen, and discharge from the vagina and anus. It doesn't affect saliva, sweat, or urine, and can't survive independently outside the body.

There is no cure for HIV, but doctors can prevent it from developing into AIDS (acquired immune deficiency syndrome) with early diagnosis and treatment. AIDS is the last stage of HIV, when the immune system is severely damaged and the body is vulnerable to life-threatening infections.

Symptoms of HIV

- Chronic fatigue and joint pain
- Coughing and shortness of breath
- Diarrhea
- Sore throat
- Fever, chills, and night sweats
- Nausea and vomiting
- Sores in the mouth or genitals; rash
- Weight loss

STD testing

Going to a sexual health clinic regularly is good practice, as some STDs don't have symptoms. If a teen has had unsafe sex, or if they are concerned they may have an STD, it's essential to book an appointment with a doctor or at the clinic as soon as possible.

Sexual health clinics are confidential and available to everyone of all genders or ages. The results of some tests may be available right away, but others might take a few weeks to come through. If the results indicate an infection, treatment will be given, and a teen's partner should be informed, as well as any previous partners, if possible.

What to expect

An STD screening might involve a blood or urine test, a sample from the urethra or the vagina, or a genital examination. You'll also be asked some questions:

- Why do you think you might have an STD?
- When did you last have sex, and have you ever had unprotected sex?
- What symptoms do you have, if any?

◁ **Worth the embarrassment**
It's normal to feel apprehensive before going in for an STD test, but getting checked regularly ensures people stay safe and healthy.

Pregnancy

Pregnancy happens as a result of unprotected sex. This might be planned, or it might be unintentional. For anyone, teen or adult, who finds out about a pregnancy, support is really important.

SEE ALSO

❰ **178–179** Dealing with conflict

❰ **198–199** Healthy relationships

❰ **228–229** Sexual reproduction

Pregnancy choices **240–241** ❱

When you can and can't get pregnant

Not every sexual encounter results in pregnancy, but it only takes one successful sperm to fertilize an egg, so it's best to be aware of how exactly a person can and can't get pregnant.

You can get pregnant:

- even if it's your first time (it's a myth that you can't).
- if it's during your period (sperm can live for five days inside the uterus until the fertile window begins).
- if the man pulls out before ejaculation (the penis can secrete a fluid before ejaculation that contains sperm).
- if contraception is used incorrectly or fails (no method of contraception is 100 percent effective).

You can't get pregnant:

- through masturbation, oral sex, or anal sex (however, pregnancy can occur if semen is ejaculated outisde the female's body and then reaches the vagina).
- if you're not having sex.

Finding out you're pregnant

The most obvious sign that someone is pregnant is a missed period. There are, however, other indicators of pregnancy, many of which can also be symptoms of premenstrual syndrome (PMS), which occurs before a period. The most reliable way to be sure is to take a pregnancy test.

◁ **Missed period**
If a person is sexually active and misses their period, it could be a sign of pregnancy. This may not be a reliable indictor for teens, however, as they often have irregular periods.

TEEN HINTS

If your partner is pregnant

Despite not carrying the baby, you and your girlfriend are both involved in the pregnancy. It's important that you're there to support your partner. You can help with any joint decisions that need to be made. It's usually also best to tell your parents, so that they can offer help and support.

△ **Morning sickness**
Nausea and/or vomiting can actually occur at any time of the day, not just in the morning.

△ **Fatigue**
Being pregnant might make some people feel unusually tired and lacking in energy or concentration.

Finding out your teen is pregnant

It can be a shock to learn that your teen or your teen's partner is pregnant. There are support groups that can help you to support them, whatever they decide to do.

- Calm, nonjudgmental support will be what your teen needs most.
- You can help them to find out all the information they'll need in order to decide what they want to do next.
- Even if you have strong views about what decision they should make, listen to them, as well as offering advice and guidance.

◁ **Providing support**
This is a time when your teen needs to hear that you love and care about them.

Telling your parents or partner

Health clinics and doctors can offer confidential advice. However, if you're pregnant (or think you are), talking to someone you trust can provide the support you need. It can be a daunting prospect, so plan when and how to talk to them.

- Telling them the news when you are doing something together, such as helping with chores, can make the conversation feel less intense.
- Keep the conversation private, unless you think it will be better to tell them in public if you are concerned about how they will react.
- Be calm and explain the situation fully; if you don't panic, they are less likely to.
- Respect their advice, but remember you make the final decision.

▷ **Food cravings**
Some people get strange cravings or aversions to certain foods, or notice strange smells and tastes.

△ **Increased breast size**
Breasts might grow and become tender to touch.

▽ **Needing the bathroom**
As pregnancy continues, there's a noticeable increase in the number of times a person needs to urinate throughout the day.

Taking a pregnancy test

Most pregnancy tests can be taken from the first day of a missed period or 21 days after an unprotected sexual encounter, although some work even sooner. Tests can be purchased in pharmacies, although some clinics will test for free. If the result is positive, a doctor's advice should be sought as soon as possible. A negative test might be false, so take a second test a few days later if the period still hasn't started.

◁ **Testing at home**
Read the packaging of each pregnancy test to ensure it is used properly.

Pregnancy choices

Deciding what do about an unexpected pregnancy can be stressful and scary. There are three main options, each with its own advantages and disadvantages.

SEE ALSO

❮ **198–199** Healthy relationships

❮ **224–225** Sex

❮ **228–229** Sexual reproduction

❮ **238–239** Pregnancy

Having choices

Whether a pregnancy is planned or unexpected, there's always a lot to think about. Deciding what to do might depend on personal values and financial circumstances, as well as study and career plans. Some people decide immediately. Others take more time. Many young women find it helpful to discuss their options with their parents, as well as with their partner. Understanding the options available, and the impact of becoming a parent, can help with the decision-making process.

MYTH BUSTER

The truth about pregnancy decisions

Keeping the baby doesn't have to ruin your future. Having and raising a child takes love, commitment, and hard work. Support and childcare aid from a partner and family helps. Many young parents have full lives, continue their education, and go on to build rewarding careers.

Deciding during your pregnancy to give a baby up for adoption is not final. Nothing is finalized until after the baby is born.

Terminating a pregnancy doesn't mean you can't get pregnant in the future. The risk of being unable to have a baby following a termination is extremely low.

Adopting and fostering

Adoption is when a baby is found new parents who bring it up as their own. After the baby is born, it might be briefly placed into foster care before going to live with those new parents. Adoption is a formal legal arrangement and once the process is completed, it can't be reversed.

Open adoption

• There is some ongoing contact between the birth parents and the adoptive family, ranging from a yearly update to regular visits.

• The identity of the adoptive parents is known to the birth parents.

Closed adoption

• There is no ongoing contact between the birth parents and the adoptive family.

• The identity of the new family is kept totally secret.

Fostering

• The baby (or child) goes to live with a different family temporarily. This may happen if the birth parents don't have enough support or are unable to look after the baby.

Keeping

Deciding to keep the baby and to be a young parent requires a lot of planning. A doctor refers the new parents to an obstetrician (a doctor who specializes in pregnancy and childbirth). In some cases, a specially trained nurse supports the parents throughout the pregnancy and during the baby's early years.

There are some key things to think about in advance to help with planning:

- Make sure everyone who will be affected is aware, including the partner, family, and friends.

- Ask the doctor if there are any local nurses and/or midwives who specialize in working with young parents.

- Look for local groups where teen parents can meet other new parents.

- Investigate what support is given to young parents at schools and colleges, so that there is as little disruption to education as possible.

- Seek help with things such as running errands or looking after the baby, if possible.

Terminating

Also known as "abortion," termination is a safe, medical way of ending a pregnancy, which is arranged by a doctor or sexual health clinic. It's possible to have a termination without friends or family knowing, if a teen is more comfortable keeping it private. However, having support from someone—such as a parent, partner, or friend—can help.

Medical termination

- This type of termination takes place within the first 10 weeks of pregnancy. Pills are prescribed to be taken 24 or 48 hours apart, which induce a miscarriage. There is no need to be in hospital.

Surgical termination

- A surgical termination takes place after the first 10 weeks of pregnancy. A doctor performs a minor procedure, in a hospital or clinic and with anaesthetic, to remove the fetus. After a certain point in a pregnancy, it can no longer be legally terminated, but the law about when this point occurs varies between countries.

Teens may have different reactions after an abortion—some may feel relieved, while others may experience sadness and distress. Medical complications are uncommon.

Pornography

Often shortened to "porn" or "porno," pornography is sexual media intended to arouse the person using it. It includes videos, photos, writing, and video games that feature sexual activity or sexual images. Some people watch porn regularly, but it can make others feel very uncomfortable.

SEE ALSO
❮ 198–199 Healthy relationships
❮ 216–217 Masturbation
❮ 220–221 Consent
❮ 224–225 Sex

What is pornography?

Images of nudity have been created throughout human history, as a form of artistic expression or occasionally to arouse the person engaging with it. Pornography tends to show naked or seminaked adults performing sexual acts. It's usually an explicit depiction of sex, and it's not typically done in an artistic way.

▷ **Types of pornographic media**
Pornographic media comes in many different forms, the most common being online videos, films, video games, and magazines.

Why people use it

Pornography is used by a range of people and for different reasons. People may use pornography by themselves, or with their partner if they are in a couple. Reasons for watching porn may include:

Exploring fantasies and what a person finds arousing.

Assisting masturbation by helping with arousal.

Watching it with a partner as part of foreplay.

Is pornography okay?

There's a lot of debate about pornography. Some people take a positive view and believe that the actors enjoy their participation, and are involved by choice. They feel that pornography can help people to embrace their sexuality. Others argue that porn typically shows sexism, unsafe sex, exploitation, and violence. They feel that actors are exploited by the production companies. They also claim that some actors may have been sexually abused in the past and so might have distorted ideas about intimacy.

△ **Personal choice**
It's important to respect individual choice, but to be aware that all countries have laws about the content of pornography, and to only use porn that complies with those laws.

Downsides of pornography

Pornography can be misused or misinterpreted, which can lead to an unhealthy relationship with sex in the real world.

"Porn sex" is often very different from "real sex": the people typically behave differently from regular people, and what they do is often very unusual, or even unpleasant and violent.

The sex or sexual acts portrayed in porn do not show sex as part of a healthy relationship. Instead, porn can lead people to think that they can treat those they have sex with as "sex objects."

Some people may feel disappointed by sex in the real world because it's not the same as sex portrayed in porn.

Female porn actors tend to have large breasts and no pubic hair, while males have large penises. This can damage people's body confidence, as most people don't look like this.

Some people become desensitized to the porn they watch and it no longer arouses them, or it desensitizes them to the pleasure of real sex.

Some people develop an unhealthy obsession with porn if they overuse it. Overwatching porn can be difficult to stop.

Pornography and the Internet

Tweens and teens are increasingly exposed to pornography online, and often before they have learned about sex or had sex themselves. They may seek out pornography intentionally, or stumble across it by accident if it appears unexpectedly on a website or in a search for educational material about sex. Such early exposure to sexually explicit images may be distressing, and is likely to leave teens misinformed about intimacy and sex as part of a healthy relationship. Young people may feel pressured to imitate activities they have seen online, or engage in risky sexual behaviors, such as not using a condom.

◁ **Online access**
Parents can set age-appropriate restrictions on phones, tablets, and computers, too, and keep the family computer in a common area. Having a conversation is essential, too, as talking about porn will help teens to approach it responsibly.

Finding balance

If a teen is concerned about their own use of porn, or is unsure if it's healthy, then talking to a friend may be useful. Having open conversations about pornography can help a teen to establish limits for what's a healthy use of porn and what isn't.

GOOD TO KNOW

Talking about pornography

- Start by asking someone you trust what they think about pornography. This allows you both to contribute as much or as little as you want.

- Ask them to keep everything confidential, but don't be ashamed or make the person you are talking to feel ashamed, either.

▷ **When and where**
Having a balanced approach to pornography includes restricting use to when and where it is appropriate.

Porn should not be used in public.

Sexting

Sexting, also known as nude selfies or nudes, is when people send naked, underwear-only, or sexually explicit pictures or videos of themselves or a part of their body. There are many risks involved, even if the sext doesn't include a person's face.

SEE ALSO
❰ **194–195** Dating
❰ **198–199** Healthy relationships
❰ **200–201** Unhealthy relationships
❰ **220–221** Consent

Why people might sext

Someone might send a sexy text, or "sext," to feel closer to their partner or because they think it's fun and flirty. If two people are happy and comfortable in their relationship, sexting is okay; however, it can still be risky.

Even if a teen trusts the person they are sexting with, if they aren't comfortable with sexting, they should feel confident enough to say no. It may seem, or people might say, that everybody else is sexting, but they aren't. If a person feels pressured or coerced by someone else to take a sext, that's not okay, and it's likely to be a sign of an unhealthy relationship. Some people may also send sexts to get someone's attention, to impress a person, or to make someone like them, but this rarely works and is more likely to put the person off them.

When sending a sext, teens should always have the consent of the other person first, as they may feel very uncomfortable about receiving an explicit image. If they say no, it's essential to respect the other person's answer.

△ **Think about it beforehand**
Not everyone feels comfortable with sending or receiving sexts, and nobody should be pressured to do so.

The risks

When a person sends a sext, it is no longer possible for them to control who sees it, no matter how much they trust the recipient of the sext. An image can be shared very quickly among a wide network of people without permission, and even posted online. When deciding whether or not to sext, it's essential to consider the risks:

Even following a good relationship, a person might share it after a breakup.

It might fall into the wrong hands, even accidentally.

A sext may eventually be seen by a person's teachers, parents, grandparents, siblings, or friends.

The recipient may not be trustworthy and could share the image with friends.

It may damage the sender's reputation and possibly affect future prospects.

People might share the image to bully, shame, or blackmail a person.

If a person is under 18 years old, taking an explicit picture of themselves is illegal, as is sharing it.

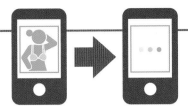

Respecting privacy

When two people decide to sext with each other, there is usually an agreement that the pictures are only for the two of them. It is critical that they treat any sexts they receive with respect. Sharing sexts without permission is a violation of trust and privacy, and there may also be legal consequences.

ALERT!

Sexting and the law

In some states, if someone is under the age of 18 and they take or share a picture of themselves naked or in a sexually explicit pose, they are creating child sex abuse images, also known as child pornography. This is illegal.

Having a copy of child pornography is also illegal, which means that the person the sext is sent to is also potentially breaking the law. The consequences could include receiving a criminal record or even being sent to prison. If someone shares a sext with you, do not send the image on. Instead, report it to a parent or teacher.

Revenge porn

Revenge porn is when someone posts online a naked or sexually explicit image or video of someone else as a way of getting back at them for something. It is most often done by someone who was recently broken up with, and they typically use images that were sent to them as sexts during the relationship. Revenge porn can also refer to a situation in which friends who have fallen out with one another share pictures they had previously been sent in confidence.

Although there are laws being written to stop revenge porn, if the picture has been posted online and seen by many people, the damage has often already been done before any legal action can be taken.

△ **Be aware of the risks**
Even if the person who first posted the image online deletes it, others may have already copied it and posted it elsewhere.

Sexting issues

If a teen has sent or received a sext and is worried about the consequences, it's important to know what to do. The first step to take is to delete the image or video from all devices where possible, and, if it appears online, to contact the site and request for it to be taken down.

◁ **Love and support**
Parents should make clear to their teen that they can come to them for help with any problem.

TEEN HINTS

Getting help

- There are things that can be done to minimize the impact, but you need to act quickly. Ask the person not to share the image and to delete it from their phone. If the image appears online, notify the site and click the link to report abuse.
- Tell your parents. They may be angry at first, but it's better for them to hear it from you rather than someone else.
- If you're being blackmailed or your image has been shared as revenge porn, contact the police.

PARENT TIPS

Giving support

- Tell your teen they can come to you in case of a problem.
- If your teen has received a sexually explicit message, discourage them from sharing and tell them to report it.
- The law is not designed to punish a teen who has taken their own picture to experiment sexually, but rather those who profit from distributing sexual images.
- If your teen is being blackmailed or has been a victim of revenge porn, contact the police.

Find out more

There is a wealth of information and support for teens and parents. Use a search engine to find out more.

Growing up

Childhelp
Online and telephone service for children offering confidential information and advice on all aspects of growing up.

Mermaids
Advice for children and young people with gender identity issues, and their parents.

Teen Line
Facts and advice on a range of issues affecting young people.

Female puberty

Girlshealth.gov
Resources for parents and children about physical and mental health during puberty.

Kids Health
Facts and advice about all aspects of puberty for parents and teens.

Breast Cancer Care
Advice on checking breasts, as well as how breasts change through puberty and adulthood.

Center for Young Women's Health
Advice and information on a huge range of health issues affecting young women, especially during puberty, from sexual health to emotional health.

Male puberty

Healthy Children
Resources for parents and children about puberty.

Kids Health
Facts and advice about all aspects of puberty for parents and teens.

Testicular Cancer Foundation
Resources on testicular cancer, from detection to treatment.

Young Men's Health
Advice and information on huge range of health issues affecting young men, from sexual health to emotional health.

Healthy body

National Eating Disorders Association
Eating disorder advice, with information and helpline.

About-Face
Resources encouraging positive self-esteem and body image, with advice on how to recognize and resist harmful media messages.

Proud2Bme
Online community created by teens to promote positive body image and encourage healthy attitudes towards food and weight.

National Sleep Foundation
Organization dedicated to the promotion of the benefits of healthy sleep.

Healthy mind

Mind
Advice and support for those with mental health problems.

Young Minds
Resources and advice on improving young people's mental health.

Anxiety and Depression Association of America
Information and support for dealing with anxiety and depression.

National Alliance on Mental Illness
An organization raising awareness and providing support on mental health issues.

Achieving potential

The College Board
An organization that supports students in their transition to college.

US Department of Education
US Government education website, with extensive information on school, higher education, and further education.

Careers.org
Information, advice and state-specific guidance on making decisions on work in the USA.

CareerOneStop
US Department of Labor resource for career advice and information, and jobs.

HomeRoom
US government education blog for information on study and education options.

Digital life

Cybersmile
Help and advice for people dealing with bullying online.

Think U Know
Advice about online safety, particularly concerning sex and relationships, for kids of all ages, and parents.

Parenting for a Digital Future
Blog about bringing up kids in the digital age.

Internet Matters
Advice on staying safe online for parents and young people.

Wider world

Drug Enforcement Administration
Facts and advice about drugs.

Alcoholics Anonymous
Recovery network for alcoholics of all ages.

Al-Anon
Support for family and friends of those suffering from alcoholism.

UN Women
The United Nations organization that works towards gender equality and the empowerment of women and girls.

StopBullying
Advice for young people and adults on how to deal with bullying.

Kidscape
Bullying and child sexual abuse help for tweens, teens, and adults.

Families

Family Lives
Support for parents and families.

USA.gov
Advice on all aspects of family, including education, abuse, and the law.

National Children's Alliance
Organization empowering local communities to serve child victims of abuse.

Relationships

Loveisrespect.org
An organization providing relationship support, particuarly dating abuse, with online help pages.

ChildLine
Advice and information on a range of topics, including relationships, mental health, and sexuality.

Scarleteen.com
Support and advice on relationships, sexuality, and sex for teens.

Sexuality

Human Rights Campaign
US civil rights organization working to achieve LGBTQ+ equality

Family Equality Council
Information and advice for LGBTQ+ parents and their children.

Coalition for Positive Sexuality
Sexuality education website for teens and young adults.

It Gets Better Project
Organization offering emotional support to LGBTQ+ people through their teen years.

Sex

American Sexual Health Association
Sexual health, well-being, and education services for young people.

Marie Stopes International
International reproductive health care and advice provider.

Advocates for Youth
Champions of young people's rights to sexual health information.

Planned Parenthood
Relationship information and advice, including safety, consent, and communication.

Glossary

abstinence
The act of refraining from having sex.

acne
Inflammation of the skin, characterized by outbreaks of whiteheads, blackheads, and other types of pimples.

addiction
An intense, often harmful urge to take a substance or do a particular activity regularly.

adolescence
When a person matures from a child into an adult. This time follows the start of puberty.

ailment
An illness.

anatomy
The structure of the body or of a body part.

anxiety
A feeling of unease that may cause a person distress.

app
A computer software program that is downloaded and installed onto a electronic device. Short for "application."

arousal
The act of being sexually excited in response to something.

asexual
A person with no sexual feelings or desire.

assertiveness
Behavior that is confident and forceful.

autonomy
Having the independence to think or act freely.

avatar
A digital representation of a person in a computer game or on an Internet forum.

bacterium
A single-celled microorganism that lives in organic material—such as a body, soil, or water. Some types of bacterium cause disease. *Plural: bacteria*

biological sex
The physical characteristics with which a person is born.

bisexual
Being sexually attracted to both males and females.

blackmail
The criminal act of demanding money from people by threatening to reveal secret or compromising information about them.

blog
A website that records the opinions, thoughts, and experiences of the writer, much like an online journal, but one that anyone can read.

body image
A person's perception of, and thoughts and feelings about, his or her physical appearance.

brainstorming
A group conference to produce ideas and solve a specific problem.

cartilage
Tough and flexible tissue that connects and supports parts of the body, such as the larynx.

cell
A microscopic living unit that forms the basic structure of the human body. There are many different types of cell, including muscle, blood, and nerve cells.

circumcision
The surgical removal of the foreskin from a male's penis, or the clitoris from a female's vulva.

cisgender
When a person's gender identity as man or woman matches the sex they were assigned at birth; the opposite of transgender.

citizenship
The state of being a citizen and legally belonging to a particular country.

clickbait
An Internet link that is designed to capture attention. When clicked on, it may direct users to sites containing viruses.

clitoris
A highly sensitive part of a female's genitals that gives sexual pleasure when stimulated.

compromise
The resolution of an argument by mutual agreement, usually with both sides making a concession.

conception
When an egg is fertilized by a sperm.

confidence
A person's self-assurance in his or her ability.

consent
A voluntary agreement or permission to do something or to allow something to happen, such as sexual intercourse.

contraception
A range of methods that can be used to prevent pregnancy. There are two types: barrier and hormone-based. Also called birth control.

cookies
Small text files that are created by a website when a user first visits it, and which are stored on the user's computer so that the website can recognize the user on future visits and track the user's preferences.

cross-cultural
Pertaining to multiple different cultures, including their ideas, values, and customs.

cross-religious
Relating to two or more different religions, including the similarities and differences in their beliefs and values.

cyberbullying
The use of technology to bully people, such as through sending them threatening emails, or posting embarrassing or unfair comments or pictures of them on social media.

defamation
The spreading of false information that hurts another person's reputation.

democracy
A political system in which the people elect representatives who rule on their behalf.

depressant
Something that reduces activity. Often used to refer to drugs such as tranquillizers and sedatives that slow down brain activity.

depression
A disorder that affects a person's

mood, typically making them feel persistently sad, dejected, and anxious.

desensitization
The lessening of a person's sensitivity and emotional response to a negative stimulus following frequent exposure to it.

digital footprint
A trail of digital data that is a record of a person's online activity.

discrimination
Treating a person unfairly as a result of prejudice, for reasons including race, gender, or religion.

divorce
The legal way of ending of a marriage.

echo chamber
A filtering system, such as that used on social media websites, whereby users are only exposed to select news and information sources based on their online activity that reinforce their already-existing opinions.

ejaculation
The sudden discharge of fluid from the genitals, usually as a result of sexual activity.

emergency contraception
A hormone-based contraception that prevents pregnancy, used only after protection has failed or following unprotected sex.

emotion
The body's instinctive response to something happening to or around a person.

empathy
The ability to see things from another person's perspective, and to understand and share his or her emotions.

endorphins
A hormone, released in the brain that lessens the feeling of pain and improves a person's mood.

equality
The state of being equal and fair, such as all people having the same rights regardless of their race or religion.

erection
The firm and enlarged state of a penis when filled with blood, often caused by sexual arousal.

erogenous zone
A highly sensitive area of the body that is packed with nerve endings, and which can cause sexual arousal when stimulated.

extremism
Having ideas and views that are extreme, or that differ considerably from what most people think to be correct or reasonable.

flaccid
The state of the penis when soft and not erect.

fertilization
The joining of sex cells (a male sperm and female egg) to create a zygote—a cluster of cells that, over time, forms a baby.

firewall
A digital security system that protects a person's computer from unauthorized access, such as from hackers.

foreplay
Intimate acts, such as kissing and touching, between two individuals that stimulate sexual arousal, sometimes (but not always) before sex.

gay
Being sexually attracted to

members of the same sex; also called homosexual.

gender
A combination of a person's biological sex, gender expression, and gender identity.

gender dysphoria
A condition in which an individual feels that their biological sex does not match their gender identity.

gender expression
The way individuals present themselves to society, through their appearance and behavior.

gender identity
The way individuals personally think, feel, and see themselves as a man, woman, or other gender.

genitals
A person's external sexual organs—the penis and testicles of a male, and a female's vulva.

germ cell
An egg or a sperm.

gestation
The period of time, from conception to birth, during which a baby develops inside a female's uterus.

gland
An organ that produces and releases chemicals, such as hormones, into the body.

grooming
When a person pretends to be someone or something that they are not, in order to earn trust and manipulate another person into doing something.

groping
When a person touches someone else in a sexual way, over or under clothing, without their consent.

gynecomastia
Enlargement of a male's "breasts" due to a change in hormone levels during puberty; often referred to as "man boobs" or "moobs."

heterosexism
The assumption that an individual is sexually attracted to people of the opposite sex.

heterosexual
A person that is sexually attracted to members of the opposite sex; also known as straight.

homophobia
Showing prejudice against people who are gay.

homosexual
A person who is sexually attracted to members of the same sex; also called gay.

hormone
A chemical (such as estrogen or testosterone) produced by the body that controls and regulates the activities of specific cells in the body.

hypothalamus
An area of the brain that triggers puberty by releasing the GnRH hormone.

identity
The distinguishing qualities and characteristics of a person, such as nationality, personality, gender, interests, and culture.

identity theft
The criminal act of obtaining and using another individual's personal details.

implantat
When a fertilized egg attaches itself to the wall of the uterus.

independence
Freedom of actions and

thoughts, without being influenced by another person.

individuality
The qualities of a person that distinguish him or her from others.

insomnia
The inability to sleep.

intimacy
Being close to or with another person emotionally or sexually.

larynx
Also called the voice box; an organ, located in the throat, that houses the vocal cords and forms a passage through which air flows to and from the lungs.

lateral thinking
The ability to solve a problem by thinking creatively or "outside the box."

LGBTQ+
Short for lesbian, gay, bisexual, trans, questioning, and others. A term used to describe and categorize the variety of different sexual identities that aren't heterosexual or straight.

logical thinking
A process whereby a person thinks through something step-by-step, in which each step is directly related in some way to the ones before and after it.

lubricant
A substance to make something slippery and reduce friction. The vagina lubricates itself when a female is sexually aroused.

malware
Malicious software that is designed to gain access to a electronic device and/or cause damage to it.

masturbation
Touching or rubbing the genitals and other body parts for sexual pleasure.

mature
A person who is fully developed and grown into an adult.

media
The term used to refer to news outlets, such as newspapers, radio, and TV broadcasting companies.

menarche
A female's first menstrual period, which starts during puberty.

menstrual care
Products designed to keep females comfortable during menstruation.

menstruation
When the lining of the uterus is discharged from the body with blood as part of her monthly menstruation cycle. It is also known as a period.

mental health
A person's psychological well-being, including their emotional and social wellness.

mental illness
A medical condition that affects a person's psychological health and disrupts their behavior, thought processes, and mood.

networking
Connecting and interacting with other people to share ideas and opinions, and to cultivate useful contacts.

obsessive-compulsive disorder (OCD)
A medical condition in which a person has thoughts or feelings that compel them to behave a certain way.

orgasm
The climax of sexual arousal, resulting in intense feelings of pleasure, usually accompanied by ejaculation in males and sometimes in females.

ovary
A female reproductive organ in which eggs (ova) are produced.

ovulation
The release of eggs (ova) from an ovary into the fallopian tube.

panic attack
An overwhelming and sudden sense of intense anxiety, which can cause certain physical symptoms such as palpitations, shortness of breath, sweating, and dizziness.

parasite
An organism that lives on or in a host, which it uses as a food source.

peer pressure
A social influence felt by individuals to be a certain way in order to fit in with their peers.

penis
The male sex organ, used for sexual pleasure and reproduction, and urination.

period
When the lining of the uterus is discharged from the body with blood as part of her monthly menstruation cycle. It is also known as menstruation.

phishing
When someone online pretends to be a financial institution in order to get someone to pass on their bank details.

phobia
A severe, often irrational, fear of something specific.

pornography
Printed or visual material that is designed to sexually excite.

pregnancy
The condition of a female who is carrying a baby.

prejudice
Preconceived assumptions that are not based in fact, and which are often untrue and unjust.

premenstrual syndrome (PMS)
A mix of symptoms, such as irritability, fatigue, and stomach pains, experienced by some females just before menstruation.

privacy
A person's seclusion from others and control over their personal information, both online and in person.

privilege
An often unearned advantage or preference given only to a particular person or group.

puberty
The time during adolescence when a person reaches sexual maturity. Characterized by many changes in the body to enable reproduction.

pubic hair
Hair that grows around the genitals.

racism
Discrimination or prejudice against an individual or group due to their racial identity.

reproduction
The biological process of procreating, in which parents produce children. Once an individual begins puberty, he or she is able to reproduce.

resilience
Having the strength to withstand and recover from change or difficulty.

safer sex
Sex using different methods, including barrier contraception, to protect against STDs and pregnancy.

scrotum
The skin sack containing the testicles.

search engine
A computer program which searches a database for information based on keywords typed in by the user.

self-confidence
A person's general trust and belief in their own abilities and judgments.

self-consciousness
A person's awkward awareness and worry over how others might perceive them.

self-esteem
An person's inner sense of self-worth, which can affect their self-confidence.

self-expression
The assertion of identity through certain behaviors or actions.

selfie
A self-portrait taken with a smartphone.

sensationalization
The exaggerated presentation of information to suggest that it is more shocking than it is in reality, in order to stimulate interest.

sex
An act of physical intimacy between two people. Also used to mean biological sex.

sexism
Discrimination or prejudice against an individual or group due to their biological sex.

sext
A naked, underwear-only, or sexually explicit picture or video message sent by the taker to another person. Also called nude selfie.

sexual identity
A person's perception of who they are attracted to.

sexual reproduction
When a male sperm and female egg join, and the chromosomes carried by each mix to produce a child.

sexuality
The interaction between a person's desires, preferences, experiences, and beliefs throughout their life.

sexually transmitted disease (STD)
A disease that can be passed from one person to another through sex.

sibling
The relationship between two children who share one or both parents.

social conscience
Having a sense of responsibility and concern for the general well-being and fair treatment of others in a society.

social norm
Unwritten rules and behaviors that are generally considered acceptable by society.

spam
Unwanted emails, messages, or ads that are sometimes used for spreading malware.

spirituality
A personal sense that something exists—such as a person's spirit or soul—beyond the physical being. Spirituality is an aspect of religious faith, but it is different from religion.

stereotype
A prevailing and oversimplified idea that is often prejudicial about a person or group.

stigma
A sense of shame due to having a certain characteristic.

stimulant
A substance that increases a person's energy or other body function. Caffeine is a stimulant, as are many other drugs.

stimulation
Something that causes something else to happen.

straight
A person that is sexually attracted to members of the opposite sex; also known as heterosexual.

stress
A feeling of worry or tension when faced with a problem, or something that causes this.

synapse
The connection between two nerve or brain cells, through which chemical signals are passed.

testicles
The two male sex glands that produce and store sperm. They are located in the scrotum.

transgender
When a person's gender identity as a man or woman is mismatched with the sex they were assigned at birth; the opposite of cisgender.

trolling
Inflammatory and offensive comments posted online with the intent to cause upset and provoke reactions.

trust
An assured confidence in someone or something.

tween
An individual who is between childhood and puberty.

United Nations (UN)
An international organization formed in 1945 to promote international cooperation, of which most of the world's countries are members.

uterus
An organ in a female's lower abdomen in which embryos develop and grow. Also known as the womb.

vaccination
The injection of a harmless version of an infection into a person to stimulate the immune system to protect them against that infection.

vagina
In females, the muscular passage between the internal sex organs and the external genitals.

virginity
The state of not having had sexual intercourse with another person.

virus
A disease-causing, nonliving microorganism that invades a cell and produces copies of itself that then invade other cells. Also describes computer programs that cause harm to computer systems.

vulva
The external parts of a female's genitals that make up the opening to the vagina.

webcam
A digital camera that allows images or videos to be transmitted over the Internet through a computer.

Index

Acknowledgments

DORLING KINDERSLEY would like to thank: David Ball and Edward
Byrne design assistance, Victoria Pyke for proofreading, and
Helen Peters for the index. Special thanks to Dr. Kristina Routh
for medical consultancy.

All images © Dorling Kindersley
For further information see: **www.dkimages.com**